# The Refutation of All Heresies

# The Refutation of All Heresies

## St. Hippolytus

# The Refutation of All Heresies

© Lighthouse Publishing 2023

Written by: Hippolytus (AD 170-236)
Translated by: Rev. J. H. MacMahon, M.A.(AD 1829-1900)
Updated into Modern U.S English: A.M. Overett (b.1960)

All rights reserved. Without limiting the rights under copyright reserved above, no part of this publication may be reproduced, stored in a retrieval system, or transmitted, in any form or by any means (electronic, mechanical, photocopying, recording or otherwise), without the prior written permission of the copyright owner of this book.

Published by
Lighthouse Publishing
SAN 257-4330
5531 Dufferin Drive
Savage, Minnesota, 55378
United States of America

www.lighthouseebooks.com

# St. Hippolytus

## Introductory Notice to Hippolytus. [a.d. 170–236.]

The first great Christian Father whose history is Roman is, nevertheless, not a Roman, but a Greek. He is the disciple of Irenaeus, and the spirit of his life-work rejects that of his master. In his personal character he so much resembles Irenaeus risen again, that the great Bishop of Lyons must be well studied and understood if we would do full justice to the conduct of Hippolytus. Especially did he follow his master's example in withstanding contemporary bishops of Rome, who, like Victor, "deserved to be blamed," but who, much more than any of their predecessors, merited rebuke alike for error in doctrine and viciousness of life.

In the year 1551, while some excavations were in progress near the ancient Church of St. Lawrence at Rome, on the Tiburtine Road, there was found an ancient statue, in marble, of a figure seated in a chair, and wearing over the Roman tunic the pallium of Tertullian's eulogy. It was in 1851, just three hundred years after its discovery, and in the year of the publication of the newly discovered Philosophumena at Oxford, that I saw it in the Vatican. As a specimen of early Christian art, it is a most interesting work, and possesses a higher merit than almost any similar production of a period subsequent to that of the Antonines. It represents a grave personage, of noble features and a high, commanding forehead, slightly bearded, his right hand resting over his heart, while under it his left arm crosses the body to reach a book placed at his side. There is no reason to doubt that this is, indeed, the statue of Hippolytus, as is stated in the inscription of Pius IV., who calls him "Saint Hippolytus, Bishop of

Portus," and states that he lived in the reign of the Emperor Alexander, i.e., Severus.

Of this there is evidence on the chair itself, which represents his episcopal cathedra, and has a modest symbol of lions at "the stays," as if borrowed from the throne of Solomon. It is a work of later date than the age of Severus, no doubt; but Wordsworth, who admirably illustrates the means by which such a statue may have been provided, gives us good reasons for supposing that it may have been the grateful tribute of contemporaries, and all the more trustworthy as a portrait of the man himself. The chair has carved upon it, no doubt for use in the Church, a calendar indicating the Paschal full moons for seven cycles of sixteen years each; answering, according to the science of the period, to similar tables in the Anglican Book of Common Prayer. It indicates the days on which Easter must fall, from a.d. 222 to a.d. 333. On the back of the chair is a list of the author's works.

Not less interesting, and vastly more important, was the discovery, at Mount Athos, in 1842, of the long-lost Philosophumena of this author, concerning which the important facts will appear below. Its learned editor, Emmanuel Miller, published it at Oxford under the name of Origen, which was inscribed on the ms. Like the Epistle of Clement, its composition in the Greek language had given it currency among the Easterns long after it was forgotten in the West; and very naturally they had ascribed to Origen an anonymous treatise containing much in coincidence with his teachings, and supplying the place of one of his works of a similar kind. It is now sufficiently established as the work of Hippolytus and has been providentially brought to light just when it was most needed. In fact, the statue rose from its grave as if to rebuke the reigning pontiff (Pius IV.), who just then imposed upon the Latin churches the novel "Creed" which bears his name; and now the Philosophumena comes forth as if to breathe a last warning to that namesake of the former Pius who, in the very teeth of its testimony, so recently forged and uttered the dogma of "papal infallibility" conferring this attribute upon himself, and retrospectively upon the very bishops of Rome whom St. Hippolytus resisted as heretics, and has transmitted to posterity, in his writings, branded with the shame alike of false doctrine and of heinous crimes. Dr. Döllinger, who for a time lent his learning and genius to an apologetic effort on behalf of the Papacy, was no doubt prepared, by this very struggle of his heart versus head, for that rejection of the new dogma which overloaded alike his intellect and his conscience, and made it impossible for him any longer to bear the lashes of Rehoboam in communion with modern Rome.

In the biographical data which will be found below, enough is supplied for the needs of the reader of the present series, who, if he wishes further to investigate the subject, will find the fullest information in the works to which reference has been made, or which will be hereafter indicated. But this is the place to recur to the much-abused passage of Irenaeus which I have discussed in a former volume. Strange to say, I was forced to correct, from a Roman-Catholic writer, the very unsatisfactory rendering of our Edinburgh editors, and to elucidate at some length the palpable absurdity of attributing to Irenaeus any other than a geographical and imperial reference to the importance of Rome, and its usefulness to the West, more especially, as its only see of apostolic origin. Quoting the Ninth Antiochian Canon, I gave good reasons for my conjecture that the Latin *convenire* represents συντρέχειν in the original; and now it remains to be noted how strongly the real meaning of Irenaeus is illustrated in the life and services of his pupil Hippolytus.

1. That neither Hippolytus nor his master had any conception that the See of Rome possesses any pre-eminent authority, to which others are obliged to defer, is conspicuously evident from the history of both. Alike they convicted Roman bishops of error, and alike they rebuked them for their misconduct.

2. Hippolytus is the author of a work called the Little Labyrinth, which, like the recently discovered Philosophumena, attributes to the Roman See anything but the "infallibility" which the quotation from Irenaeus is so ingeniously wrested to sustain. How he did not understand the passage is, therefore, sufficiently apparent. Let us next inquire what appears, from his conduct, to be the true understanding of Irenaeus.

3. I have shown, in the elucidation already referred to, how Irenaeus affirms that Rome is the city which everybody visits from all parts, and that Christians, resorting thither, because it is the Imperial City, carry into it the testimony of all other churches. Thus, it becomes a competent witness to the *quod ab omnibus*, because it cannot be ignorant of what all the churches teach with one accord. This argument, therefore, reverses the modern Roman dogma; primitive Rome received orthodoxy instead of prescribing it. She embosomed the Catholic testimony brought into it from all the churches and gave it forth as reflected light; not primarily her own, but what she faithfully preserved in coincidence with older and more learned churches than herself. Doubtless she had

been planted and watered by St. Paul and St. Peter; but doubtless, also, she had been expressly warned by the former of her liability 5 to error and to final severance from apostolic communion. Hippolytus lived at a critical moment, when this awful admonition seemed about to be realized.

4. Now, then, from Portus and from Lyons, Hippolytus brought into Rome the Catholic doctrine, and convicted two of its bishops of pernicious heresies and evil living. And thus, as Irenaeus teaches, the faith was preserved in Rome by the testimony of those from every side resorting thither, not by any prerogative of the See itself. All this will appear clearly enough as the student proceeds in the examination of this volume. But it is now time to avail ourselves of the information given us by the translator in his Introductory Notice, as follows:—

The entire of The Refutation of all Heresies, with the exception of book i., was found in a ms. brought from a convent on Mount Athos so recently as the year 1842. The discoverer of this treasure—for treasure it certainly is—was Minöides Mynas, an erudite Greek, who had visited his native country in search of ancient mss., by direction of M. Abel Villemain, Minister of Public Instruction under Louis Philippe. The French Government have thus the credit of being instrumental in bringing to light this valuable work, while the University of Oxford shares the distinction by being its earliest publishers. The Refutation was printed at the Clarendon Press in 1851, under the editorship of M. Emmanuel Miller, whose labors have proved serviceable to all subsequent commentators. One generally acknowledged mistake was committed by Miller in ascribing the work to Origen. He was right in affirming that the discovered ms.

was the continuation of the fragment, The Philosophumena, inserted in the Benedictine copy of Origen's works. In the volume, however, containing the Philosophumena, we have dissertations by Huet, in which he questions Origen's authorship in favor of Epiphanius. Heuman attributed the Philosophumena to Didymus of Alexandria, Gale to Aetius; and it, with the rest of The Refutation, Fessler and Baur ascribed to Caius, but the Abbe Jellabert to Tertullian. The last hypothesis is untenable, if for no other reason, because the work is in Greek. In many respects, Caius, who was a presbyter of Rome in the time of Victor and Zephyrinus, would seem the probable author; but a fatal argument—one applicable to those named above, except Epiphanius—against Caius is his not being, as the author of The Refutation in the Proœmium declares himself to be, a bishop. Epiphanius no doubt filled the episcopal office; but when we have a large work of his on the heresies, with a summary, it would seem scarcely probable that he composed likewise, on the same topic, an extended treatise like the present, with two abridgments. Whatever diversity of opinion, however, existed as to these claimants, most critics, though not all, now agree in denying the authorship of Origen. Neither the style nor tone of The Refutation is Origenian. Its compilatory process is foreign to Origen's plan of composition; while the subject matter itself, for many reasons, would not be likely to have occupied the pen of the Alexandrine Father. It is almost impossible but that Origen would have made some allusions in The Refutation to his other writings, or in them to it. Not only, however, is there no such allusion, but the derivation of the word "Ebionites," in The Refutation, and an expressed belief in the (orthodox) doctrine of eternal punishment, are at variance with Origen's authorship. Again, no work answering the description is awarded to Origen in catalogues of his extant or lost writings. These arguments are strengthened by the facts, that Origen was never a bishop, and that he did not reside for any length of time at Rome. He once paid a hurried visit to the capital of the West, whereas the author of The Refutation asserts his presence at Rome during the occurrence of events which occupied a period of some twenty years. And not only was he a spectator but took part in these transactions in such an official and authoritative manner as Origen could never have assumed, either at Rome or elsewhere.

In this state of the controversy, commentators turned their attention towards Hippolytus, in favor of whose authorship the majority of modern scholars have decided. The arguments that have led to this conclusion, and those alleged by others against it, could not be adequately discussed in a notice like the present. Suffice it to say, that such names as Jacobi, Gieseler, Duncker, Schneidewin, Bernays, Bunsen, Wordsworth, and Döllinger, support the claims of Hippolytus. The testimony of Dr. Döllinger, considering the extent of his theological learning, and in particular his intimate acquaintance with the apostolic period in church history, virtually, we submit, decides the question.

For a biography of Hippolytus, we have not much authentic materials. There can be no reasonable doubt but that he was a bishop and passed the greater portion of his life in Rome and its vicinity. This assertion corresponds with the conclusion adopted by Dr. Döllinger, who, however, refuses to allow that Hippolytus was, as is generally maintained, Bishop of Portus, a harbor of Rome at the northern mouth of the Tiber, opposite Ostia.

However, it is satisfactory to establish, and especially upon such eminent authority as that of Dr. Döllinger, the fact of Hippolytus' connection with the Western Church, not only because it bears on the investigation of the authorship of The Refutation, the writer of which affirms his personal observation of what he records as occurring in his own time at Rome, but also because it overthrows the hypothesis of those who contend that there were more Hippolytuses than one—Dr. Döllinger shows that there is only one historical Hippolytus—or that the East, and not Italy, was the sphere of his episcopal labors. Thus, Le Moyne, in the seventeenth century, a French writer resident in Leyden, ingeniously argues that Hippolytus was bishop of Portus Romanorum (Aden), in Arabia. Le Moyne's theory was adopted by some celebrities, viz., Dupin, Tillemont, Spanheim, Basnage, and our own Dr. Cave. To this position are opposed, among others, the names of Nicephorus, Syncellus, Baronius, Bellarmine, Dodwell, Beveridge, Bull, and Archbishop Ussher. The judgment and critical accuracy of Ussher is, on a point of this kind, of the highest value. Wherefore the question of Hippolytus being bishop of Portus near Rome would also appear established, for the reasons laid down in Bunsen's Letters to Archdeacon Hare, and Canon Wordsworth's St. Hippolytus. The mind of inquirers appears to have been primarily unsettled in consequence of Eusebius' mentioning Hippolytus (Ecclesiast. Hist., vi. 10) in company with Beryllus (of Bostra), an Arabian, expressing at the same time his uncertainty as to where Hippolytus was bishop. This indecision is easily explained and cannot invalidate the tradition and historical testimony which assign the bishopric of Portus near Rome to Hippolytus, a saint and martyr of the

Church. Of his martyrdom, though the fact itself is certain, the details, furnished in Prudentius' hymn, are not historic. Thus, the mode of Hippolytus' death is stated by Prudentius to have been identical with that of Hippolytus the son of Theseus, who was torn limb from limb by being tied to wild horses. St. Hippolytus, however, is known on historical testimony to have been thrown into a canal and drowned; but whether the scene of his martyrdom was Sardinia, to which he was undoubtedly banished along with the Roman bishop Pontianus, or Rome, or Portus, has not as yet been definitively proved. The time of his martyrdom, however, is probably a year or two, perhaps less or more, after the commencement of the reign of Maximin the Thracian, that is, somewhere about a.d. 235–39. This enables us to determine the age of Hippolytus; and as some statements in The Refutation evince the work to be the composition of an old man, and as the work itself was written after the death of Callistus in a.d. 222, this would transfer the period of his birth to not very long after the last half of the second century.

The contents of The Refutation, as they originally stood, seem to have been arranged 7 thus: The first book (which we have) contained an account of the different schools of ancient philosophers; the second (which is missing), the doctrines and mysteries of the Egyptians; the third (likewise missing), the Chaldean science and astrology; and the fourth (the beginning of which is missing), the system of the Chaldean horoscope, and the magical rites and incantations of the Babylonian Theurgists. Next came the portion of the work relating more immediately to the heresies of the Church, which is contained in books v.–ix. The tenth book is the résumé of the entire, together with the exposition of the author's own religious opinions. The heresies enumerated by Hippolytus comprehend a period starting from an age prior to the composition of St. John's Gospel and terminating with the death of Callistus. The heresies are explained according to chronological development and may be ranged under five leading schools: (1) The Ophites; (2) Simonists; (3) Basilidians; (4) Docetæ; (5) Noetians. Hippolytus ascends to the origin of heresy, not only in assigning heterodoxy a derivative nature from heathenism, but in pointing out in the Gnosis elements of abnormal opinions antecedent to the promulgation of Christianity. We have thus a most interesting account of the early heresies, which in some respects supplies many desiderata in the ecclesiastical history of this epoch.

We can scarcely over-estimate the value of The Refutation, on account of the propinquity of its author to the apostolic age. Hippolytus was a disciple of St. Irenaeus, St. Irenaeus of St. Polycarp, St. Polycarp of St. John. Indeed, one fact of grave importance connected with the writings of St. John, is elicited from Hippolytus' Refutation. The passage given out of Basilides' work, containing a quotation by the heretic from St. John i. 9, settles the period of the composition of the fourth Gospel, as of greater antiquity by at least thirty years than is allowed to it by the Tübingen school. It is therefore obvious that Basilides formed his system out of the prologue of St. John's Gospel; thus, forever setting at rest the allegation of these critics, that St. John's Gospel was written at a later date, and assigned an apostolic author, in order to silence the Basilidian Gnostics. In the case of Irenaeus, too, The Refutation has restored the Greek text of much of his book Against Heresies, hitherto only known to us in a Latin version. Nor is the value of

Hippolytus' work seriously impaired, even on the supposition of the authorship not being proved, —a concession, however, in no wise justified by the evidence. Whoever the writer of The Refutation be, he belonged to the early portion of the third century, formed his compilations from primitive sources, made conscientious preparation for his undertaking, delivered statements confirmed by early writers of note, and lastly, in the execution of his task, furnished indubitable marks of information and research, and of having thoroughly mastered the relations and affinities, each to other, of the various heresies of the first two and a quarter centuries. These heresies, whether deducible from attempts to Christianize the philosophy of Paganism, or to interpret the Doctrines and Life of our Lord by the tenets of Gnosticism and Oriental speculation generally, or to create a compromise with the pretensions of Judaism, — these heresies, amid all their complexity and diversity, St. Hippolytus reduces to one common ground of censure— antagonism to Holy Scripture. Heresy, thus branded, he leaves to wither under the condemnatory sentence of the Church.

The Refutation of All Heresies.

[Translated by the Rev. J. H. MacMahon, M.A.]

Book I. ————————————

Contents.

The following are the contents of the first book of The Refutation of all Heresies. We propose to furnish an account of the tenets of natural philosophers, and who these are, as well as the tenets of moral philosophers, and who these are; and thirdly, the tenets of logicians, and who these logicians are. Among natural philosophers may be enumerated Thales, Pythagoras, Empedocles, Heraclitus, Anaximander, Anaximenes, Anaxagoras, Archelaus, Parmenides, Leucippus, Democritus, Xenophanes, Ecphantus, Hippo. Among moral philosophers are Socrates, pupil of Archelaus the physicist, (and) Plato the pupil of Socrates. This (speculator) combined three systems of philosophy. Among logicians is Aristotle, pupil of Plato. He systematized the art of dialectics. Among the Stoic (logicians) were Chrysippus (and) Zeno. Epicurus, however, advanced an opinion almost contrary to all philosophers. Pyrrho was an Academic; this (speculator) taught the incomprehensibility of everything. The Brahmins among the Indians, and the Druids among the Celts, and Hesiod (devoted themselves to philosophic pursuits).

The Prœmium. —Motives for Undertaking the Refutation; Exposure of the Ancient Mysteries; Plan of the Work; Completeness of the Refutation; Value of the Treatise to Future Ages.

We must not overlook any figment devised by those denominated philosophers among the Greeks. For even their incoherent tenets must be received as worthy of credit, on account of the excessive madness of the heretics, who, from the observance of silence, and from concealing their own ineffable mysteries, have by many been supposed worshippers of God. We have likewise, on a former occasion, expounded the doctrines of these briefly, not illustrating them with any degree of minuteness, but refuting them in coarse digest; not having considered it requisite to bring to light their secret doctrines, in order that, when we have explained their tenets by enigmas, they, becoming ashamed, lest also, by our divulging their mysteries, we should convict them of atheism, might be induced to desist in some 10 degree from their unreasonable opinion and their profane attempt. But since I perceive that they have not been abashed by our forbearance, and have made no account of how God is long-suffering, though blasphemed by them, in order that either from shame they may repent, or should they persevere, be justly condemned, I am forced to proceed in my intention of exposing those secret mysteries of theirs, which, to the initiated, with a vast amount of plausibility they deliver who are not accustomed first to disclose (to any one), till, by keeping such in suspense during a period (of necessary preparation), and by rendering him blasphemous towards the true God they have acquired complete ascendancy over him, and perceive him eagerly panting after the promised disclosure. And then, when they have tested him to be enslaved by sin, they initiate him, putting him in possession of the perfection of wicked things. Previously, however, they bind him with an oath neither to divulge (the mysteries), nor to hold communication with any person whatsoever, unless he first undergoes similar subjection, though, when the doctrine has been simply delivered (to any one), there was no longer any need of an oath. For he who was content to submit to the necessary purgation, and so receive the perfect mysteries of these men, by the very act itself, as well as in reference to his own conscience, will feel himself sufficiently under an obligation not to divulge to others; for if he once disclose wickedness of this description to any man, he would neither be reckoned among men, nor be deemed worthy to behold the light, since not even irrational animals would attempt such an enormity, as we shall explain when we come to treat of such topics.

Since, however, reason compels us to plunge into the very depth of narrative, we conceive we should not be silent, but, expounding the tenets of the several schools with minuteness, we shall evince reserve in nothing. Now it seems expedient, even at the expense of a more protracted investigation, not to shrink from labor; for we shall leave behind us no trifling auxiliary to human life against the recurrence of error, when all are made to behold, in an obvious light, the clandestine rites of these men, and the secret orgies which, retaining under their management, they deliver to the initiated only. But none will refute these, save the Holy Spirit bequeathed unto the Church, which the Apostles, having in the first instance received, have transmitted to those who have rightly believed. But we, as being their successors, and as participators in this grace, high-priesthood, and office of teaching, as well as being reputed guardians of the Church, must not be found deficient in vigilance, or disposed to suppress correct doctrine. Not even, however, laboring with every energy of body and soul, do we tire in our attempt adequately to render our Divine Benefactor a fitting return; and yet withal we do not so requite Him in a becoming manner, except we are not remiss in discharging the trust committed to us, but careful to complete the measure of our particular opportunity, and to impart to all without grudging whatever the Holy Ghost supplies, not only bringing to light, by means of our refutation, matters foreign (to our subject), but also whatsoever things the truth has received by the grace of the Father, and ministered to men. These also, illustrating by argument and creating testimony by letters, we shall unabashedly proclaim.

In order, then, as we have already stated, that we may prove them atheists, both in opinion and their mode (of treating a question) and in fact, and (in order to show) whence it is that their attempted theories have accrued unto them, and that they have endeavored to establish their tenets, taking nothing from the holy Scriptures—nor is it from preserving the succession of any saint that they have hurried headlong into these opinions;—but that their doctrines have derived their origin from the wisdom of the Greeks, from the conclusions of those who have formed systems of philosophy, and from would-be mysteries, and the vagaries of astrologers,—it seems, then, advisable, in the first instance, by explaining the opinions advanced by the philosophers of the Greeks, to satisfy our readers that such are of greater antiquity than these (heresies), and more deserving of reverence in reference to their views respecting the divinity; in the next place, to compare each heresy with the system of each speculator, so as to show that the earliest champion of the heresy availing himself of these attempted theories, has turned them to advantage by appropriating their principles, and, impelled from these into worse, has constructed his own doctrine. The undertaking admittedly is full of labor, and (is one) requiring extended research. We shall not, however, be wanting in exertion; for afterwards it will be a source of joy, just like an athlete obtaining with much toil the crown, or a merchant after a huge swell of sea compassing gain, or a husbandman after sweat of brow enjoying the fruits, or a prophet after reproaches and insults seeing his predictions turning out true. In the commencement, therefore, we shall declare who first, among the Greeks, pointed out (the principles of) natural philosophy. For from these especially have they furtively taken their views who have first propounded these heresies, as we shall subsequently prove when we come to compare them one with another. Assigning to each of those who take the lead among philosophers their own peculiar tenets, we shall publicly exhibit these heresiarchs as naked and unseemly.

Chapter I.—Thales; His Physics and Theology; Founder of Greek Astronomy.

It is said that Thales of Miletus, one of the seven wise men, first attempted to frame a system of natural philosophy. This person said that some such thing as water is the generative principle of the universe, and its end;—for that out of this, solidified and again dissolved, all things consist, and that all things are supported on it; from which also arise both earthquakes and changes of the winds and atmospheric movements, and that all things are both produced and are in a state of flux corresponding with the nature of the primary author of generation;—and that the Deity is that which has neither beginning nor end. This person, having been occupied with a hypothesis and investigation concerning the stars, became the earliest author to the Greeks of this kind of learning. And he, looking towards heaven, alleging that he was carefully examining supernal objects, fell into a well; and a certain maid, by name Thratta, remarked of him derisively, that while intent on beholding things in heaven, he did not know what was at his feet. And he lived about the time of Crœsus.

Chapter II. —Pythagoras; His Cosmogony; Rules of His Sect; Discoverer of Physiognomy; His Philosophy of Numbers; His System of the Transmigration of Souls; Zaratas on Demons; Why Pythagoras Forbade the Eating of Beans; The Mode of Living Adopted by His Disciples.

But there was also, not far from these times, another philosophy which Pythagoras originated (who some say was a native of Samos), which they have denominated Italian, because that Pythagoras, flying from Polycrates the king of Samos, took up his residence in a city of Italy, and there passed the entire of his remaining years. And they who received in succession his doctrine, did not much differ from the same opinion. And this person, instituting an investigation concerning natural phenomena, combined together astronomy, and geometry, and music. And so, he proclaimed that the Deity is a monad; and carefully acquainting himself with the nature of number, he affirmed that the world sings, and that its system corresponds with harmony, and he first resolved the motion of the seven stars into rhythm and melody. And being astonished at the management of the entire fabric, he required that at first his disciples should keep silence, as if persons coming into the world initiated in (the secrets of) the universe; next, when it seemed that they were sufficiently conversant with his mode of teaching his doctrine, and could forcibly philosophize concerning the stars and nature, then, considering them pure, he enjoins them to speak. This man distributed his pupils in two orders, and called the one esoteric, but the other exoteric. And to the former he confided more advanced doctrines, and to the latter a more moderate amount of instruction.

And he also touched on magic—as they say—and himself discovered an art of physiogony, laying down as a basis certain numbers and measures, saying that they comprised the principle of arithmetical philosophy by composition after this manner. The first number became an originating principle, which is one, indefinable, incomprehensible, having in itself all numbers that, according to plurality, can go on ad infinitum. But the primary monad became a principle of numbers, according to substance, —which is a male monad, begetting after the manner of a parent all the rest of the numbers. Secondly, the duad is a female number, and the same also is by arithmeticians termed even. Thirdly, the triad is a male number. This also has been classified by arithmeticians under the denomination uneven. And in addition to all these is the tetrad, a female number; and the same also is called even, because it is female. Therefore, all the numbers that have been derived from the genus are four; but number is the indefinite genus, from which was constituted, according to them, the perfect number, viz., the decade. For one, two, three, four, become ten, if its proper denomination be preserved essentially for each of the numbers. Pythagoras affirmed this to be a sacred quaternion, source of everlasting nature, having, as it were, roots in itself; and that from this number all the numbers receive their originating principle. For eleven, and twelve, and the rest, partake of the origin of existence from ten. Of this decade, the perfect number, there are termed four divisions, — namely, number, monad, square, (and) cube. And the connections and blending of these are performed, according to nature, for the generation of growth completing the productive number. For when the square itself is multiplied into itself, a biquadratic is the result. But when the square is multiplied into the cube, the result is the product of a square and cube; and when the cube is multiplied into the cube, the product of two cubes is the result. So that all the numbers from which the production of existing (numbers) arises, are seven, —namely, number, monad, square, cube, biquadratic, quadratic-cube, cubo-cube.

This philosopher likewise said that the soul is immortal, and that it subsists in successive bodies. Wherefore he asserted that before the Trojan era he was Æthalides, and during the Trojan epoch Euphorbus, and subsequent to this Hermotimus of Samos, and after him Pyrrhus of Delos; fifth, Pythagoras. And Diodorus the Eretrian, and Aristoxenus the musician, assert that Pythagoras came to Zaratas the Chaldean, and that he explained to him that there are two original causes of things, father and mother, and that father is light, but mother darkness; and that of the light the parts are hot, dry, not heavy, light, swift; but of darkness, cold, moist, weighty, slow; and that out of all these, from female and male, the world consists. But the world, he says, is a musical harmony; wherefore, also, that the sun performs a circuit in accordance with harmony. And as regards the things that are produced from earth and the cosmical system, they maintain that Zaratas makes the following statements: that there are two demons, the one celestial and the other terrestrial; and that the terrestrial sends up a production from earth, and that this is water; and that the celestial is a fire, partaking of the nature of air, hot and cold. And he therefore affirms that none of these destroys or sullies the soul, for these constitute the substance of all things. And he is reported to have ordered his followers not to eat beans, because that Zaratas said that, at the origin and concretion of all things, when the earth was still undergoing its process of solidification, and that of putrefaction had set in, the bean was produced. And of this he mentions the following indication, that if any one, after having chewed a bean without the husk, places it opposite the sun for a certain period, —for this immediately will aid in the result,—it yields the smell of human seed. And he mentions also another clearer instance to be this: if, when the bean is blossoming, we take the bean and its flower, and deposit them in a jar, smear this over, and bury it in the ground, and after a few days uncover it, we shall see it wearing the appearance, first of a woman's pudendum, and after this, when closely examined, of the head of a child growing in along with it. This person, being burned along with his disciples in Croton, a town of Italy, perished. And this was a habit with him, whenever one repaired to him with a view of becoming his follower, (the candidate disciple was compelled) to sell his possessions, and lodge the money sealed with Pythagoras, and he continued in silence to undergo instruction, sometimes for three, but sometimes for five years. And again, on being released, he was permitted to associate with the rest, and remained as a disciple, and took his meals along with them; if otherwise, however, he received back his property, and was rejected. These persons, then, were styled Esoteric Pythagoreans, whereas the rest, Pythagoristæ.

Among his followers, however, who escaped the conflagration were Lysis and Archippus, and the servant of Pythagoras, Zamolxis, who also is said to have taught the Celtic Druids to cultivate the philosophy of Pythagoras. And they assert that Pythagoras learned from the Egyptians his system of numbers and measures; and being struck by the plausible, fanciful, and not easily revealed wisdom of the priests, he himself likewise, in imitation of them, enjoined silence, and made his disciples lead a solitary life in underground chapels.

Chapter III. —Empedocles; His Twofold Cause; Tenet of Transmigration.

But Empedocles, born after these, advanced likewise many statements respecting the nature of demons, to the effect that, being very numerous, they pass their time in managing earthly concerns. This person affirmed the originating principle of the universe to be discord and friendship, and that the intelligible fire of the monad is the Deity, and that all things consist of fire, and will be resolved into fire; with which opinion the Stoics likewise almost agree, expecting a conflagration. But most of all does he concur with the tenet of transition of souls from body to body, expressing himself thus: —

"For surely both youth and maid I was, And shrub, and bird, and fish, from ocean stray'd."

This (philosopher) maintained the transmutation of all souls into any description of animal. For Pythagoras, the instructor of these (sages), asserted that himself had been Euphorbus, who served in the expedition against Ilium, alleging that he recognized his shield. The foregoing are the tenets of Empedocles.

Chapter IV. —Heraclitus; His Universal Dogmatism; His Theory of Flux; Other Systems.

But Heraclitus, a natural philosopher of Ephesus, surrendered himself to universal grief, condemning the ignorance of the entire of life, and of all men; nay, commiserating the (very) existence of mortals, for he asserted that he himself knew everything, whereas the rest of mankind nothing. But he also advanced statements almost in concert with Empedocles, saying that the originating principle of all things is discord and friendship, and that the Deity is a fire endued with intelligence, and that all things are borne one upon another, and never are at a standstill; and just as Empedocles, he affirmed that the entire locality about us is full of evil things, and that these evil things reach as far as the moon, being extended from the quarter situated around the earth, and that they do not advance further, inasmuch as the entire space above the moon is more pure. So also, it seemed to Heraclitus.

After these arose also other natural philosophers, whose opinions we have not deemed it necessary to declare, (inasmuch as) they present no diversity to those already specified. Since, however, upon the whole, a not inconsiderable school has sprung (from thence), and many natural philosophers subsequently have arisen from them, each advancing different accounts of the nature of the universe, it seems also to us advisable, that, explaining the philosophy that has come down by succession from Pythagoras, we should recur to the opinions entertained by those living after the time of Thales, and that, furnishing a narrative of these, we should approach the consideration of the ethical and logical philosophy which Socrates and Aristotle originated, the former ethical, and the latter logical.

Chapter V.—Anaximander; His Theory of the Infinite; His Astronomic Opinions; His Physics.

Anaximander, then, was the hearer of Thales. Anaximander was son of Praxiadas, and a native of

Miletus. This man said that the originating principle of existing things is a certain constitution of the Infinite, out of which the heavens are generated, and the worlds therein; and that this principle is eternal and undecaying and comprising all the worlds. And he speaks of time as something of limited generation, and subsistence, and destruction. This person declared the Infinite to be an originating principle and element of existing things, being the first to employ such a denomination of the originating principle. But, moreover, he asserted that there is an eternal motion, by the agency of which it happens that the heavens are generated; but that the earth is poised aloft, upheld by nothing, continuing (so) on account of its equal distance from all (the heavenly bodies); and that the figure of it is curved, circular, similar to a column of stone. And one of the surfaces we tread upon, but the other is opposite. And that the stars are a circle of fire, separated from the fire, which is in the vicinity of the world, and encompassed by air. And that certain atmospheric exhalations arise in places where the stars shine; wherefore, also, when these exhalations are obstructed, that eclipses take place. And that the moon sometimes appears full and sometimes waning, according to the obstruction or opening of its (orbital) paths. But that the circle of the sun is twenty-seven times larger than the moon, and that the sun is situated in the highest (quarter of the firmament); whereas the orbs of the fixed stars in the lowest. And that animals are produced (in moisture) by evaporation from the sun. And that man was, originally, similar to a different animal, that is, a fish. And that winds are caused by the separation of very rarified exhalations of the atmosphere, and by their motion after they have been condensed. And that rain arises from earth's giving back (the vapors which it receives) from the (clouds) under the sun. And that there are flashes of lightning when the wind coming down severs the clouds. This person was born in the third year of the xlii. Olympiad.

Chapter VI. —Anaximenes; His System of "An Infinite Air;" His Views of Astronomy and Natural Phenomena.

But Anaximenes, who himself was also a native of Miletus, and son of Eurystratus, affirmed that the originating principle is infinite air, out of which are generated things existing, those which have existed, and those that will be, as well as gods and divine (entities), and that the rest arise from the offspring of this. But that there is such a species of air, when it is most even, which is imperceptible to vision, but capable of being manifested by cold and heat, and moisture and motion, and that it is continually in motion; for that whatsoever things undergo alteration, do not change if there is not motion. For that it presents a different appearance according as it is condensed and attenuated, for when it is dissolved into what is more attenuated that fire is produced, and that when it is moderately condensed again into air that a cloud is formed from the air by virtue of the contraction; but when condensed still more, water, (and) that when the condensation is carried still further, earth is formed; and when condensed to the very highest degree, stones. Wherefore, that the dominant principles of generation are contraries, —namely, heat and cold. And that the expanded earth is wafted along upon the air, and in like manner both sun and moon and the rest of the stars; for all things being of the nature of fire, are wafted about through the expanse of space, upon the air. And that the stars are produced from earth by reason of the mist which arises from this earth; and when this is attenuated, that fire is produced, and that the stars consist of the fire which is being borne aloft. But also, that there are terrestrial natures in the region of the stars carried on along with them. And he says that the stars do not move under the earth, as some have supposed, but around the earth, just as a cap is turned round our head; and that the sun is hid, not by being under the earth, but because covered by the higher portions of the earth, and on account of the greater distance that he is from us. But that the stars do not emit heat on account of the length of distance; and that the winds are produced when the condensed air, becoming rarified, is borne on; and that when collected and thickened still further, clouds are generated, and thus a change made into water. And that hail is produced when the water borne down from the clouds becomes congealed; and that snow is generated when these very clouds, being more moist, acquire congelation; and that lightning is caused when the clouds are parted by force of the winds; for when these are sundered there is produced a brilliant and fiery flash. And that a rainbow is produced by reason of the rays of the sun falling on the collected air. And that an earthquake takes place when the earth is altered into a larger (bulk) by heat and cold. These indeed, then, were the opinions of Anaximenes. This (philosopher) flourished about the first year of the lviii. Olympiad.

Chapter VII. —Anaxagoras; His Theory of Mind; Recognizes an Efficient Cause; His Cosmogony and Astronomy.

After this (thinker) comes Anaxagoras, son of Hegesibulus, a native of Clazomenæ. This person affirmed the originating principle of the universe to be mind and matter; mind being the efficient cause, whereas matter that which was being formed. For all things coming into existence simultaneously, mind supervening introduced order. And material principles, he says, are infinite; even the smaller of these are infinite. And that all things partake of motion by being moved by mind, and that similar bodies coalesce. And that celestial bodies were arranged by orbicular motion. That, therefore, what was thick and moist, and dark and cold, and all things heavy, came together into the center, from the solidification of which earth derived support; but that the things opposite to these—namely, heat and brilliancy, and dryness and lightness—hurried impetuously into the farther portion of the atmosphere. And that the earth is in figure plane; and that it continues suspended aloft, by reason of its magnitude, and by reason of there being no vacuum, and by reason of the air, which was most powerful, bearing along the wafted earth. But that among moist substances on earth, was the sea, and the waters in it; and when these evaporated (from the sun), or had settled under, that the ocean was formed in this manner, as well as from the rivers that from time-to-time flow into it. And that the rivers also derive support from the rains and from the actual waters in the earth; for that this is hollow and contains water in its caverns. And that the Nile is inundated in summer, by reason of the waters carried down into it from the snows in northern (latitudes). And that the sun and moon and all the stars are fiery stones, that were rolled round by the rotation of the atmosphere. And that beneath the stars are sun and moon, and certain invisible bodies that are carried along with us; and that we have no perception of the heat of the stars, both on account of their being so far away, and on account of their distance from the earth; and further, they are not to the same degree hot as the sun, on account of their occupying a colder situation. And that the moon, being lower than the sun, is nearer us. And that the sun surpasses the Peloponnesus in size. And that the moon has not light of its own, but from the sun. But that the revolution of the stars takes place under the earth. And that the moon is eclipsed when the earth is interposed, and occasionally also those (stars) that are underneath the moon. And that the sun (is eclipsed) when, at the beginning of the month, the moon is interposed. And that the solstices are caused by both sun and moon being repulsed by the air. And that the moon is often turned, by its not being able to make head against the cold. This person was the first to frame definitions regarding eclipses and illuminations. And he affirmed that the moon is earthy and has in it plains and ravines. And that the milky way is a reflection of the light of the stars which do not derive their radiance from the sun; and that the stars, coursing (the firmament) as shooting sparks, arise out of the motion of the pole. And that winds are caused when the atmosphere is rarified by the sun, and by those burning orbs that advance under the pole and are borne from (it). And that thunder and lightning are caused by heat falling on the clouds. And that earthquakes are produced by the air above falling on that under the earth;

for when this is moved, that the earth also, being wafted by it, is shaken. And that animals originally came into existence in moisture, and after this one from another; and that males are procreated when the seed secreted from the right parts adhered to the right parts of the womb, and that females are born when the contrary took place. This philosopher flourished in the first year of the lxxxviii. Olympiad, at which time they say that Plato also was born. They maintain that Anaxagoras was likewise prescient.

Chapter VIII. —Archelaus; System Akin to that of Anaxagoras; His Origin of the Earth and of Animals; Other Systems.

Archelaus was by birth an Athenian, and son of Apollodorus. This person, similarly with Anaxagoras, asserted the mixture of matter, and enunciated his first principles in the same manner. This philosopher, however, held that there is inherent immediately in mind a certain mixture; and that the originating principle of motion is the mutual separation of heat and cold, and that the heat is moved, and that the cold remains at rest. And that the water, being dissolved, flows towards the center, where the scorched air and earth are produced, of which the one is borne upwards and the other remains beneath. And that the earth is at rest, and that on this account it came into existence; and that it lies in the center, being no part, so to speak, of the universe, delivered from the conflagration; and that from this, first in a state of ignition, is the nature of the stars, of which indeed the largest is the sun, and next to this the moon; and of the rest some less, but some greater. And he says that the heaven was inclined at an angle, and so that the sun diffused light over the earth, and made the atmosphere transparent, and the ground dry; for that at first it was a sea, inasmuch as it is lofty at the horizon and hollow in the middle. And he adduces, as an indication of the hollowness, that the sun does not rise and set to all at the same time, which ought to happen if the earth was even. And with regard to animals, he affirms that the earth, being originally fire in its lower part, where the heat and cold were intermingled, both the rest of animals made their appearance, numerous and dissimilar, all having the same food, being nourished from mud; and their existence was of short duration, but afterwards also generation from one another arose unto them; and men were separated from the rest (of the animal creation), and they appointed rulers, and laws, and arts, and cities, and the rest. And he asserts that mind is innate in all animals alike; for that each, according to the difference of their physical constitution, employed (mind), at one time slower, at another faster.

Natural philosophy, then, continued from Thales until Archelaus. Socrates was the hearer of this (latter philosopher). There are, however, also very many others, introducing various opinions respecting both the divinity and the nature of the universe; and if we were disposed to adduce all the opinions of these, it would be necessary to compose a vast quantity of books. But, reminding the reader of those whom we especially ought—who are deserving of mention from their fame, and from being, so to speak, the leaders to those who have subsequently framed systems of philosophy, and from their supplying them with a starting-point towards such undertakings—let us hasten on our investigations towards what remains for consideration.

Chapter IX. —Parmenides; His Theory of "Unity;" His Eschatology.

For Parmenides likewise supposes the universe to be one, both eternal and unbegotten, and of a spherical form. And neither did he escape the opinion of the great body (of speculators), affirming fire and earth to be the originating principles of the universe—the earth as matter, but the fire as cause, even an efficient one. He asserted that the world would be destroyed, but in what way he does not mention. The same (philosopher), however, affirmed the universe to be eternal, and not generated, and of spherical form and homogeneous, but not having a figure in itself, and immoveable and limited.

Chapter X.—Leucippus; His Atomic Theory.

But Leucippus, an associate of Zeno, did not maintain the same opinion, but affirms things to be infinite, and always in motion, and that generation and change exist continuously. And he affirms plenitude and vacuum to be elements. And he asserts that worlds are produced when many bodies are congregated and flow together from the surrounding space to a common point, so that by mutual contact they made substances of the same figure and similar in form come into connection; and when thus intertwined, there are transmutations into other bodies, and that created things wax and wane through necessity. But what the nature of necessity is, (Parmenides) did not define.

## Chapter XI. —Democritus; His Duality of Principles; His Cosmogony.

And Democritus was an acquaintance of Leucippus. Democritus, son of Damasippus, a native of Abdera, conferring with many gymnosophists among the Indians, and with priests in Egypt, and with astrologers and magi in Babylon, (propounded his system). Now he makes statements similarly with Leucippus concerning elements, viz., plenitude and vacuum, denominating plenitude entity, and vacuum nonentity; and this he asserted, since existing things are continually moved in the vacuum. And he maintained worlds to be infinite and varying in bulk; and that in some there is neither sun nor moon, while in others that they are larger than with us, and with others more numerous. And that intervals between worlds are unequal; and that in one quarter of space (worlds) are more numerous, and in another less so; and that some of them increase in bulk, but that others attain their full size, while others dwindle away and that in one quarter they are coming into existence, whilst in another they are failing; and that they are destroyed by clashing one with another. And that some worlds are destitute of animals and plants, and every species of moisture. And that the earth of our world was created before that of the stars, and that the moon is underneath; next (to it) the sun; then the fixed stars. And that (neither) the planets nor these (fixed stars) possess an equal elevation. And that the world flourishes, until no longer it can receive anything from without. This (philosopher) turned all things into ridicule, as if all the concerns of humanity were deserving of laughter.

Chapter XII. —Xenophanes; His Skepticism; His Notions of God and Nature; Believes in a Flood.

But Xenophanes, a native of Colophon, was son of Orthomenes. This man survived to the time of Cyrus. This (philosopher) first asserted that there is no possibility of comprehending anything, expressing himself thus: —

"For if for the most part of perfection man may speak, Yet he knows it not himself, and in all attains surmise."

And he affirms that nothing is generated or perishes, or is moved; and that the universe, being one, is beyond change. But he says that the deity is eternal, and one and altogether homogeneous and limited, and of a spherical form, and endued with perception in all parts. And that the sun exists during each day from a conglomeration of small sparks, and that the earth is infinite, and is surrounded neither by an atmosphere nor by the heaven. And that there are infinite suns and moons, and that all things spring from earth. This man affirmed that the sea is salt, on account of the many mixtures that flow into it. Metrodorus, however, from the fact of its being filtered through earth, asserts that it is on account of this that it is made salt. And Xenophanes is of opinion that there had been a mixture of the earth with the sea, and that in process of time it was disengaged from the moisture, alleging that he could produce such proofs as the following: that in the midst of earth, and in mountains, shells are discovered; and also in Syracuse he affirms was found in the quarries the print of a fish and of seals, and in Paros an image of a laurel in the bottom of a stone, and in

Melita parts of all sorts of marine animals. And he says that these were generated when all things originally were embedded in mud, and that an impression of them was dried in the mud, but that all men had perished when the earth, being precipitated into the sea, was converted into mud; then, again, that it originated generation, and that this overthrow occurred to all worlds.

Chapter XIII. —Ecphantus; His Skepticism; Tenet of Infinity.

One Ecphantus, a native of Syracuse, affirmed that it is not possible to attain a true knowledge of things. He defines, however, as he thinks, primary bodies to be indivisible, and that there are three variations of these, viz., bulk, figure, capacity, from which are generated the objects of sense. But that there is a determinable multitude of these, and that this is infinite. And that bodies are moved neither by weight nor by impact, but by divine power, which he calls mind and soul; and that of this the world is a representation; wherefore also it has been made in the form of a sphere by divine power. And that the earth in the middle of the cosmical system is moved round its own center towards the east.

Chapter XIV. —Hippo; His Duality of Principles; His Psychology.

Hippo, a native of Rhegium, asserted as originating principles, coldness, for instance water, and heat, for instance fire. And that fire, when produced by water, subdued the power of its generator, and formed the world. And the soul, he said, is sometimes brain, but sometimes water; for that also the seed is that which appears to us to arise out of moisture, from which, he says, the soul is produced.

So far, then, we think we have sufficiently adduced (the opinions of) these; wherefore, inasmuch as we have adequately gone in review through the tenets of physical speculators, it seems to remain that we now turn to Socrates and Plato, who gave especial preference to moral philosophy.

Chapter XV. —Socrates; His Philosophy Reproduced by Plato.

Socrates, then, was a hearer of Archelaus, the natural philosopher; and he, reverencing the rule, "Know thyself," and having assembled a large school, had Plato (there), who was far superior to all his pupils. (Socrates) himself left no writings after him. Plato, however, taking notes of all his (lectures on) wisdom, established a school, combining together natural, ethical, (and) logical (philosophy). But the points Plato determined are these following.

Chapter XVI. —Plato; Threefold Classification of Principles; His Idea of God; Different Opinions Regarding His Theology and Psychology; His Eschatology and System of Metempsychosis; His Ethical Doctrines; Notions on the Free-Will Question.

Plato (lays down) that there are three originating principles of the universe, (namely) God, and matter, and exemplar; God as the Maker and Regulator of this universe, and the Being who exercises providence over it;

but matter, as that which underlies all (phenomena), which (matter) he styles both receptive and a nurse, out of the arrangement of which proceeded the four elements of which the world consists; (I mean) fire, air, earth, water, from which all the rest of what are denominated concrete substances, as well as animals and plants, have been formed. And that the exemplar, which he likewise calls ideas, is the intelligence of the Deity, to which, as to an image in the soul, the Deity attending, fabricated all things. God, he says, is both incorporeal and shapeless, and comprehensible by wise men solely; whereas matter is body potentially, but with potentiality not as yet passing into action, for being itself without form and without quality, by assuming forms and qualities, it became body. That matter, therefore, is an originating principle, and coeval with the Deity, and that in this respect the world is uncreated. For (Plato) affirms that (the world) was made out of it. And that (the attribute of) imperishableness necessarily belongs to (literally "follows") that which is uncreated. So far forth, however, as body is supposed to be compounded out of both many qualities and ideas, so far forth it is both created and perishable. But some of the followers of Plato mingled both of these, employing some such example as the following: That as a wagon can always continue undestroyed, though undergoing partial repairs from time to time, so that even the parts each in turn perish, yet itself remains always complete; so after this manner the world also, although in parts it perishes, yet the things that are removed, being repaired, and equivalents for them being introduced, it remains eternal.

Some maintain that Plato asserts the Deity to be one, ingenerable and incorruptible, as he says in The Laws: "God, therefore, as the ancient account has it, possesses both the beginning, and end, and middle of all things." Thus, he shows God to be one, on account of His having pervaded all things. Others, however, maintain that Plato affirms the existence of many gods indefinitely, when he uses these words: "God of gods, of whom I am both the Creator and Father." But others say that he speaks of a definite number of deities in the following passage: "Therefore the mighty Jupiter, wheeling his swift chariot in heaven;" and when he enumerates the offspring of the children of heaven and earth. But others assert that (Plato) constituted the gods as generable; and on account of their having been produced, that altogether they were subject to the necessity of corruption, but that on account of the will of God they are immortal, (maintaining this) in the passage already quoted, where, to the words, "God of gods, of whom I am Creator and Father," he adds, "indissoluble through the fiat of My will;" so that if (God) were disposed that these should be dissolved, they would easily be dissolved.

And he admits natures (such as those) of demons, and says that some of them are good, but others worthless. And some affirm that he states the soul to be uncreated and immortal, when he uses the following words, "Every soul is immortal, for that which is always moved is immortal;" and when he demonstrates that the soul is self-moved, and capable of originating motion. Others, however, (say that Plato asserted that the soul was) created but rendered imperishable through the will of God. But some (will have it that he considered the soul) a composite (essence), and generable and corruptible; for even he supposes that there is a receptacle for it, and that it possesses a luminous body, but that everything generated involves a necessity of corruption. Those, however, who assert the immortality of the soul are especially strengthened in their opinion by those passages (in Plato's writings), where he says, that both there are judgments after death, and tribunals of justice in Hades, and that the virtuous (souls) receive a good reward, while the wicked (ones) suitable punishment. Some notwithstanding assert, that he also acknowledges a transition of souls from one body to another, and that different souls, those that were marked out for such a purpose, pass into different bodies, according to the desert of each, and that after certain definite periods they are sent up into this world to furnish once more a proof of their choice. Others, however, (do not admit this to be his doctrine, but will have it that Plato affirms that the souls) obtain a place according to the desert of each; and they employ as a testimony the saying of his, that some good men are with Jove, and that others are ranging abroad (through heaven) with other gods; whereas that others are involved in eternal punishments, as many as during this life have committed wicked and unjust deeds.

And people affirm that Plato says that some things are without a mean, that others have a mean, that others are a mean. (For example, that) waking and sleep, and such like, are conditions without an intermediate state; but that there are things that had means, for instance virtue and vice; and there are means (between extremes), for instance grey between white and black, or some other color. And they say that he affirms that the things pertaining to the soul are absolutely alone good, but that the things pertaining to the body, and those external (to it), are not any longer absolutely good, but reputed blessings. And that frequently he names these means also, for that it is possible to use them both well and ill. Some virtues, therefore, he says, are extremes in regard of intrinsic worth, but in regard of their essential nature means, for nothing is more estimable than virtue. But whatever excels or falls short of these terminates in vice. For instance, he says that there are four virtues—prudence, temperance, justice, fortitude—and that on each of these is attendant two vices, according to excess and defect: for example, on prudence, recklessness according to defect, and knavery according to excess; and on temperance, licentiousness according to defect, stupidity according to excess; and on justice, foregoing a claim according to defect, unduly pressing it according to excess; and on fortitude, cowardice according to defect, foolhardiness according to excess. And that these virtues, when inherent in a man, render him perfect, and afford him happiness. And happiness, he says, is assimilation to the Deity, as far as this is possible; and that assimilation to God takes place when anyone combines holiness and justice with prudence. For this he supposes the end of supreme wisdom and virtue. And he affirms that the virtues follow one another in turn, and are uniform, and are never antagonistic to each other; whereas that vices are multiform, and sometimes follow one the other, and sometimes are antagonistic to each other. He asserts that fate exists; not, to be sure, that all things are produced according to fate, but that there is even something in our power, as in the passages where he says, "The fault is his who chooses, God is blameless;" and "the following law of Adrasteia." And thus some (contend for his upholding) a system of fate, whereas others one of free-will. He asserts, however, that sins are involuntary. For into what is most glorious of the things in our power, which is the soul, no one would (deliberately) admit what is vicious, that is, transgression, but that from ignorance and an erroneous conception of virtue, supposing that they were achieving something honorable, they pass into vice. And his doctrine on this point is most clear in The Republic, where he says, "But, again, you presume to assert that vice is disgraceful and abhorred of God; how then, I may ask, would one choose such an evil thing? He, you reply, (would do so) who is worsted by pleasures. Therefore, this also is involuntary, if to gain a victory be voluntary; so that, in every point of view, the committing an act of turpitude, reason proves to be involuntary." Someone, however, in opposition to this (Plato), advances the contrary statement, "Why then are men punished if they sin involuntary?" But he replies that he himself also, as soon as possible, may be emancipated from vice, and undergo punishment. For that the undergoing punishment is not an evil, but a good thing, if it is likely to prove a purification of evils; and that the rest of mankind, hearing of it, may not transgress, but guard against such an error. (Plato, however, maintains) that the nature of evil is neither created by the Deity, nor possesses subsistence of itself, but that it derives existence from contrariety to what is good, and from attendance upon it, either by excess and defect, as we have previously affirmed concerning the virtues. Plato unquestionably then, as we have already stated, collecting together the three departments of universal philosophy, in this manner formed his speculative system.

Chapter XVII. —Aristotle; Duality of Principles; His Categories; His Psychology; His Ethical Doctrines; Origin of the Epithet "Peripatetic."

Aristotle, who was a pupil of this (Plato), reduced philosophy into an art, and was distinguished rather for his proficiency in logical science, supposing as the elements of all things substance and accident; that there is one substance underlying all things, but nine accidents,—namely, quantity, quality, relation, where, when, possession, posture, action, passion; and that substance is of some such description as God, man, and each of the beings that can fall under a similar denomination. But in regard of accidents, quality is seen in, for instance, white, black; and quantity, for instance two cubits, three cubits; and relation, for instance father, son; and where, for instance at Athens, Megara; and when, for instance during the tenth Olympiad; and possession, for instance to have acquired; and action, for instance to write, and in general to evince any practical powers; and posture, for instance to lie down; and passion, for instance to be struck. He also supposes that some things have means, but that others are without means, as we have declared concerning Plato likewise. And in most points, he is in agreement with Plato, except the opinion concerning soul. For Plato affirms it to be immortal, but Aristotle that it involves permanence; and after these things, that this also vanishes in the fifth body, which he supposes, along with the other four (elements), —viz., fire, and earth, and water, and air,—to be a something more subtle (than these), of the nature of spirit. Plato therefore says, that the only really good things are those pertaining to the soul, and that they are sufficient for happiness; whereas Aristotle introduces a threefold classification of good things, and asserts that the wise man is not perfect, unless there are present to him both the good things of the body and those extrinsic to it. The former are beauty, strength, vigor of the senses, soundness; while the things extrinsic (to the body) are wealth, nobility, glory, power, peace, friendship. And the inner qualities of the soul he classifies, as it was the opinion of Plato, under prudence, temperance, justice, fortitude. This (philosopher) also affirms that evils arise according to an opposition of the things that are good, and that they exist beneath the quarter around the moon but reach no farther beyond the moon; and that the soul of the entire world is immortal, and that the world itself is eternal, but that (the soul) in an individual, as we have before stated, vanishes (in the fifth body). This (speculator), then holding discussions in the Lyceum, drew up from time to time his system of philosophy; but Zeno (held his school) in the porch called Poecilé. And the followers of Zeno obtained their name from the place—that is, from Stoa— (i.e., a porch), being styled Stoics, whereas Aristotle's followers (were denominated) from their mode of employing themselves while teaching. For since they were accustomed walking about in the Lyceum to pursue their investigations, on this account they were called Peripatetics. These indeed, then, were the doctrines of Aristotle.

Chapter XVIII. —The Stoics; Their Superiority in Logic; Fatalists; Their Doctrine of Conflagrations.

The Stoics themselves also imparted growth to philosophy, in respect of a greater development of the art of syllogism, and included almost everything under definitions, both Chrysippus and Zeno being coincident in opinion on this point. And they likewise supposed God to be the one originating principle of all things, being a body of the utmost refinement, and that His providential care pervaded everything; and these speculators were positive about the existence of fate everywhere, employing some such example as the following: that just as a dog, supposing him attached to a car, if indeed he is disposed to follow, both is drawn, or follows voluntarily, making an exercise also of free power, in combination with necessity, that is, fate; but if he may not be disposed to follow, he will altogether be coerced to do so. And the same, of course, holds good in the case of men. For though not willing to follow, they will altogether be compelled to enter upon what has been decreed for them. (The Stoics), however, assert that the soul abides after death, but that it is a body, and that such is formed from the refrigeration of the surrounding atmosphere; wherefore, also, that it was called psyche (i.e., soul). And they acknowledge likewise, that there is a transition of souls from one body to another, that is, for those souls for whom this migration has been destined. And they accept the doctrine, that there will be a conflagration, a purification of this world, some say the entire of it, but others a portion, and that (the world) itself is undergoing partial destruction; and this all but corruption, and the generation from it of another world, they term purgation. And they assume the existence of all bodies, and that body does not pass-through body, but that a refraction takes place, and that all things involve plenitude, and that there is no vacuum. The foregoing are the opinions of the Stoics also.

Chapter XIX. —Epicurus; Adopts the Democritic Atomism; Denial of Divine Providence; The Principle of His Ethical System.

Epicurus, however, advanced an opinion almost contrary to all. He supposed, as originating principles of all things, atoms and vacuity. He considered vacuity as the place that would contain the things that will exist, and atoms the matter out of which all things could be formed; and that from the concourse of atoms both the Deity derived existence, and all the elements, and all things inherent in them, as well as animals and other (creatures); so that nothing was generated or existed, unless it be from atoms. And he affirmed that these atoms were composed of extremely small particles, in which there could not exist either a point or a sign, or any division; wherefore also he called them atoms. Acknowledging the Deity to be eternal and incorruptible, he says that God has providential care for nothing, and that there is no such thing at all as providence or fate, but that all things are made by chance. For that the Deity reposed in the intermundane spaces, (as they) are thus styled by him; for outside the world he determined that there is a certain habitation of God, denominated "the intermundane spaces," and that the Deity surrendered Himself to pleasure, and took His ease in the midst of supreme happiness; and that neither has He any concerns of business, nor does He devote His attention to them. As a consequence, on these opinions, he also propounded his theory concerning wise men, asserting that the end of wisdom is pleasure. Different persons, however, received the term "pleasure" in different acceptations; for some (among the Gentiles understood) the passions, but others the satisfaction resulting from virtue. And he concluded that the souls of men are dissolved along with their bodies, just as also they were produced along with them, for that they are blood, and that when this has gone forth or been altered, the entire man perishes; and in keeping with this tenet, (Epicurus maintained) that there are neither trials in Hades, nor tribunals of justice; so that whatsoever any one may commit in this life, that, provided he may escape detection, he is altogether beyond any liability of trial (for it in a future state). In this way, then, Epicurus also formed his opinions.

Chapter XX. —The Academics; Difference of Opinion Among Them.

And another opinion of the philosophers was called that of the Academics, on account of those holding their discussions in the Academy, of whom the founder Pyrrho, from whom they were called Pyrrhonean philosophers, first introduced the notion of the incomprehensibility of all things, so as to (be ready to) attempt an argument on either side of a question, but not to assert anything for certain; for that there is nothing of things intelligible or sensible true, but that they appear to men to be so; and that all substance is in a state of flux and change, and never continues in the same (condition). Some followers, then, of the Academics say that one ought not to declare an opinion on the principle of anything, but simply making the attempt to give it up; whereas others subjoined the formulary "not rather" (this than that), saying that the fire is not rather fire than anything else. But they did not declare what this is, but what sort it is.

Chapter XXI. —The Brachmans; Their Mode of Life; Ideas of Deity; Different Sorts Of; Their Ethical Notions.

But there is also with the Indians a sect composed of those philosophizing among the Brachmans. They spend a contented existence, abstain both from living creatures and all cooked food, being satisfied with fruits; and not gathering these from the trees, but carrying off those that have fallen to the earth. They subsist upon them, drinking the water of the river Tazabena. But they pass their life naked, affirming that the body has been constituted a covering to the soul by the Deity. These affirm that God is light, not such as one sees, nor such as the sun and fire; but to them the Deity is discourse, not that which finds expression in articulate sounds, but that of the knowledge through which the secret mysteries of nature are perceived by the wise. And this light which they say is discourse, their god, they assert that the Brachmans only know on account of their alone rejecting all vanity of opinion which is the soul's ultimate covering. These despise death, and always in their own peculiar language call God by the name which we have mentioned previously, and they send up hymns (to him). But neither are there women among them, nor do they beget children. But they who aim at a life similar to these, after they have crossed over to the country on the opposite side of the river, continue to reside there, returning no more; and these also are called Brachmans. But they do not pass their life similarly, for there are also in the place women, of whom those that dwell there are born, and in turn beget children. And this discourse which they name God they assert to be corporeal, and enveloped in a body outside himself, just as if one were wearing a sheep's skin, but that on divesting himself of body that he would appear clear to the eye. But the Brachmans say that there is a conflict in the body that surrounds them, (and they consider that the body is for them full of conflicts); in opposition to which, as if marshalled for battle against enemies, they contend, as we have already explained. And they say that all men are captive to their own congenital struggles, viz., sensuality and inchastity, gluttony, anger, joy, sorrow, concupiscence, and such like. And he who has reared a trophy over these, alone goes to God; wherefore the Brachmans deify Dandamis, to whom Alexander the Macedonian paid a visit, as one who had proved victorious in the bodily conflict. But they bear down on Calanus as having profanely withdrawn from their philosophy. But the Brachmans, putting off the body, like fishes jumping out of water into the pure air, behold the sun.

Chapter XXII. —The Druids; Progenitors of Their System.

And the Celtic Druids investigated to the very highest point the Pythagorean philosophy, after Zamolxis, by birth a Thracian, a servant of Pythagoras, became to them the originator of this discipline. Now after the death of Pythagoras, Zamolxis, repairing thither, became to them the originator of this philosophy. The Celts esteem these as prophets and seers, on account of their foretelling to them certain (events), from calculations and numbers by the Pythagorean art; on the methods of which very art also we shall not keep silence, since also from these some have presumed to introduce heresies; but the Druids resort to magical rites likewise.

Chapter XXIII. —Hesiod; The Nine Muses; The Hesiodic Cosmogony; The Ancient Speculators, Materialists; Derivative Character of the Heresies from Heathen Philosophy.

But Hesiod the poet asserts himself also that he thus heard from the Muses concerning nature, and that the Muses are the daughters of Jupiter. For when for nine nights and days together, Jupiter, through excess of passion, had uninterruptedly lain with Mnemosyne, that Mnemosyne conceived in one womb those nine Muses, becoming pregnant with one during each night. Having then summoned the nine Muses from Pieria, that is, Olympus, he exhorted them to undergo instruction: —

"How first both gods and earth were made,
And rivers, and boundless deep, and ocean's surge,
And glittering stars, and spacious heaven above;
How they grasped the crown and shared the glory,
And how at first they held the many-valed Olympus.
These (truths), ye Muses, tell me of, saith he,
From first, and next which of them first arose.
Chaos, no doubt, the very first, arose; but next
Wide-stretching Earth, ever the throne secure of all
Immortals, who hold the peaks of white Olympus;
And breezy Tartarus in wide earth's recess;
And Love, who is most beauteous of the gods immortal,
Chasing care away from all the gods and men,
Quells in breasts the mind and counsel sage.
But Erebus from Chaos and gloomy Night arose;

And, in turn, from Night both Air and Day were born;
But primal Earth, equal to self in sooth begot
The stormy sky to veil it round on every side,
Ever to be for happy gods a throne secure.
And forth she brought the towering hills, the pleasant haunts
Of nymphs who dwell throughout the woody heights.
And also barren Sea begat the surge-tossed
Flood, apart from luscious Love; but next
Embracing Heaven, she Ocean bred with eddies deep,
And Cæus, and Crius, and Hyperian, and Iapetus,
And Thia, and Rhea, and Themis, and Mnemosyne,
And gold-crowned Phœbe, and comely Tethys.
But after these was born last the wiley Cronus,
Fiercest of sons; but he abhorred his blooming sire,
And in turn the Cyclops bred, who owned a savage breast."

And all the rest of the giants from Cronus, Hesiod enumerates, and somewhere afterwards that Jupiter was born of Rhea. All these, then, made the foregoing statements in their doctrine regarding both the nature and generation of the universe. But all, sinking below what is divine, busied themselves concerning the substance of existing things, being astonished at the magnitude of creation, and supposing that it constituted the Deity, each speculator selecting in preference a different portion of the world; failing, however, to discern the God and maker of these.

The opinions, therefore, of those who have attempted to frame systems of philosophy among the Greeks, I consider that we have sufficiently explained; and from these the heretics, taking occasion, have endeavored to establish the tenets that will be after a short time declared. It seems, however, expedient, that first explaining the mystical rites and whatever imaginary doctrines some have laboriously framed concerning the stars, or magnitudes, to declare these; for heretics likewise, taking occasion from them, are considered by the multitude to utter prodigies. Next in order we shall elucidate the feeble opinions advanced by these.

Books II. And III. Are Awanting.

Book IV.

Chapter I.—System of the Astrologers; Sidereal Influence; Configuration of the Stars.

But in each zodiacal sign they call limits of the stars those in which each of the stars, from any one quarter to another, can exert the greatest amount of influence; in regard of which there is among them, according to their writings, no mere casual divergency of opinion. But they say that the stars are attended as if by satellites when they are in the midst of other stars, in continuity with the signs of the Zodiac; as if, when any particular star may have occupied the first portions of the same sign of the Zodiac, and another the last, and another those portions in the middle, that which is in the middle is said to be guarded by those holding the portions at the extremities. And they are said to look upon one another, and to be in conjunction with one another, as if appearing in a triangular or quadrangular figure. They assume, therefore, the figure of a triangle, and look upon one another, which have an intervening distance extending for three zodiacal signs; and they assume the figure of a square those which have an interval extending for two signs. But as the underlying parts sympathize with the head, and the head with the underlying parts, so also things terrestrial with superlunar objects. But there is of these a certain difference and want of sympathy, so that they do not involve one and the same point of juncture.

Chapter II. —Doctrines Concerning Æons; The Chaldean Astrology; Heresy Derivable from It.

Employing these (as analogies), Euphrates the Peratic, and Acembes the Carystian, and the rest of the crowd of these (speculators), imposing names different from the doctrine of the truth, speak of a sedition of Æons, and of a revolt of good powers over to evil (ones), and of the concord of good with wicked (Æons), calling them Toparchai and Proastioi, and very many other names. But the entire of this heresy, as attempted by them, I shall explain and refute when we come to treat of the subject of these (Æons). But now, lest anyone suppose the opinions propounded by the Chaldeans respecting astrological doctrine to be trustworthy and secure, we shall not hesitate to furnish a brief refutation respecting these, establishing that the futile art is calculated both to deceive and blind the soul indulging in vain expectations, rather than to profit it. And we urge our case with these, not according to any experience of the art, but from knowledge based on practical principles. Those who have cultivated the art, becoming disciples of the Chaldeans, and communicating mysteries as if strange and astonishing to men, having changed the names (merely), have from this source concocted their heresy. But since, estimating the astrological art as a powerful one, and availing themselves of the testimonies adduced by its patrons, they wish to gain reliance for their own attempted conclusions, we shall at present, as it has seemed expedient, prove the astrological art to be untenable, as our intention next is to invalidate also the Peratic system, as a branch growing out of an unstable root.

Chapter III. —The Horoscope the Foundation of Astrology; Indiscoverability of the Horoscope; Therefore the Futility of the Chaldean Art.

The originating principle, and, as it were, foundation, of the entire art, is fixing the horoscope. For from this are derived the rest of the cardinal points, as well as the declinations and ascensions, the triangles and squares, and the configurations of the stars in accordance with these; and from all these the predictions are taken. Whence, if the horoscope be removed, it necessarily follows that neither any celestial object is recognizable in the meridian, or at the horizon, or in the point of the heavens opposite the meridian; but if these be not comprehended, the entire system of the Chaldeans vanishes along with (them). But that the sign of the horoscope is indiscoverable by them, we may show by a variety of arguments. For in order that this (horoscope) may be found, it is first requisite that the (time of) birth of the person falling under inspection should be firmly fixed; and secondly, that the horoscope which is to signify this should be infallible; and thirdly, that the ascension of the zodiacal sign should be observed with accuracy. For from (the moment) of birth the ascension of the zodiacal sign rising in the heaven should be closely watched, since the

Chaldeans, determining (from this) the horoscope, frame the configuration of the stars in accordance with the ascension (of the sign); and they term this—disposition, in accordance with which they devise their predictions. But neither is it possible to take the birth of persons, falling under consideration, as I shall explain, nor is the horoscope infallible, nor is the rising zodiacal sign apprehended with accuracy.

How it is, then, that the system of the Chaldeans is unstable, let us now declare. Having, then, previously marked it out for investigation, they draw the birth of persons falling under consideration from, unquestionably, the depositing of the seed, and (from) conception or from parturition. And if one will attempt to take (the horoscope) from conception, the accurate account of this is incomprehensible, the time (occupied) passing quickly, and naturally (so). For we are not able to say whether conception takes place upon the transference of the seed or not. For this can happen even as quick as thought, just also as leaven, when put into heated jars, immediately is reduced to a glutinous state. But conception can also (take place) after a lapse of duration. For there being an interval from the mouth of the womb to the fundament, where physicians say conceptions take place, it is altogether the nature of the seed deposited to occupy some time in traversing this interval. The Chaldeans, therefore, being ignorant of the quantity of duration to a nicety, never will comprehend the (moment of) conception; the seed at one time being injected straight forward, and falling at one spot upon actual parts of the womb well-disposed for conception, and at another time dropping into it dispersedly, and being collected into one place by uterine energies. Now, while these matters are unknown, (namely), as to when the first takes place, and when the second, and how much time is spent in that particular conception, and how much in this; while, I say, ignorance on these points prevails on the part of these (astrologers), an accurate comprehension of conception is put out of the question. And if, as some natural philosophers have asserted, the seed, remaining stationary first, and undergoing alteration in the womb, then enters the (womb's) opened blood-vessels, as the seeds of the earth sink into the ground; from this it will follow, that those who are not acquainted with the quantity of time occupied by the change, will not be aware of the precise moment of conception either. And, moreover, as women differ from one another in the other parts of the body, both as regards energy and in other respects, so also (it is reasonable to suppose that they differ from one another) in respect of energy of womb, some conceiving quicker, and others slower. And this is not strange, since also women, when themselves compared with themselves, at times are observed having a strong disposition towards conception, but at times with no such tendency. And when this is so, it is impossible to say with accuracy when the deposited seed coalesces, in order that from this time the Chaldeans may fix the horoscope of the birth.

Chapter IV. —Impossibility of Fixing the Horoscope; Failure of an Attempt to Do This at the Period of Birth.

For this reason, it is impossible to fix the horoscope from the (period of) conception. But neither can this be done from (that of) birth. For, in the first place, there exists the difficulty as to when it can be declared that there is a birth; whether it is when the fetus begins to incline towards the orifice, or when it may project a little, or when it may be borne to the ground. Neither is it in each of these cases possible to comprehend the precise moment of parturition, or to define the time. For also on account of disposition of soul, and on account of suitableness of body, and on account of choice of the parts, and on account of experience in the midwife, and other endless causes, the time is not the same at which the fetus inclines towards the orifice, when the membranes are ruptured, or when it projects a little, or is deposited on the ground; but the period is different in the case of different individuals. And when the Chaldeans are not able definitely and accurately to calculate this, they will fail, as they ought, to determine the period of emergence.

That, then, the Chaldeans profess to be acquainted with the horoscope at the periods of birth, but in reality, do not know it, is evident from these considerations. But that neither is their horoscope infallible, it is easy to conclude. For when they allege that the person sitting beside the woman in travail at the time of parturition gives, by striking a metallic rim, a sign to the Chaldean, who from an elevated place is contemplating the stars, and he, looking towards heaven, marks down the rising zodiacal sign; in the first place, we shall prove to them, that when parturition happens indefinitely, as we have shown a little before, neither is it easy to signify this (birth) by striking the metallic rim. However, grant that the birth is comprehensible, yet neither is it possible to signify this at the exact time; for as the noise of the metallic plate is capable of being divided by a longer time and one protracted, in reference to perception, it happens that the sound is carried to the height (with proportionate delay). And the following proof may be observed in the case of those felling timber at a distance. For a sufficiently long time after the descent of the axe, the sound of the stroke is heard, so that it takes a longer time to reach the listener. And for this reason, therefore, it is not possible for the Chaldeans accurately to take the time of the rising zodiacal sign, and consequently the time when one can make the horoscope with truth. And not only does more time seem to elapse after parturition, when he who is sitting beside the woman in labor strikes the metallic plate, and next after the sound reaches the listener, that is, the person who has gone up to the elevated position; but also, while he is glancing around and looking to ascertain in which of the zodiacal signs is the moon, and in which appears each of the rest of the stars, it necessarily follows that there is a different position in regard of the stars, the motion of the pole whirling them on with incalculable velocity, before what is seen in the heavens is carefully adjusted to the moment when the person is born.

Chapter V.—Another Method of Fixing the Horoscope at Birth; Equally Futile; Use of the Clepsydra in Astrology; The Predictions of the Chaldeans Not Verified.

In this way, the art practiced by the Chaldeans will be shown to be unstable. Should anyone, however, allege that, by questions put to him who inquires from the Chaldeans, the birth can be ascertained, not even by this plan is it possible to arrive at the precise period. For if, supposing any such attention on their part in reference to their art to be on record, even these do not attain—as we have proved—unto accuracy either, how, we ask, can an unsophisticated individual comprehend precisely the time of parturition, in order that the Chaldean acquiring the requisite information from this person may set the horoscope correctly? But neither from the appearance of the horizon will the rising star seem the same everywhere; but in one place its declination will be supposed to be the horoscope, and in another the ascension (will be thought) the horoscope, according as the places come into view, being either lower or higher. Wherefore, also, from this quarter an accurate prediction will not appear, since many may be born throughout the entire world at the same hour, each from a different direction observing the stars.

But the supposed comprehension (of the period of parturition) by means of clepsydras is likewise futile. For the contents of the jar will not flow out at the same time when it is full as when it is half empty; yet, according to their own account, the pole itself by a single impulse is whirled along at an equable velocity. If, however, evading the argument, they should affirm that they do not take the time precisely, but as it happens in any particular latitude, they will be refuted almost by the sidereal influences themselves. For those who have been born at the same time do not spend the same life, but some, for example, have been made kings, and others have grown old in fetters. There has been born nonequal, at all events, to Alexander the Macedonian, though many were brought forth along with him throughout the earth; (and) none equal to the philosopher Plato. Wherefore the Chaldean, examining the time of the birth in any particular latitude, will not be able to say accurately, whether a person born at this time will be prosperous. Many, I take it, born at this time, have been unfortunate, so that the similarity according to dispositions is futile.

Having, then, by different reasons and various methods, refuted the ineffectual mode of examination adopted by the Chaldeans, neither shall we omit this, namely, to show that their predictions will eventuate in inexplicable difficulties. For if, as the mathematicians assert, it is necessary that one born under the barb of Sagittarius' arrow should meet with a violent death, how was it that so many myriads of the Barbarians that fought with the Greeks at Marathon or Salamis were simultaneously slaughtered? For unquestionably there was not the same horoscope in the case, at all events, of them all. And again, it is said that one born under the urn of Aquarius will suffer shipwreck: (yet) how is it that so many of the Greeks that returned from Troy were overwhelmed in the deep around the indented shores of Eubœa? For it is incredible that all, distant from one another by a long interval of duration, should have been born under the urn of Aquarius. For it is not reasonable to say, that frequently, for one whose fate it was to be destroyed in the sea, all who were with him in the same vessel should perish. For why should the doom of this man subdue the (destinies) of all? Nay, but why, on account of one for whom it was allotted to die on land, should not all be preserved?

Chapter VI. —Zodiacal Influence; Origin of Sidereal Names.

But since also they frame an account concerning the action of the zodiacal signs, to which they say the creatures that are procreated are assimilated, neither shall we omit this: as, for instance, that one born in Leo will be brave; and that one born in Virgo will have long straight hair, be of a fair complexion, childless, modest. These statements, however, and others similar to them, are rather deserving of laughter than serious consideration. For, according to them, it is possible for no Ethiopian to be born in Virgo; otherwise, he would allow that such a one is white, with long straight hair and the rest. But I am rather of opinion, that the ancients imposed the names of received animals upon certain specified stars, for the purpose of knowing them better, not from any similarity of nature; for what have the seven stars, distant one from another, in common with a bear, or the five stars with the head of a dragon?—in regard of which Aratus says:—

"But two his temples, and two his eyes, and one beneath Reaches the end of the huge monster's jaw."

Chapter VII. —Practical Absurdity of the Chaldaic Art; Development of the Art.

In this manner also, that these points are not deserving so much labor, is evident to those who prefer to think correctly, and do not attend to the bombast of the Chaldeans, who consign monarchs to utter obscurity, by perfecting cowardice in them, and rouse private individuals to dare great exploits. But if anyone, surrendering himself to evil, is guilty of delinquency, he who has been thus deceived does not become a teacher to all whom the Chaldeans are disposed to mislead by their mistakes. (Far from it); (these astrologers) impel the minds (of their dupes, as they would have them), into endless perturbation, (when) they affirm that a configuration of the same stars could not return to a similar position, otherwise than by the renewal of the Great Year, through a space of seven thousand seven hundred and seventy and seven years. How then, I ask, will human observation for one birth be able to harmonize with so many ages; and this not once, (but oftentimes, when a destruction of the world, as some have stated, would intercept the progress of this Great Year; or a terrestrial convulsion, though partial, would utterly break the continuity of the historical tradition)? The Chaldaic art must necessarily be refuted by a greater number of arguments, although we have been reminding (our readers) of it on account of other circumstances, not peculiarly on account of the art itself.

Since, however, we have determined to omit none of the opinions advanced by Gentile philosophers, on account of the notorious knavery of the heretics, let us see what they also say who have attempted to propound doctrines concerning magnitudes,—who, observing the fruitless labor of the majority (of speculators), where each after a different fashion coined his own falsehoods and attained celebrity, have ventured to make some greater assertion, in order that they might be highly magnified by those who mightily extol their contemptible lies. These suppose the existence of circles, and measures, and triangles, and squares, both in twofold and threefold array. Their argumentation, however, in regard of this matter, is extensive, yet it is not necessary in reference to the subject which we have taken in hand.

Chapter VIII. —Prodigies of the Astrologers; System of the Astronomers; Chaldean Doctrine of Circles; Distances of the Heavenly Bodies.

I reckon it then sufficient to declare the prodigies detailed by these men. Wherefore, employing condensed accounts of what they affirm, I shall turn my attention to the other points (that remain to be considered). Now they make the following statements. The Creator communicated pre-eminent power to the orbital motion of the identical and similar (circle), for He permitted the revolution of it to be one and indivisible; but after dividing this internally into six parts, (and thus having formed) seven unequal circles, according to each interval of a twofold and threefold dimension, He commanded, since there were three of each, that the circles should travel in orbits contrary to one another, three indeed (out of the aggregate of seven) being whirled along with equal velocity, and four of them with a speed dissimilar to each other and to the remaining three, yet (all) according to a definite principle. For he affirms that the mastery was communicated to the orbital motion of the same (circle), not only since it embraces the motion of the other, that, is, the erratic stars, but because also it possesses so great mastery, that is, so great power, that even it leads round, along with itself, by a peculiar strength of its own, those heavenly bodies—that is, the erratic stars—that are whirled along in contrary directions from west to east, and, in like manner, from east to west.

And he asserts that this motion was allowed to be one and indivisible, in the first place, inasmuch as the revolutions of all the fixed stars were accomplished in equal periods of time and were not distinguished according to greater or less portions of duration. In the next place, they all present the same phase as that which belongs to the outermost motion, whereas the erratic stars have been distributed into greater and varying periods for the accomplishment of their movements, and into unequal distances from earth. And he asserts that the motion in six parts of the other has been distributed probably into seven circles. For as many as are sections of each (circle)—I allude to monads of the sections—become segments; for example, if the division be by one section, there will be two segments; if by two, three segments; and so, if anything be cut into six parts, there will be seven segments. And he says that the distances of these are alternately arranged both in double and triple order, there being three of each, —a principle which, he has attempted to prove, holds good of the composition of the soul likewise, as depending upon the seven numbers. For among them there are from the monad three double (numbers), viz., 2, 4, 8, and three triple ones, viz., 3, 9, 27. But the diameter of Earth is 80,108 stadii; and the perimeter of Earth, 250,543 stadii; and the distance also from the surface of the Earth to the lunar circle, Aristarchus the Samian computes at 8,000,178 stadii, but Apollonius 5,000,000, whereas Archimedes computes it at 5,544,130. And from the lunar to solar circle, (according to the last authority,) are 50,262,065 stadii; and from this to the circle of Venus, 20,272,065 stadii; and from this to the circle of Mercury, 50,817,165 stadii; and from this to the circle of Mars, 40,541,108 29 stadii; and from this to the circle of Jupiter, 20,275,065 stadii; and from this to the circle of Saturn, 40,372,065 stadii; and from this to the Zodiac and the furthest periphery, 20,082,005 stadii.

Chapter IX. —Further Astronomic Calculations.

The mutual distances of the circles and spheres, and the depths, are rendered by Archimedes. He takes the perimeter of the Zodiac at 447,310,000 stadii; so that it follows that a straight line from the center of the Earth to the most outward superficies would be the sixth of the aforesaid number, but that the line from the surface of the Earth on which we tread to the Zodiac would be a sixth of the aforesaid number, less by four myriads of stadii, which is the distance from the center of the Earth to its surface. And from the circle of Saturn to the Earth he says the distance is 2,226,912,711 stadii; and from the circle of Jupiter to Earth, 202,770,646 stadii; and from the circle of Mars to Earth, 132,418,581. From the Sun to Earth, 121,604,454; and from Mercury to the Earth, 526,882,259; and from Venus to Earth, 50,815,160.

Chapter X.—Theory of Stellar Motion and Distance in Accordance with Harmony.

Concerning the Moon, however, a statement has been previously made. The distances and profundities of the spheres Archimedes thus renders; but a different declaration regarding them has been made by Hipparchus; and a different one still by Apollonius the mathematician. It is sufficient, however, for us, following the Platonic opinion, to suppose twofold and threefold distances from one another of the erratic stars; for the doctrine is thus preserved of the composition of the universe out of harmony, on concordant principles in keeping with these distances. The numbers, however, advanced by Archimedes, and the accounts rendered by the rest concerning the distances, if they be not on principles of symphony,—that is, the double and triple (distances) spoken of by Plato,—but are discovered independent of harmonies, would not preserve the doctrine of the formation of the universe according to harmony. For it is neither credible nor possible that the distances of these should be both contrary to some reasonable plan, and independent of harmonious and proportional principles, except perhaps only the Moon, on account of wanings and the shadow of the Earth, in regard also of the distance of which alone—that is, the lunar (planet) from earth—one may trust Archimedes. It will, however, be easy for those who, according to the Platonic dogma itself, adopt this distance to comprehend by numerical calculation (intervals) according to what is double and triple, as Plato requires, and the rest of the distances. If then, according to Archimedes, the Moon is distant from the surface of the Earth 5,544,130 stadii, by increasing these numbers double and triple, (it will be) easy to find also the distances of the rest, as if subtracting one part of the number of stadii which the Moon is distant from the Earth.

But because the rest of the numbers—those alleged by Archimedes concerning the distance of the erratic stars—are not based on principles of concord, it is easy to understand—that is, for those who attend to the matter—how the numbers are mutually related, and on what principles they depend. That, however, they should not be in harmony and symphony—I mean those that are parts of the world which consists according to harmony—this is impossible. Since, therefore, the first number which the Moon is distant from the earth is 5,544,130, the second number which the Sun is distant from the Moon being 50,272,065, subsists by a greater computation than ninefold. But the higher number in reference to this, being 20,272,065, is (comprised) in a greater computation than half. The number, however, superior to this, which is 50,817,165, is contained in a greater computation than half. But the number superior to this, which is 40,541,108, is contained in a less computation than two-fifths. But the number superior to this, which is 20,275,065, is contained in a greater computation than half. The final number, however, which is 40,372,065, is comprised in a less computation than double.

Chapter XI. —Theory of the Size of the Heavenly Bodies in Accordance with Numerical Harmonies.

These (numerical) relations, therefore, the greater than ninefold, and less than half, and greater than double, and less than two-fifths, and greater than half, and less than double, are beyond all symphonies, from which not any proportionate or harmonic system could be produced. But the whole world, and the parts of it, are in all respects similarly framed in conformity with proportion and harmony. The proportionate and harmonic relations, however, are preserved—as we have previously stated—by double and triple intervals. If, therefore, we consider Archimedes reliable in the case of only the first distance, that from the Moon to the Earth, it is easy also to find the rest (of the intervals), by multiplying (them) by double and treble. Let then the distance, according to Archimedes, from Earth to Moon be 5,544,130 stadii; there will therefore be the double number of this of stadii which the Sun is distant from the Moon, viz. 11,088,260. But the Sun is distant from the Earth 16,632,390 stadii;

and Venus is likewise distant from the Sun 16,632,390 stadii, but from the Earth 33,264,780 stadii; and Mercury is distant from Venus 22,176,520 stadii, but from Earth 55,441,300 stadii; and Mars is distant from Mercury 49,897,170 stadii, and from Earth 105,338,470 stadii; and Jupiter is distant from Mars 44,353,040 stadii, but from Earth 149,691,510 stadii; Saturn is distant from Jupiter 149,691,510 stadii, but from Earth 299,383,020 stadii.

Chapter XII. —Waste of Mental Energy in the Systems of the Astrologers.

Who will not feel astonishment at the exertion of so much deep thought with so much toil? This Ptolemy, however—a careful investigator of these matters—does not seem to me to be useless; but only this grieves (one), that being recently born, he could not be of service to the sons of the giants, who, being ignorant of these measures, and supposing that the heights of heaven were near, endeavored in vain to construct a tower. And so, if at that time he were present to explain to them these measures, they would not have made the daring attempt ineffectually. But if anyone profess not to have confidence in this (astronomer's calculations), let him by measuring be persuaded (of their accuracy); for in reference to those incredulous on the point, one cannot have a more manifest proof than this. O, pride of vain-toiling soul, and incredible belief, that Ptolemy should be considered pre-eminently wise among those who have cultivated similar wisdom!

Chapter XIII. —Mention of the Heretic Colarbasus; Alliance Between Heresy and the Pythagorean Philosophy.

Certain, adhering partly to these, as if having propounded great conclusions, and supposed things worthy of reason, have framed enormous and endless heresies; and one of these is Colarbasus, who attempts to explain religion by measures and numbers. And others there are (who act) in like manner, whose tenets we shall explain when we commence to speak of what concerns those who give heed to Pythagorean calculation as possible; and uttering vain prophecies, hastily assume as secure the philosophy by numbers and elements. Now certain (speculators), appropriating similar reasonings from these, deceive unsophisticated individuals, alleging themselves endued with foresight; sometimes, after uttering many predictions, happening on a single fulfilment, and not abashed by many failures, but making their boast in this one. Neither shall I pass over the witless philosophy of these men; but, after explaining it, I shall prove that those who attempt to form a system of religion out of these (aforesaid elements), are disciples of a school weak and full of knavery.

Chapter XIV. —System of the Arithmeticians; Predictions Through Calculations; Numerical Roots; Transference of These Doctrines to Letters; Examples in Particular Names; Different Methods of Calculation; Prescience Possible by These.

Those, then, who suppose that they prophesy by means of calculations and numbers, and elements and names, constitute the origin of their attempted system to be as follows. They affirm that there is a root of each of the numbers; in the case of thousands, so many monads as there are thousands: for example, the root of six thousand, six monads; of seven thousand, seven monads; of eight thousand, eight monads; and in the case of the rest, in like manner, according to the same (proportion). And in the case of hundreds, as many hundreds as there are, so many monads are the root of them: for instance, of seven hundred there are seven hundreds; the root of these is seven monads: of six hundred, six hundreds; the root of these, six monads. And it is similar respecting decades: for of eighty (the root is) eight monads; and of sixty, six monads; of forty, four monads; of ten, one monad. And in the case of monads, the monads themselves are a root: for instance, of nine, nine; of eight, eight; of seven, seven. In this way, also, ought we therefore to act in the case of the elements (of words), for each letter has been arranged according to a certain number: for instance, the letter n according to fifty monads; but of fifty monads five is the root, and the root of the letter n is (therefore) five. Grant that from some name we take certain roots of it. For instance, (from) the name Agamemnon, there is of the a, one monad; and of the g, three monads; and of the other a, one monad; of the m, four monads; of the e, five monads; of the m, four monads; of the n, five monads; of the (long) o, eight monads; of the n, five monads; which, brought together into one series, will be 1, 3, 1, 4, 5, 4, 5, 8, 5; and these added together make up 36 monads. Again, they take the roots of these, and they become three in the case of the number thirty, but actually six in the case of the number six. The three and the six, then, added together, constitute nine; but the root of nine is nine: therefore, the name Agamemnon terminates in the root nine. Let us do the same with another name—Hector. The name (H)ector has five letters—e, and k, and t, and o, and r. The roots of these are 5, 2, 3, 8, 1; and these added together make up 19 monads. Again, of the ten the root is one; and of the nine, nine; which added together make up ten: the root of ten is a monad. The name Hector, therefore, when made the subject of computation, has formed a root, namely a monad. It would, however, be easier to conduct the calculation thus: Divide the ascertained roots from the letters—as now in the case of the name Hector we have found nineteen monads—into nine, and treat what remains over as roots. For example, if I divide 19 into 9, the remainder is 1, for 9 times 2 are 18, and there is a remaining monad: for if I subtract 18 from 19, there is a remaining monad; so that the root of the name Hector will be a monad. Again, of the name Patroclus these numbers are roots: 8, 1, 3, 1, 7, 2, 3, 7, 2; added together, they make up 34 monads. And of these the remainder is 7 monads: of the 30, 3; and of the 4, 4. Seven monads, therefore, are the root of the name Patroclus.

    Those, then, that conduct their calculations according to the rule of the number nine, take the ninth part of the aggregate number of roots, and define what is left over as the sum of the roots. They, on the other hand, (who conduct their calculations) according to the rule of the number seven, take the seventh (part of the aggregate number of roots); for example, in the case of the name Patroclus, the aggregate in the matter of roots is 34 monads. This divided into seven parts makes four, which (multiplied into each other) are 28. There are six remaining monads; (so that a person using this method) says, according to the rule of the number seven, that six monads are the root of the name Patroclus. If, however, it be 43, (six) taken seven times, he says, are 42, for seven times six are 42, and one is the remainder. A monad, therefore, is the root of the number 43, according to the rule of the number seven. But one ought to observe if the assumed number, when divided, has no remainder; for example, if from any name, after having added together the roots, I find, to give an instance, 36 monads. But the number 36 divided into nine makes exactly 4 enneads; for nine times 4 are 36, and nothing is over. It is evident, then, that the actual root is 9. And again, dividing the number forty-five, we find nine and nothing over—for nine times five are forty-five, and nothing remains; (wherefore) in the case of such they assert the root itself to be nine. And as regards the number seven, the case is similar: if, for example we divide 28 into 7, we have nothing over; for seven times four are 28, and nothing remains; (wherefore) they say that seven is the root. But when one computes names, and finds the same letter occurring twice, he calculates it once; for instance, the name Patroclus has the pa twice, and the o twice: they therefore calculate the a once and the o once. According to this, then, the roots will be 8, 1, 3, 1, 7, 2, 3, 2, and added together they make 27 monads; and the root of the name will be, according to the rule of the number nine, nine itself, but according to the rule of the number seven, six. In like manner, (the name) Sarpedon, when made the subject of calculation, produces as a root, according to the rule of the number nine, two monads. Patroclus, however, produces nine monads; Patroclus gains the victory. For when one number is uneven, but the other even, the uneven number, if it is larger, prevails. But again, when there is an even number, eight, and five an uneven number, the eight prevails, for it is larger. If, however, there were two numbers, for example, both of them even, or both of them odd, the smaller prevails. But how does (the name) Sarpedon, according to the rule of the number nine, make two monads, since the letter (long) o is omitted? For when there may be in a name the letter (long) o and (long) e, they leave out the (long) o, using one letter, because they say both are equipollent; and the same must not be computed twice over, as has been above declared. Again, (the name) Ajax makes four monads; (but the name) Hector, according to the rule of the ninth number, makes one monad. And the tetrad is even, whereas the monad odd. And in the case of such, we say, the greater prevails—Ajax gains the victory. Again, Alexander and Menelaus (may be adduced as examples). Alexander has a proper name (Paris). But Paris, according to the rule of the number nine, makes four monads; and Menelaus, according to the rule of the number nine, makes nine monads. The nine, however, conquer the four (monads): for it has been declared, when the one number is odd and the other even, the greater prevails; but when both are even or both odd, the less (prevails). Again, Amycus and Polydeuces (may be adduced as examples). Amycus, according to the rule of the number nine, makes two monads, and Polydeuces, however, seven: Polydeuces gains the victory. Ajax and Ulysses contended at the funeral games. Ajax, according to the rule of the number nine, makes four monads; Ulysses, according to the rule of the number nine, (makes) eight. Is there, then, not any annexed, and (is there) not a proper name for Ulysses? for he has gained the victory. According to the numbers, no doubt, Ajax is victorious, but history hands down the name of Ulysses as the conqueror. Achilles and

Hector (may be adduced as examples). Achilles, according to the rule of the number nine, makes four monads; Hector one: Achilles gains the victory. Again, Achilles and Asteropæus (are instances). Achilles makes four monads, Asteropæus three: Achilles conquers. Again, Menelaus and Euphorbus (may be adduced as examples). Menelaus has nine monads, Euphorbus eight: Menelaus gains the victory. Some, however, according to the rule of the number seven, employ the vowels only, but others distinguish by themselves the vowels, and by themselves the semi-vowels, and by themselves the mutes; and, having formed three orders, they take the roots by themselves of the vowels, and by themselves of the semi-vowels, and by themselves of the mutes, and they compare each apart. Others, however, do not employ even these customary numbers, but different ones: for instance, as an example, they do not wish to allow that the letter p has as a root 8 monads, but 5, and that the (letter) x (si) has as a root four monads; and turning in every direction, they discover nothing sound. When, however, they contend about the second (letter), from each name they take away the first letter; but when they contend about the third (letter), they take away two letters of each name, and calculating the rest, compare them.

Chapter XV. —Quibbles of the Numerical Theorists; The Art of the Frontispicists (Physiognomy); Connection of This Art with Astrology; Type of Those Born Under Aries.

I think that there has been clearly expounded the mind of arithmeticians, who, by means of numbers and of names, suppose that they interpret life. Now I perceive that these, enjoying leisure, and being trained in calculation, have been desirous that, through the art delivered to them from childhood, they, acquiring celebrity, should be styled prophets. And they, measuring the letters up (and) down, have wandered into trifling. For if they fail, they say, in putting forward the difficulty, perhaps this name was not a family one, but imposed, as also lighting in the instance they argue in the case of (the names) Ulysses and Ajax. Who, taking occasion from this astonishing philosophy, and desirous of being styled "Heresiarch," will not be extolled?

But since, also, there is another more profound art among the all-wise speculators of the Greeks—to whom heretical individuals boast that they attach themselves as disciples, on account of their employing the opinions of these (ancient philosophers) in reference to the doctrines attempted (to be established) by themselves, as shall a little afterwards be proved; but this is an art of divination, by examination of the forehead or rather, I should say, it is madness: yet we shall not be silent as regards this (system). There are some who ascribe to the stars figures that mold the ideas and dispositions of men, assigning the reason of this to births (that have taken place) under particular stars; they thus express themselves: Those who are born under Aries will be of the following kind: long head, red hair, contracted eyebrows, pointed forehead, eyes grey and lively, drawn cheeks, long-nosed, expanded nostrils, thin lips, tapering chin, wide mouth. These, he says, will partake of the following nature: cautious, subtle, perspicuous, prudent, indulgent, gentle, over-anxious, persons of secret resolves fitted for every undertaking, prevailing more by prudence than strength, deriders for the time being, scholars, trustworthy, contentious, quarrelers in a fray, concupiscent, inflamed with unnatural lust, reflective, estranged from their own homes, giving dissatisfaction in everything, accusers, like madmen in their cups, scorners, year by year losing something serviceable in friendship through goodness; they, in the majority of cases, end their days in a foreign land.

Chapter XVI. —Type of Those Born Under Taurus.

Those, however, who are born in Taurus will be of the following description: round head, thick hair, broad forehead, square eyes, and large black eyebrows; in a white man, thin veins, sanguine, long eyelids, coarse huge ears, round mouths, thick nose, round nostrils, thick lips, strong in the upper parts, formed straight from the legs. The same are by nature pleasing, reflective, of a goodly disposition, devout, just, uncouth, complaisant, laborers from twelve years, quarrelsome, dull. The stomach of these is small, they are quickly filled, forming many designs, prudent, niggardly towards themselves, liberal towards others, beneficent, of a slow body: they are partly sorrowful, heedless as regards friendship, useful on account of mind, unfortunate.

Chapter XVII. —Type of Those Born Under Gemini.

Those who are born in Gemini will be of the following description: red countenance, size not very large, evenly proportioned limbs, black eyes as if anointed with oil, cheeks turned down, and large mouth, contracted eyebrows; they conquer all things, they retain whatever possessions they acquire, they are extremely rich, penurious, miserly of what is peculiarly their own, profuse in the pleasures of women, equitable, musical, liars. And the same by nature are learned, reflective, inquisitive, arriving at their own decisions, concupiscent, sparing of what belongs to themselves, liberal, quiet, prudent, crafty, they form many designs, calculators, accusers, importunate, not prosperous, they are beloved by the fair sex, merchants; as regards friendship, not to any considerable extent useful.

Chapter XVIII. —Type of Those Born Under Cancer.

Those born in Cancer are of the following description: size not large, hair like a dog, of a reddish color, small mouth, round head, pointed forehead, grey eyes, sufficiently beautiful, limbs somewhat varying. The same by nature are wicked, crafty, proficient in plans, insatiable, stingy, ungracious, illiberal, useless, forgetful; they neither restore what is another's, nor do they ask back what is their own; as regards friendship, useful.

Chapter XIX. —Type of Those Born Under Leo.

Those born in Leo are of the following description: round head, reddish hair, huge wrinkled forehead, coarse ears, large development of neck, partly bald, red complexion, grey eyes, large jaws, coarse mouth, gross in the upper parts, huge breast, the under limbs tapering. The same are by nature persons who allow nothing to interfere with their own decision, pleasing themselves, irascible, passionate, scorners, obstinate, forming no design, not loquacious, indolent, making an improper use of leisure, familiar, wholly abandoned to pleasures of women, adulterers, immodest, in faith untrue, importunate, daring, penurious, spoliators, remarkable; as regards fellowship, useful; as regards friendship, useless.

Chapter XX. —Type of Those Born Under Virgo.

Those born in Virgo are of the following description: fair appearance, eyes not large, fascinating, dark, compact eyebrows, cheerful, swimmers; they are, however, slight in frame, beautiful in aspect, with hair prettily adjusted, large forehead, prominent nose. The same by nature are docile, moderate, intelligent, sportive, rational, slow to speak, forming many plans; in regard of a favor, importunate; gladly observing everything; and well-disposed pupils, they master whatever they learn; moderate, scorners, victims of unnatural lusts, companionable, of a noble soul, despisers, careless in practical matters, attending to instruction, more honorable in what concerns others than what relates to themselves; as regards friendship, useful.

Chapter XXI. —Type of Those Born Under Libra.

Those born in Libra will be of the following description: hair thin, drooping, reddish and longish, forehead pointed (and) wrinkled, fair compact eyebrows, beautiful eyes, dark pupils, long thin ears, head inclined, wide mouth. The same by nature are intelligent, God☐fearing, communicative to one another, traders, toilers, not retaining gain, liars, not of an amiable disposition, in business or principle true, free-spoken, beneficent, illiterate, deceivers, friendly, careless, (to whom it is not profitable to do any act of injustice); they are scorners, scoffers, satirical, illustrious, listeners, and nothing succeeds with these; as regards friendship, useful.

Chapter XXII. —Type of Those Born Under Scorpio.

Those born in Scorpio are of the following description: a maidenish countenance, comely, pungent, blackish hair, well-shaped eyes, forehead not broad, and sharp nostril, small contracted ears, wrinkled foreheads, narrow eyebrows, drawn cheeks. The same by nature are crafty, sedulous, liars, communicating their particular designs to no one, of a deceitful spirit, wicked, scorners, victims to adultery, well-grown, docile; as regards friendship, useless.

Chapter XXIII. —Type of Those Born Under Sagittarius.

Those born in Sagittarius will be of the following description: great length, square forehead, profuse eyebrows, indicative of strength, well-arranged projection of hair, reddish (in complexion). The same by nature are gracious, as educated persons, simple, beneficent; given to unnatural lusts, companionable, toil-worn, lovers, beloved, jovial in their cups, clean, passionate, careless, wicked; as regards friendship, useless; scorners, with noble souls, insolent, crafty; for fellowship, useful.

Chapter XXIV. —Type of Those Born Under Capricorn.

Those born in Capricorn will be of the following description: reddish body, projection of greyish hair, round mouth, eyes as of an eagle, contracted brows, open forehead, somewhat bald, in the upper parts of the body endued with more strength. The same by nature are philosophic, scorners, and scoffers at the existing state of things, passionate, persons that can make concessions, honorable, beneficent, lovers of the practice of music, passionate in their cups, mirthful, familiar, talkative, given to unnatural lusts, genial, amiable, quarrelsome lovers, for fellowship well disposed.

Chapter XXV. —Type of Those Born Under Aquarius.

Those born in Aquarius will be of the following description: square in size, of a diminutive body; sharp, small, fierce eyes; imperious, ungenial, severe, readily making acquisitions, for friendship and fellowship well disposed; moreover, for maritime enterprises they make voyages, and perish. The same by nature are taciturn, modest, sociable, adulterers, penurious, practiced in business, tumultuous, pure, well-disposed, honorable, large eyebrows; frequently they are born in the midst of trifling events, but (in after life) follow a different pursuit; though they may have shown kindness to anyone, still no one returns them thanks.

Chapter XXVI. —Type of Those Born Under Pisces.

Those born in Pisces will be of the following description: of moderate dimensions, pointed forehead like fishes, shaggy hair, frequently they become soon grey. The same by nature are of exalted soul, simple, passionate, penurious, talkative; in the first period of life they will be drowsy; they are desirous of managing business by themselves, of high repute, venturesome, emulous, accusers, changing their locality, lovers, dancers; for friendship, useful.

Chapter XXVII. —Futility of This Theory of Stellar Influence.

Since, therefore, we have explained the astonishing wisdom of these men, and have not concealed their overwrought art of divination by means of contemplation, neither shall I be silent as regards (undertakings) in the case of which those that are deceived act foolishly. For, comparing the forms and dispositions of men with names of stars, how impotent their system is! For we know that those originally conversant with such investigations have called the stars by names given in reference to propriety of signification and facility for future recognition. For what similarity is there of these (heavenly bodies) with the likeness of animals, or what community of nature as regards conduct and energy (is there in the two cases), that one should allege that a person born in Leo should be irascible, and one born in Virgo moderate, or one born in Cancer wicked, but that those born in...

Chapter XXVIII. —System of the Magicians; Incantations of Demons; Secret Magical Rites.

... And (the sorcerer), taking (a paper), directs the inquirer to write down with water whatever questions he may desire to have asked from the demons. Then, folding up the paper, and delivering it to the attendant, he sends him away to commit it to the flames, that the ascending smoke may waft the letters to demons. While, however, the attendant is executing this order, (the sorcerer) first removes equal portions of the paper, and on some more parts of it he pretends that demons write in Hebrew characters. Then burning an incense of the Egyptian magicians, termed Cyphi, he takes these (portions of paper) away, and places them near the incense. But (that paper) which the inquirer happens to have written (upon), having placed on the coals, he has burned. Then (the sorcerer), appearing to be borne away under divine influence, (and) hurrying into a corner (of the house), utters a loud and harsh cry, and unintelligible to all...and orders all those present to enter, crying out (at the same time), and invoking Phryn, or some other demon. But after passing into the house, and when those that were present stood side by side, the sorcerer, flinging the attendant upon a bed, utters to him several words, partly in the Greek, and partly, as it were, the Hebrew language, (embodying) the customary incantations employed by the magicians. (The attendant), however, goes away to make the inquiry. And within (the house), into a vessel full of water (the sorcerer) infusing copperas mixture, and melting the drug, having with it sprinkled the paper that forsooth had (the characters upon it) obliterated, he forces the latent and concealed letters to come once more into light; and by these he ascertains what the inquirer has written down. And if one writes with copperas mixture likewise, and having ground a gall nut, use its vapor as a fumigator, the concealed letters would become plain. And if one writes with milk, (and) then scorch the paper, and scraping it, sprinkle and rub (what is thus scraped off) upon the letters traced with the milk, these will become plain. And urine likewise, and sauce of brine, and juice of euphorbia, and of a fig, produce a similar result. But when (the sorcerer) has ascertained the question in this mode, he makes provision for the manner in which he ought to give the reply. And next he orders those that are present to enter, holding laurel branches and shaking them, and uttering cries, and invoking the demon Phryn. For also it becomes these to invoke him; and it is worthy that they make this request from demons, which they do not wish of themselves to put forward, having lost their minds. The confused noise, however, and the tumult, prevent them directing attention to those things which it is supposed (the sorcerer) does in secret. But what these are, the present is a fair opportunity for us to declare.

Considerable darkness, then, prevails. For the (sorcerer) affirms that it is impossible for mortal nature to behold divine things, for that to hold converse (with these mysteries) is sufficient. Making, however, the attendant lie down (upon the couch), head foremost, and placing by each side two of those little tablets, upon which had been inscribed in, forsooth, Hebrew characters, as it were names of demons, he says that (a demon) will deposit the rest in their ears. But this (statement) is requisite, in order that some instrument may be placed beside the ears of the attendant, by which it is possible that he signify everything which he chooses. First, however, he produces a sound that the (attendant) youth may be terrified; and secondly, he makes a humming noise; then, thirdly, he speaks through the instrument what he wishes the youth to say, and remains in expectation of the issue of the affair; next, he makes those present remain still, and directs the (attendant) to signify, what he has heard from the demons. But the instrument that is placed beside his ears is a natural instrument, viz., the windpipe of long-necked cranes, or storks, or swans. And if none of these is at hand, there are also some different artificial instruments (employed); for certain pipes of brass, ten in number, (and) fitting into one another, terminating in a narrow point, are adapted (for the purpose), and through these is spoken into the ear whatsoever the (magician) wishes. And the youth hearing these (words) with terror as uttered by demons, when ordered, speaks them out. If anyone, however, putting around a stick a moist hide, and having dried it and drawn it together, close it up, and by removing the rod fashion the hide into the form of a pipe, he attains a similar end. Should any of these, however, be not at hand, he takes a book, and, opening it inside, stretches it out as far as he think requisite, (and thus) achieves the same result.

But if he knows beforehand that one is present who is about to ask a question, he is the more ready for all (contingencies). If, however, he may also previously ascertain the question, he writes (it) with the drug, and, as being prepared, he is considered more skillful, on account of having clearly written out what is (about) being asked. If, however, he is ignorant of the question, he forms conjectures, and puts forth something capable of a doubtful and varied interpretation, in order that the oracular response, being originally unintelligible, may serve for numerous purposes, and in the issue of events the prediction may be considered correspondent with what actually occurs. Next, having filled a vessel with water, he puts down (into it) the paper, as if uninscribed, at the same time infusing along with it copperas mixture. For in this way the paper written upon floats upwards (to the surface), bearing the response. Accordingly, there ensue frequently to the attendant formidable fancies, for also he strikes blows plentifully on the terrified (bystanders). For, casting incense into the fire, he again operates after the following method. Covering a lump of what are called "fossil salts" with Etruscan wax and dividing the piece itself of incense into two parts, he throws in a grain of salt; and again joining (the piece) together, and placing it on the burning coals, he leaves it there. And when this is consumed, the salts, bounding upwards, create the impression of, as it were, a strange vision taking place. And the dark-blue dye which has been deposited in the incense produces a blood-red flame, as we have already declared. But (the sorcerer) makes a scarlet liquid, by mixing wax with alkanet, and, as I said, depositing the wax in the incense. And he makes the coals be moved, placing underneath powdered alum; and when this is dissolved and swells up like bubbles, the coals are moved.

Chapter XXIX. —Display of Different Eggs.

But different eggs they display after this manner. Perforating the top at both ends, and extracting the white, (and) having again dipped it, throw in some minium and some writing ink. Close, however, the openings with refined scrapings of the eggs, smearing them with fig-juice.

### Chapter XXX. —Self-Slaughter of Sheep.

By those who cause sheep to cut off their own heads, the following plan is adopted. Secretly smearing the throat (of the animal) with a cauterizing drug, he places a sword near, and leaves it there. The sheep, desirous of scratching himself, rushes against the blade, and in the act of rubbing is slaughtered, while the head is almost severed from the trunk. There is, however, a compound of the drug, bryony and salt and squills, made up in equal parts. In order that the person bringing the drug may escape notice, he carries a box with two compartments constructed of horn, the visible one of which contains frankincense, but the secret one (the aforesaid) drug. He, however, likewise insinuates into the ears of the sheep about to meet death quicksilver; but this is a poisonous drug.

### Chapter XXXI. —Method of Poisoning Goats.

And if one smear the ears of goats over with cerate, they say that they expire a little afterwards, by having their breathing obstructed. For this to them is the way—as these affirm—of their drawing their breath in an act of respiration. And a ram, they assert, dies, if one bends back (its neck) opposite the sun. And they accomplish the burning of a house, by daubing it over with the juice of a certain fish called dactylus. And this effect, which it has by reason of the seawater, is very useful. Likewise foam of the ocean is boiled in an earthen jar along with some sweet ingredients; and if you apply a lighted candle to this while in a seething state, it catches the fire and is consumed; and (yet though the mixture) be poured upon the head, it does not burn it at all. If, however, you also smear it over with heated resin, it is consumed far more effectually. But he accomplishes his object better still, if also he takes some sulfur.

Chapter XXXII. —Imitations of Thunder, and Other Illusions.

Thunder is produced in many ways; for stones very numerous and unusually large, being rolled downwards along wooden planks, fall upon plates of brass, and cause a sound similar to thunder. And also, around the thin plank with which carders thicken cloth, they coil a thin rope; and then drawing away the cord with a whirr, they spin the plank round, and in its revolution it emits a sound like thunder. These farces, verily, are played off thus.

There are, however, other practices which I shall explain, which those who execute these ludicrous performances estimate as great exploits. Placing a cauldron full of pitch upon burning coals, when it boils up, (though) laying their hands down upon it, they are not burned; nay, even while walking on coals of fire with naked feet, they are not scorched. But also setting a pyramid of stone on a hearth, (the sorcerer) makes it get on fire, and from the mouth it disgorges a volume of smoke, and that of a fiery description. Then also putting a linen cloth upon a pot of water, throwing on (at the same time) a quantity of blazing coals, (the magician) keeps the linen cloth unconsumed. Creating also darkness in the

## The Refutation of All Heresies

house, (the sorcerer) alleges that he can introduce gods or demons; and if any requires him to show Æsculapius, he uses an invocation couched in the following words:—

"The child once slain, again of Phœbus deathless made,
I call to come, and aid my sacrificial rites;
Who, also, once the countless tribes of fleeting dead,
In ever-mournful homes of Tartarus wide,
The fatal billow breasting, and the inky flood
Surmounting, where all of mortal mould must float,
Torn, beside the lake, with endless grief and woe,
Thyself didst snatch from gloomy Proserpine.
Or whether the seat of Holy Thrace thou haunt, or lovely Pergamos, or besides Ionian Epidaurus,
The chief of seers, O happy God, invites thee here."

Chapter XXXIII. —The Burning Æsculapius; Tricks with Fire.

But after he discontinues uttering these jests, a fiery Æsculapius appears upon the floor. Then, placing in the midst a pot full of water, he invokes all the deities, and they are present. For anyone who is by, glancing into the pot, will behold them all, and Diana leading on her baying hounds. We shall not, however, shrink from narrating the account (of the devices) of these men, how they attempt (to accomplish their jugglery). For (the magician) lays his hand upon the cauldron of pitch, which is in, as it were, a boiling state; and throwing in (at the same time) vinegar and nitre and moist pitch, he kindles a fire beneath the cauldron. The vinegar, however, being mixed along with the nitre, on receiving a small accession of heat, moves the pitch, so as to cause bubbles to rise to the surface, and afford the mere semblance of a seething (pot). The (sorcerer), however, previously washes his hands frequently in brine; the consequence being, that the contents of the cauldron do not in any wise, though in reality boiling, burn him very much. But if, having smeared his hands with a tincture of myrtle and nitre and myrrh, along with vinegar, he washes them in brine frequently, he is not scorched: and he does not burn his feet, provided he smear them with isinglass and a salamander.

As regards, however, the burning like a taper of the pyramid, though composed of stone, the cause of this is the following. Chalky earth is fashioned into the shape of a pyramid, but its color is that of a milk-white stone, and it is prepared after this fashion. Having anointed the piece of clay with plenty of oil, and put it upon coals, and baked it, by smearing it afresh, and scorching it a second and third time, and frequently, (the sorcerer) contrives that it can be burned, even though he should plunge it in water; for it contains in itself abundance of oil. The hearth, however, is spontaneously kindled, while the magician pours out a libation, by having lime instead of ashes burning underneath, and refined frankincense and a large quantity of tow, and a bundle of anointed tapers and of gall nuts, hollow within, and supplied with (concealed) fire. And after some delay, (the sorcerer) makes (the pyramid) emit smoke from the mouth, by both putting fire in the gall nut, and encircling it with tow, and blowing into the mouth. The linen cloth, however, that has been placed round the cauldron, (and) on which he deposits the coals, on account of the underlying brine, would not be burned; besides, that it has itself been washed in brine, and then smeared with the white of an egg, along with moist alum. And if, likewise, one mix in these the juice of houseleek along with vinegar, and for a long time previously smear it (with this preparation), after being washed in this drug, it continues altogether fire-proof.

Chapter XXXIV. —The Illusion of the Sealed Letters; Object in Detailing These Juggleries.

After, then, we have succinctly explained the powers of the secret arts practiced among these (magicians), and have shown their easy plan for the acquisition of knowledge, neither are we disposed to be silent on the following point, which is a necessary one,— how that, loosing the seals, they restore the sealed letters, with the actual seals themselves. Melting pitch, resin, and sulfur, and moreover asphalt, in equal parts, (and) forming the ointment into a figure, they keep it by them. When, however, it is time to loose a small tablet, smearing with oil their tongue, next with the latter anointing the seal, (and) heating the drug with a moderate fire, (the sorcerers) place it upon the seal; and they leave it there until it has acquired complete consistence, and they use it in this condition as a seal. But they say, likewise, that wax itself with fir-wood gum possesses a similar potency, as well as two parts of mastich with one part of dry asphalt. But sulfur also by itself effects the purpose tolerably well, and flower of gypsum strained with water, and of gum. Now this (last mixture) certainly answers most admirably also for sealing molten lead. And that which is accomplished by the Tuscan wax, and refuse of resin, and pitch, and asphalt, and mastich, and powdered spar, all being boiled together in equal parts, is superior to the rest of the drugs which I have mentioned, while that which is affected by the gum is not inferior. In this manner, then, also, they attempt to loose the seals, endeavoring to learn the letters written within.

These contrivances, however, I hesitated to narrate in this book, perceiving the danger lest, perchance, any knavish person, taking occasion (from my account), should attempt (to practice these juggleries). Solicitude, however, for many young persons, who could be preserved from such practices, has persuaded me to teach and publish, for security's sake, (the foregoing statements). For although one person may make use of these for gaining instruction in evil, in this way somebody else will, by being instructed (in these practices), be preserved from them. And the magicians themselves, corrupters of life, will be ashamed in plying their art. And learning these points that have been previously elucidated by us, they will possibly be restrained from their folly. But that this seal may not be broken, let me seal it with hog's lard and hair mixed with wax.

Chapter XXXV. —The Divination by a Cauldron; Illusion of Fiery Demons; Specimen of a Magical Invocation.

But neither shall I be silent respecting that piece of knavery of these (sorcerers), which consists in the divination by means of the cauldron. For, making a closed chamber, and anointing the ceiling with cyanus for present use, they introduce certain vessels of cyanus, and stretch them upwards. The cauldron, however, full of water, is placed in the middle on the ground; and the reflection of the cyanus falling upon it, presents the appearance of heaven. But the floor also has a certain concealed aperture, on which the cauldron is laid, having been (previously, supplied with a bottom of crystal, while itself is composed of stone. Underneath, however, unnoticed (by the spectators), is a compartment, into which the accomplices, assembling, appear invested with the figures of such gods and demons as the magician wishes to exhibit. Now the dupe, beholding these, becomes astonished at the knavery of the magician, and subsequently believes all things that are likely to be stated by him. But (the sorcerer) produces a burning demon, by tracing on the wall whatever figure he wishes, and then covertly smearing it with a drug mixed according to this manner, viz., of Laconian and Zacynthian asphalt, — while next, as if under the influence of prophetic frenzy, he moves the lamp towards the wall. The drug, however, is burned with considerable splendor. And that a fiery Hecate seems to career through air, he contrives in the mode following. Concealing a certain accomplice in a place which he wishes, (and) taking aside his dupes, he persuades them (to believe himself), alleging that he will exhibit a flaming demon riding through the air. Now he exhorts them immediately to keep their eyes fixed until they see the flame in the air, and that (then), veiling themselves, they should fall on their face until he himself should call them; and after having given them these instructions, he, on a moonless night, in verses speaks thus: —

"Infernal, and earthy, and supernal Bombo, come! Saint of streets, and brilliant one, that strays by night;
Foe of radiance, but friend and mate of gloom;
In howl of dogs rejoicing, and in crimson gore,
Wading 'mid corpses through tombs of lifeless dust,

Panting for blood; with fear convulsing men.
Gorgo, and Mormo, and Luna, and of many shapes,
Come, propitious, to our sacrificial rites!"

Chapter XXXVI. —Mode of Managing an Apparition.

And while speaking these words, fire is seen borne through the air; but the (spectators) being horrified at the strange apparition, (and) covering their eyes, fling themselves speechless to earth. But the success of the artifice is enhanced by the following contrivance. The accomplice whom I have spoken of as being concealed, when he hears the incantation ceasing, holding a kite or hawk enveloped with tow, sets fire to it and releases it. The bird, however, frightened by the flame, is borne aloft, and makes a (proportionably) quicker flight, which these deluded persons beholding, conceal themselves, as if they had seen something divine. The winged creature, however, being whirled round by the fire, is borne whithersoever chance may have it, and burns now the houses, and now the courtyards. Such is the divination of the sorcerers.

Chapter XXXVII. —Illusive Appearance of the Moon.

And they make moon and stars appear on the ceiling after this manner. In the central part of the ceiling, having fastened a mirror, placing a dish full of water equally (with the mirror) in the central portion of the floor, and setting in a central place likewise a candle, emitting a faint light from a higher position than the dish,—in this way, by reflection, (the magician) causes the moon to appear by the mirror. But frequently, also, they suspend on high from the ceiling, at a distance, a drum, but which, being covered with some garment, is concealed by the accomplice, in order that (the heavenly body) may not appear before the (proper) time. And afterwards placing a candle (within the drum), when the magician gives the signal to the accomplice, he removes so much of the covering as may be sufficient for effecting an imitation representing the figure of the moon as it is at that particular time. He smears, however, the luminous parts of the drum with cinnabar and gum; and having pared around the neck and bottom of a flagon of glass ready behind, he puts a candle in it, and places around it some of the requisite contrivances for making the figures shine, which some one of the accomplices has concealed on high; and on receiving the signal, he throws down from above the contrivances, so to make the moon appear descending from the sky.

And the same result is achieved by means of a jar in sylvan localities. For it is by means of a jar that the tricks in a house are performed. For having set up an altar, subsequently is (placed upon it) the jar, having a lighted lamp; when, however, there are a greater number of lamps, no such sight is displayed. After then the enchanter invokes the moon, he orders all the lights to be extinguished, yet that one be left faintly burning; and then the light, that which streams from the jar, is reflected on the ceiling, and furnishes to those present a representation of the moon; the mouth of the jar being kept covered for the time which it would seem to require, in order that the representation of full moon should be exhibited on the ceiling.

Chapter XXXVIII. —Illusive Appearance of the Stars.

But the scales of fishes—for instance, the seahorse—cause the stars to appear to be the scales being steeped in a mixture of water and gum, and fastened on the ceiling at intervals.

Chapter XXXIX. —Imitation of an Earthquake.

The sensation of an earthquake they cause in such a way, as that all things seem set in motion; ordure of a weasel burned with a magnet upon coals (has this effect).

Chapter XL. —Trick with the Liver.

And they exhibit a liver seemingly bearing an inscription in this manner. With the left hand he writes what he wishes, appending it to the question, and the letters are traced with gall juice and strong vinegar. Then taking up the liver, retaining it in the left hand, he makes some delay, and then it draws away the impression, and it is supposed to have, as it were, writing upon it.

Chapter XLI. —Making a Skull Speak.

But putting a skull on the ground, they make it speak in this manner. The skull itself is made out of the caul of an ox; and when fashioned into the requisite figure, by means of Etruscan wax and prepared gum, (and) when this membrane is placed around, it presents the appearance of a skull, which seems to all to speak when the contrivance operates; in the same manner as we have explained in the case of the (attendant) youths, when, having procured the windpipe of a crane, or some such long-necked animal, and attaching it covertly to the skull, the accomplice utters what he wishes. And when he desires (the skull) to become invisible, he appears as if burning incense, placing around, (for this purpose,) a quantity of coals; and when the wax catches the heat of these, it melts, and in this way the skull is supposed to become invisible.

Chapter XLII. —The Fraud of the Foregoing Practices; Their Connection with Heresy.

These are the deeds of the magicians, and innumerable other such (tricks) there are which work on the credulity of the dupes, by fair balanced words, and the appearance of plausible acts. And the heresiarchs, astonished at the art of these (sorcerers), have imitated them, partly by delivering their doctrines in secrecy and darkness, and partly by advancing (these tenets) as their own. For this reason, being desirous of warning the multitude, we have been the more painstaking, in order not to omit any expedient practiced by the magicians, for those who may be disposed to be deceived. We have been however drawn, not unreasonably, into a detail of some of the secret (mysteries) of the sorcerers, which are not very requisite, to be sure, in reference to the subject taken in hand; yet, for the purpose of guarding against the villainous and incoherent art of magicians, may be supposed useful. Since, therefore, as far as delineation is feasible, we have explained the opinions of all (speculators), exerting especial attention towards the elucidation of the opinions introduced as novelties by the heresiarchs; (opinions) which, as far as piety is concerned, are futile and spurious, and which are not, even among themselves, perhaps deemed worthy of serious consideration. (Having pursued this course of inquiry), it seems expedient that, by means of a compendious discourse, we should recall to the (reader's) memory statements that have been previously made.

Chapter XLIII. —Recapitulation of Theologies and Cosmogonies; System of the Persians; Of the Babylonians; The Egyptian Notion of Deity; Their Theology Based on a Theory of Numbers; Their System of Cosmogony.

Among all those who throughout the earth, as philosophers and theologians, have carried on investigations, has prevailed diversity of opinion278 concerning the Deity, as to His essence or nature. For some affirm Him to be fire, and some spirit, and some water, while others say that He is earth. And each of the elements labors under some deficiency, and one is worsted by the other. To the wise men of the world, this, however, has occurred, which is obvious to persons possessing intelligence; (I mean) that, beholding the stupendous works of creation, they were confused respecting the substance of existing things, supposing that these were too vast to admit of deriving generation from another, and at the same time (asserting) that neither the universe itself is God. As far as theology was concerned, they declared, however, a single cause for things that fall under the cognizance of vision, each supposing the cause which he adjudged the most reasonable; and so, when gazing on the objects made by God, and on those which are the most insignificant in comparison with His overpowering majesty, not, however, being able to extend the mind to the magnitude of God as He really is, they deified these (works of the external world).

But the Persians, supposing that they had penetrated more within the confines of the truth, asserted that the Deity is luminous, a light contained in air. The Babylonians, however, affirmed that the Deity is dark, which very opinion also appears the consequence of the other; for day follows night, and night day. Do not the Egyptians, however, who suppose themselves more ancient than all, speak of the power of the Deity? (This power they estimate by) calculating these intervals of the parts (of the zodiac; and, as if) by a most divine inspiration, they asserted that the Deity is an indivisible monad, both itself generating itself, and that out of this were formed all things. For this, say they, being unbegotten, produces the succeeding numbers; for instance, the monad, superadded into itself, generates the duad; and in like manner, when superadded (into duad, triad, and so forth), produces the triad and tetrad, up to the decade, which is the beginning and end of numbers. Wherefore it is that the first and tenth monad is generated, on account of the decade being equipollent, and being reckoned for a monad, and (because) this multiplied ten times will become a hundred, and again becomes a monad, and the hundred multiplied ten times will produce a thousand, and this will be a monad. In this manner also the thousand multiplied ten times make up the full sum of a myriad; in like manner will it be a monad. But by a comparison of indivisible quantities, the kindred numbers of the monad comprehend 3, 5, 7, 9.

There is also, however, a more natural relation of a different number to the monad, according to the arrangement of the orbit of six days' duration, (that is), of the duad, according to the position and division of even numbers. But the kindred number is 4 and 8. These, however, taking from the monad of the numbers an idea of virtue, progressed up to the four elements; (I allude), of course, to spirit, and fire, and water, and earth. And out of these having made the world, (God) framed it an ermaphrodite, and allocated two elements for the upper hemisphere, namely spirit and fire; and this is styled the hemisphere of the monad, (a hemisphere) beneficent, and ascending, and masculine. For, being composed of small particles, the monad soars into the most rarified and purest part of the atmosphere; and the other two elements, earth and water, being more gross, he assigned to the duad; and this is termed the descending hemisphere, both feminine and mischievous. And likewise, again, the upper elements themselves, when compared one with another, comprise in one another both male and female for fruitfulness and increase of the whole creation. And the fire is masculine, and the spirit feminine. And again, the water is masculine, and the earth feminine. And so, from the beginning fire consorted with spirit, and water with earth. For as the power of spirit is fire, so also that of earth is water...and the elements themselves, when computed and resolved by subtraction of enneads, terminate properly, some of them in the masculine number, and others of them in the feminine. And, again, the ennead is subtracted for this cause, because the three hundred and sixty parts of the entire (circle) consist of enneads, and for this reason the four regions of the world are circumscribed by ninety perfect parts. And light has been appropriated to the monad, and darkness to the duad, and life to light, according to nature, and death to the duad. And to life (has been appropriated) justice, and to death, injustice. Wherefore everything generated among masculine numbers is beneficent, while that (produced) among feminine (numbers) is mischievous. For instance, they pursue their calculations thus: monad—that we may commence from this—becomes 361, which (numbers) terminate in a monad by the subtraction of the ennead. In like manner, reckon thus: Duad becomes 605; take away the enneads, it ends in a duad, and each reverts into its own peculiar (function).

Chapter XLIV. —Egyptian Theory of Nature; Their Amulets.

For the monad, therefore, as being beneficent, they assert that there are consequently names ascending, and beneficent, and masculine, and carefully observed, terminating in an uneven number; whereas that those terminating in the even number have been supposed to be both descending, and feminine and malicious. For they affirm that nature is made up of contraries, namely bad and good, as right and left, light and darkness, night and day, life and death. And moreover, they make this assertion, that they have calculated the word "Deity," (and found that it reverts into a pentad with an ennead subtracted). Now this name is an even number, and when it is written down (on some material) they attach it to the body and accomplish cures by it. In this manner, likewise, a certain herb, terminating in this number, being similarly fastened around (the frame), operates by reason of a similar calculation of the number. Nay, even a doctor cures sickly people by a similar calculation. If, however, the calculation is contrary, it does not heal with facility. Persons attending to these numbers reckon as many as are homogeneous according to this principle; some, however, according to vowels alone; whereas others according to the entire number. Such also is the wisdom of the Egyptians, by which, as they boast, they suppose that they cognize the divine nature.

Chapter XLV. —Use of the Foregoing Discussions.

It appears, then, that these speculations also have been sufficiently explained by us. But since I think that I have omitted no opinion found in this earthly and groveling Wisdom, I perceive that the solicitude expended by us on these subjects has not been useless. For we observe that our discourse has been serviceable not only for a refutation of heresies, but also in reference to those who entertain these opinions. Now these, when they encounter the extreme care evinced by us, will even be struck with admiration of our earnestness, and will not despise our industry and condemn Christians as fools when they discern the opinions to which they themselves have stupidly accorded their belief. And furthermore, those who, desirous of learning, addict themselves to the truth, will be assisted by our discourse to become, when they have learned the fundamental principles of the heresies, more intelligent not only for the easy refutation of those who have attempted to deceive them, but that also, when they have ascertained the avowed opinions of the wise men, and have been made acquainted with them, that they shall neither be confused by them as ignorant persons would, nor become the dupes of certain individuals acting as if from some authority; nay, more than this, they shall be on their guard against those that are allowing themselves to become victims to these delusions.

Chapter XLVI. —The Astrotheosophists; Aratus Imitated by the Heresiarchs; His System of the Disposition of the Stars.

Having sufficiently explained these opinions, let us next pass on to a consideration of the subject taken in hand, in order that, by proving what we have determined concerning heresies, and by compelling their (champions) to return to these several (speculators) their peculiar tenets, we may show the heresiarchs destitute (of a system); and by proclaiming the folly of those who are persuaded (by these heterodox tenets), we shall prevail on them to retrace their course to the serene haven of the truth. In order, however, that the statements about to follow may seem clearer to the readers, it is expedient also to declare the opinions advanced by Aratus concerning the disposition of the stars of the heavens. (And this is necessary), inasmuch as some persons, assimilating these (doctrines) to those declared by the Scriptures, convert (the holy writings) into allegories, and endeavor to seduce the mind of those who give heed to their (tenets), drawing them on by plausible words into the admission of whatever opinions they wish, (and) exhibiting a strange marvel, as if the assertions made by them were fixed among the stars. They, however, gazing intently on the very extraordinary wonder, admirers as they are of trifles, are fascinated like a bird called the owl, which example it is proper to mention, on account of the statements that are about to follow. The animal (I speak of) is, however, not very different from an eagle, either in size or figure, and it is captured in the following way:— The hunter of these birds, when he sees a flock of them lighting anywhere, shaking his hands, at a distance pretends to dance, and so by little and little draws near the birds. But they, struck with amazement at the strange sight, are rendered unobservant of everything passing around them. But others of the party, who have come into the country equipped for such a purpose, coming from behind upon the birds, easily lay hold on them as they are gazing on the dancer.

Wherefore I desire that no one, astonished by similar wonders of those who interpret the (aspect of) heaven, should, like the owl, be taken captive. For the knavery practiced by such speculators may be considered dancing and silliness, but not truth. Aratus, therefore, expresses himself thus: —

"Just as many are they; hither and thither they roll
Day by day o'er heav'n, endless, ever, (that is, every star),
Yet this declines not even little; but thus exactly
E'er remains with axis fixed and poised in every part
Holds earth midway, and heaven itself around conducts."

Chapter XLVII. —Opinions of the Heretics Borrowed from Aratus.

Aratus says that there are in the sky revolving, that is, gyrating stars, because from east to west, and west to east, they journey perpetually, (and) in an orbicular figure. And he says that there revolves towards "The

Bears" themselves, like some stream of a river, an enormous and prodigious monster, (the) Serpent; and that this is what the devil says in the book of Job to the Deity, when (Satan) uses these words: "I have traversed earth under heaven, and have gone around (it)," that is, that I have been turned around, and thereby have been able to survey the worlds. For they suppose that towards the North Pole is situated the Dragon, the Serpent, from the highest pole looking upon all (the objects), and gazing on all the works of creation, in order that nothing of the things that are being made may escape his notice. For though all the stars in the firmament set, the pole of this (luminary) alone never sets, but, careering high above the horizon, surveys and beholds all things, and none of the works of creation, he says, can escape his notice.

"Where chiefly
Settings mingle and risings one with other."

(Here Aratus) says that the head of this (constellation) is placed. For towards the west and east of the two hemispheres is situated the head of the Dragon, in order, he says, that nothing may escape his notice throughout the same quarter, either of objects in the west or those in the east, but that the Beast may know all things at the same time. And near the head itself of the Dragon is the appearance of a man, conspicuous by means of the stars, which Aratus styles a wearied image, and like one oppressed with labor, and he is denominated "Engonasis." Aratus then affirms that he does not know what this toil is, and what this prodigy is that revolves in heaven. The heretics, however, wishing by means of this account of the stars to establish their own doctrines, (and) with more than ordinary earnestness devoting their attention to these (astronomic systems), assert that Engonasis is Adam, according to the commandment of God as Moses declared, guarding the head of the Dragon, and the Dragon (guarding) his heel. For so Aratus expresses himself: —

"The right-foot's track of the Dragon fierce possessing."

Chapter XLVIII. —Invention of the Lyre; Allegorizing the Appearance and Position of the Stars; Origin of the Phoenicians; The Logos Identified by Aratus with the Constellation Canis; Influence of Canis on Fertility and Life Generally.

And (Aratus) says that (the constellations) Lyra and Corona have been placed on both sides near him, — now I mean Engonasis,—but that he bends the knee, and stretches forth both hands, as if making a confession of sin. And that the lyre is a musical instrument fashioned by Logos while still altogether an infant, and that Logos is the same as he who is denominated Mercury among the Greeks. And Aratus, with regard to the construction of the lyre, observes: —

"Then, further, also near the cradle,
Hermes pierced it through, and said, Call it Lyre."

It consists of seven strings, signifying by these seven strings the entire harmony and construction of the world as it is melodiously constituted. For in six days the world was made, and (the Creator) rested on the seventh. If then, says (Aratus), Adam, acknowledging (his guilt) and guarding the head of the Beast, according to the commandment of the Deity, will imitate Lyra, that is, obey the Logos of God, that is, submit to the law, he will receive Corona that is situated near him. If, however, he neglects his duty, he shall be hurled downwards in company with the Beast that lies underneath, and shall have, he says, his portion with the Beast. And Engonasis seems on both sides to extend his hands, and on one to touch Lyra, and on the other Corona—and this is his confession; —so that it is possible to distinguish him by means of this (sidereal) configuration itself. But Corona nevertheless is plotted against, and forcibly drawn away by another beast, a smaller Dragon, which is the offspring of him who is guarded by the foot of Engonasis. A man also stands firmly grasping with both hands and dragging towards the space behind the Serpent from Corona; and he does not permit the Beast to touch Corona. though making a violent effort to do so. And Aratus styles him Anguitenens, because he restrains the impetuosity of the Serpent in his attempt to reach Corona. But Logos, he says, is he who, in the figure of a man, hinders the Beast from reaching Corona, commiserating him who is being plotted against by the Dragon and his offspring simultaneously.

These (constellations), "The Bears," however, he says, are two hebdomads, composed of seven stars, images of two creations. For the first creation, he affirms, is that according to Adam in labors, this is he who is seen "on his knees" (Engonasis). The second creation, however, is that according to Christ, by which we are regenerated; and this is Anguitenens, who struggles against the Beast, and hinders him from reaching Corona, which is reserved for the man. But "The Great Bear" is, he says, Helice, symbol of a mighty world towards which the Greeks steer their course, that is, for which they are being disciplined. And, wafted by the waves of life, they follow onwards, (having in prospect) some such revolving world or discipline or wisdom which conducts those back that follow in pursuit of such a world. For the term Helice seems to signify a certain circling and revolution towards the same points. There is likewise a certain other "Small Bear" (Cynosuris), as it were some image of the second creation—that formed according to God. For few, he says, there are that journey by the narrow path. But they assert that Cynosuris is narrow, towards which Aratus says that the Sidonians navigate. But Aratus has spoken partly of the Sidonians, (but means) the Phoenicians, on account of the existence of the admirable wisdom of the Phoenicians. The Greeks, however, assert that they are Phoenicians, who have migrated from (the shores of) the Red Sea into this country where they even at present dwell, for this is the opinion of Herodotus. Now Cynosura, he says, is this (lesser) Bear, the second creation; the one of limited dimensions, the narrow way, and not Helice. For he does not lead them back, but guides forward by a straight path, those that follow him being (the tail) of Canis. For Canis is the Logos, partly guarding and preserving the flock, that is plotted against by the wolves; and partly like a dog, hunting the beasts from the creation, and destroying them; and partly producing all things, and being what they express by the name "Cyon" (Canis), that is, generator. Hence it is said, Aratus has spoken of the rising of Canis, expressing himself thus: "When, however, Canis has risen, no longer do the crops miss." This is what he says: Plants that have been put into the earth up to the period of Canis' rising, frequently, though not having struck root, are yet covered with a profusion of leaves, and afford indications to spectators that they will be productive, and that they appear full of life, (though in reality) not having vitality in themselves from the root. But when the rising of Canis takes place, the living are separated from the dead by Canis; for whatsoever plants have not taken root, really undergo putrefaction. This Canis, therefore, he says, as being a certain divine Logos, has been appointed judge of quick and dead. And as (the influence of) Canis is observable in the vegetable productions of this world, so in plants of celestial growth—in men—is beheld the (power of the) Logos. From some such cause, then, Cynosura, the second creation, is set in the firmament as an image of a creation by the Logos. The Dragon, however, in the center reclines between the two creations, preventing a transition of whatever things are from the great creation to the small creation; and in guarding those that are fixed in the (great) creation, as for instance Engonasis, observing (at the same time) how and in what manner each is constituted in the small creation. And (the Dragon) himself is watched at the head, he says, by Anguitenens. This image, he affirms, is fixed in heaven, being a certain wisdom to those capable of discerning it. If, however, this is obscure, by means of some other image, he says the creation teaches (men) to philosophize, in regard to which Aratus has expressed himself thus: —

"Neither of Cepheus Iasidas are we the wretched brood."

Chapter XLIX. —Symbol of the Creature; And of Spirit; And of the Different Orders of Animals.

But Aratus says, near this (constellation) is Cepheus, and Cassiepea, and Andromeda, and Perseus, great lineaments of the creation to those who are able to discern them. For he asserts that Cepheus is Adam, Cassiepea Eve, Andromeda the soul of both of these, Perseus the Logos, winged offspring of Jove, and Cetos the plotting monster. Not to any of these, but to Andromeda only does he repair, who slays the Beast; from whom, likewise taking unto himself Andromeda, who had been delivered (and) chained to the Beast, the Logos—that is, Perseus—achieves, he says, her liberation. Perseus, however, is the winged axle that pierces both poles through the center of the earth and turns the world round. The spirit also, that which is in the world, is (symbolized by) Cycnus, a bird—a musical animal near "The Bears"—type of the Divine Spirit, because that when it approaches the end itself of life, it alone is fitted by nature to sing, on departing with good hope from the wicked creation, (and) offering up hymns unto God. But crabs, and bulls, and lions, and rams, and goats, and kids, and as many other beasts as have their names used for denominating the stars in the firmament, are, he says, images, and exemplars from which the creation, subject to change, obtaining (the different) species, becomes replete with animals of this description.

Chapter L.—Folly of Astrology.

Employing these accounts, (the heretics) think to deceive as many of these as devote themselves over-sedulously to the astrologers, from thence striving to construct a system of religion that is widely divergent from the thoughts of these (speculators). Wherefore, beloved, let us avoid the habit of admiring trifles, secured by which the bird (styled) the owl (is captured). For these and other such speculations are, (as it were), dancing, and not Truth. For neither do the stars yield these points of information; but men of their own accord, for the designation of certain stars, thus called them by names, in order that they might become to them easily distinguishable. For what similarity with a bear or lion, or kid, or waterman, or Cepheus, or Andromeda, or the specters that have names given them in Hades, have the stars that are scattered over the firmament—for we must remember that these men, and the titles themselves, came into existence long after the origin of man,—(what, I say, is in common between the two), that the heretics, astonished at the marvel, should thus strive by means of such discourses to strengthen their own opinions?

Chapter LI.—The Hebdomadarii; System of the Arithmeticians; Pressed into the Service of Heresy; Instances Of, in Simon and Valentinus; The Nature of the Universe Deducible from the Physiology of the Brain.

But since almost every heresy (that has sprung up) through the arithmetical art has discovered measures of hebdomads and certain projections of Æons, each rending the art differently, while whatever variation prevailed was in the names merely; and (since) Pythagoras became the instructor of these, first introducing numbers of this sort among the Greeks from Egypt, it seems expedient not to omit even this, but, after we have given a compendious elucidation, to approach the demonstration of those things that we propose to investigate.

Arithmeticians and geometers arose, to whom especially Pythagoras first seems to have furnished principles. And from numbers that can continually progress ad infinitum by multiplication, and from figures, these derived their first principles, as capable of being discerned by reason alone; for a principle of geometry, as one may perceive, is an indivisible point. From that point, however, by means of the art, the generation of endless figures from the point is discovered. For the point being drawn into length becomes a line, after being thus continued, having a point for its extremity. And a line flowing out into breadth begets a surface, and the limits of the surface are lines; but a surface flowing out into breadth becomes body. And when what is solid has in this manner derived existence from, altogether, the smallest point, the nature of a huge body is constituted; and this is what Simon expresses thus: "The little will be great, being as a point, and the great illimitable." Now this coincides with the geometrical doctrine of a point.

But of the arithmetical art, which by composition contains philosophy, number became a first principle, which is an indefinable and incomprehensible (entity), comprising in itself all the numbers that can go on ad infinitum by aggregation. But the first monad became a principle, according to substance, of the numbers, which (principle) is a male monad, pro-creating paternally all the rest of the numbers. Secondly, the duad is a female number, which by the arithmeticians is also itself denominated even. Thirdly, the triad is a male number; this also it has been the usual custom of arithmeticians to style odd. In addition to all these, the tetrad is a female number; and this same, because it is feminine, is likewise denominated even. All the numbers therefore, taken generically, are four—number, however, as regards genus, is indefinite—from which, according to their system, is formed the perfect number—I mean the decade. For one, two, three, four, become ten—as has been previously proved—if the proper denomination be preserved, according to substance, for each of the numbers. This is the sacred quaternion, according to Pythagoras, having in itself roots of an endless nature, that is, all other numbers; for eleven, and twelve, and the rest, derive the principle of generation from the ten. Of this decade—the perfect number—there are called four parts—number, monad, power, cube—whose connections and mixtures take place for the generation of increase, according to nature completing the productive number. For when the square is multiplied into itself, it becomes a biquadratic; but when the square is multiplied into a cube, it becomes the product of a quadratic and cube; but when a cube is multiplied into a cube, it becomes the product of cube multiplied by cube. Wherefore all the numbers are seven; so that the generation of things produced may be from the hebdomad—which is number, monad, power, cube, biquadratic, product of quadratic multiplied by cube, product of cube multiplied by cube.

Of this hebdomad Simon and Valentinus, having altered the names, detailed marvelous stories, from thence hastily adopting a system for themselves. For Simon employs his denominations thus: Mind, Intelligence, Name, Voice, Ratiocination, Reflection; and He who stood, stands, will stand. And Valentinus (enumerates them thus): Mind, Truth, Word, Life, Man, Church, and the Father, reckoned along with these, according to the same principles as those advanced by the cultivators of arithmetical philosophy. And (heresiarchs) admiring, as if unknown to the multitude, (this philosophy, and) following it, have framed heterodox doctrines devised by themselves.

Some indeed, then, attempt likewise to form the hebdomads from the medical (art), being astonished at the dissection of the brain, asserting that the substance of the universe and the power of procreation and the Godhead could be ascertained from the arrangement of the brain. For the brain, being the dominant portion of the entire body, reposes calm and unmoved, containing within itself the spirit. Such an account, then, is not incredible, but widely differs from the conclusions which these (heretics) attempt to deduce from it. For the brain, on being dissected, has within it what may be called a vaulted chamber. And on either side of this are thin membranes, which they term little wings. Now these are gently moved by the spirit, and in turn propel towards the cerebellum the spirit, which, careering through a certain blood vessel like a reed, advances towards the pineal gland. And near this is situated the entrance of the cerebellum, which admits the current of spirit, and distributes it into what is styled the spinal marrow. But from them the whole frame participates in the spiritual energy, inasmuch as all the arteries, like a branch, are fastened on from this blood vessel, the extremity of which terminates in the genital blood vessels, whence all the (animal) seeds proceeding from the brain through the loin are secreted (in the seminal glands). The form, however, of the brain is like the head of a serpent, respecting which a lengthened discussion is maintained by the professors of knowledge, falsely so named, as we shall prove. Six other coupling ligaments grow out of the brain, which, traversing round the head, and having their termination in (the head) itself, hold bodies together; but the seventh (ligament) proceeds from the cerebellum to the lower parts of the rest of the frame, as we have declared.

And respecting this there is an enlarged discussion, whence both Simon and Valentinus will be found both to have derived from this source starting points for their opinions, and, though they may not acknowledge it, to be in the first instance liars, then heretics. Since, then, it appears that we have sufficiently explained these tenets likewise, and that all the reputed opinions of this earthly philosophy have been comprised in four books; it seems expedient to proceed to a consideration of the disciples of these men, nay rather, those who have furtively appropriated their doctrines.

Book V.

Contents.

The following are the contents of the fifth book of the Refutation of all Heresies: —

What the assertions are of the Naasseni, who style themselves Gnostics, and that they advance those opinions which the Philosophers of the Greeks previously propounded, as well as those who have handed down mystical (rites), from (both of) whom the Naasseni taking occasion, have constructed their heresies.

And what are the tenets of the Peratæ, and that their system is not framed by them out of the holy Scriptures, but from astrological art.

What is the doctrine of the Sethians, and that, purloining their theories from the wise men among the

Greeks, they have patched together their own system out of shreds of opinion taken from Musæus, and Linus, and Orpheus.

What are the tenets of Justinus, and that his system is framed by him, not out of the holy Scriptures, but from the detail of marvels furnished by Herodotus the historian.

Chapter I.—Recapitulation; Characteristics of Heresy; Origin of the Name Naasseni; The System of the Naasseni.

I think that in the four preceding books I have very elaborately explained the opinions propounded by all the speculators among both Greeks and Barbarians, respecting the Divine Nature and the creation of the world; and not even have I omitted the consideration of their systems of magic. So that I have for my readers undergone no ordinary amount of toil, in my anxiety to urge many forward into a desire of learning, and into steadfastness of knowledge in regard of the truth. It remains, therefore, to hasten on to the refutation of the heresies; but it is for the purpose of furnishing this (refutation) that we have put forward the statements already made by us. For from philosophers the heresiarchs deriving starting points, (and) like cobblers patching together, according to their own particular interpretation, the blunders of the ancients, have advanced them as novelties to those that are capable of being deceived, as we shall prove in the following books. In the remainder (of our work), the opportunity invites us to approach the treatment of our proposed subjects, and to begin from those who have presumed to celebrate a serpent, the originator of the error (in question), through certain expressions devised by the energy of his own (ingenuity). The priests, then, and champions of the system, have been first those who have been called Naasseni, being so denominated from the Hebrew language, for the serpent is called naas (in Hebrew). Subsequently, however, they have styled themselves Gnostics, alleging that they alone have sounded the depths of knowledge. Now, from the system of these (speculators), many, detaching parts, have constructed a heresy which, though with several subdivisions, is essentially one, and they explain precisely the same (tenets); though conveyed under the guise of different opinions, as the following discussion, according as it progresses, will prove.

These (Naasseni), then, according to the system advanced by them, magnify, (as the originating cause) of all things else, a man and a son of man. And this man is a hermaphrodite and is denominated among them Adam; and hymns many and various are made to him. The hymns however—to be brief—are couched among them in some such form as this: "From thee (comes) father, and through thee (comes) mother, two names immortal, progenitors of Æons, O denizen of heaven, thou illustrious man." But they divide him as Geryon into three parts. For, say they, of this man one part is rational, another psychical, another earthly. And they suppose that the knowledge of him is the originating principle of the capacity for a knowledge of God, expressing themselves thus: "The originating principle of perfection is the knowledge of man, while the knowledge of God is absolute perfection." All these qualities, however—rational, and psychical, and earthly—have, (the Naassene) says, retired and descended into one man simultaneously—Jesus, who was born of Mary. And these three men (the Naassene) says, are in the habit of speaking (through Jesus) at the same time together, each from their own proper substances to those peculiarly their own. For, according to these, there are three kinds of all existent things—angelic, psychical, earthly; and there are three churches—angelic, psychical, earthly; and the names of these are elect, called, captive.

Chapter II.—Naasseni Ascribe Their System, Through Mariamne, to James the Lord's Brother; Really Traceable to the Ancient Mysteries; Their Psychology as Given in the "Gospel According to Thomas;" Assyrian Theory of the Soul; The Systems of the Naasseni and the Assyrians Compared; Support Drawn by the Naasseni from the Phrygian and Egyptian Mysteries; The Mysteries of Isis; These Mysteries Allegorized by the Naasseni.

These are the heads of very numerous discourses which (the Naassene) asserts James the brother of the Lord handed down to Mariamne. In order, then, that these impious (heretics) may no longer belie Mariamne or James, or the Savior Himself, let us come to the mystic rites (whence these have derived their figment),—to a consideration, if it seems right, of both the Barbarian and Grecian (mysteries),—and let us see how these (heretics), collecting together the secret and ineffable mysteries of all the Gentiles, are uttering falsehoods against Christ, and are making dupes of those who are not acquainted with these orgies of the Gentiles. For since the foundation of the doctrine with them is the man Adam, and they say that concerning him it has been written, "Who shall declare his generation?" learn how, partly deriving from the

Gentiles the undiscoverable and diversified generation of the man, they fictitiously apply it to Christ.

"Now earth," say the Greeks, "gave forth a man, (earth) first bearing a goodly gift, wishing to become mother not of plants devoid of sense, nor beasts without reason, but of a gentle and highly favored creature." "It, however, is difficult," (the Naassene) says, "to ascertain whether Alalcomeneus, first of men, rose upon the Bœotians over Lake Cephisus; or whether it were the Idæan Curetes, a divine race; or the Phrygian Corybantes, whom first the sun beheld springing up after the manner of the growth of trees; or whether Arcadia brought forth Pelasgus, of greater antiquity than the moon; or Eleusis (produced) Diaulus, an inhabitant of Raria; or Lemnus begot Cabirus, fair child of secret orgies; or Pallene (brought forth) the Phlegræan Alcyoneus, oldest of the giants. But the Libyans affirm that Iarbas, firstborn, on emerging from arid plains, commenced eating the sweet acorn of Jupiter. But the Nile of the Egyptians," he says, "up to this day fertilizing mud, (and therefore) generating animals, renders up living bodies, which acquire flesh from moist vapor." The Assyrians, however, say that fish-eating Oanneswas (the first man, and) produced among themselves. The Chaldeans, however, say that this Adam is the man whom alone earth brought forth. And that he lay inanimate, unmoved, (and) still as a statue; being an image of him who is above, who is celebrated as the man Adam, having been begotten by many powers, concerning whom individually is an enlarged discussion.

In order, therefore, that finally the Great Man from above may be overpowered, "from whom," as they say, "the whole family named on earth and in the heavens has been formed, to him was given also a soul, that through the soul he might suffer; and that the enslaved image may be punished of the Great and most Glorious and Perfect Man, for even so they call him. Again, then, they ask what is the soul, and whence, and what kind in its nature, that, coming to the man and moving him, it should enslave and punish the image of the Perfect Man. They do not, however, (on this point) institute an inquiry from the Scriptures but ask this (question) also from the mystic (rites). And they affirm that the soul is very difficult to discover, and hard to understand; for it does not remain in the same figure or the same form invariably, or in one passive condition, that either one could express it by a sign, or comprehend it substantially.

But they have these varied changes (of the soul) set down in the gospel inscribed "according to the Egyptians." They are, then, in doubt, as all the rest of men among the Gentiles, whether (the soul) is at all from something pre-existent, or whether from the self-produced (one), or from a widespread Chaos. And first they fly for refuge to the mysteries of the Assyrians, perceiving the threefold division of the man; for the Assyrians first advanced the opinion that the soul has three parts, and yet (is essentially) one. For of soul, say they, is every nature desirous, and each in a different manner. For soul is cause of all things made; all things that are nourished, (the Naassene) says, and that grow, require soul. For it is not possible, he says, to obtain any nourishment or growth where soul is not present. For even stones, he affirms, are animated, for they possess what is capable of increase; but increase would not at any time take place without nourishment, for it is by accession that things which are being increased grow, but accession is the nourishment of things that are nurtured. Every nature, then, (the Naasene) says, of things celestial, and earthly, and infernal, desires a soul. And an entity of this description the Assyrians call Adonis or Endymion; and when it is styled Adonis, Venus, he says, loves and desires the soul when styled by such a name. But Venus is production, according to them. But whenever Proserpine or Cora becomes enamored with Adonis, there results, he says, a certain mortal soul separated from Venus (that is, from generation). But should the Moon pass into concupiscence for Endymion, and into love of her form, the nature, he says, of the higher beings requires a soul likewise. But if, he says, the mother of the gods emasculate Attis, and herself has this (person) as an object of affection, the blessed nature, he says, of the supernal and everlasting (beings) alone recalls the male power of the soul to itself.

For (the Naassene) says, there is the hermaphrodite man. According to this account of theirs, the intercourse of woman with man is demonstrated, in conformity with such teaching, to be an exceedingly wicked and filthy (practice). For, says (the Naassene), Attis has been emasculated, that is, he has passed over from the earthly parts of the nether world to the everlasting substance above, where, he says, there is neither female or male, but a new creature, a new man, which is hermaphrodite. As to where, however, they use the expression "above," I shall show when I come to the proper place (for treating this subject). But they assert that, by their account, they testify that Rhea is not absolutely isolated, but—for so I may say—the universal creature; and this they declare to be what is affirmed by the Word. "For the invisible things of Him are seen from the creation of the world, being understood by the things that are made by Him, even His eternal power and

Godhead, for the purpose of leaving them without excuse. Wherefore, knowing God, they glorified Him not as God, nor gave Him thanks; but their foolish heart was rendered vain. For, professing themselves to be wise, they became fools, and changed the glory of the uncorruptible God into images of the likeness of corruptible man, and of birds, and four-footed beasts, and creeping things. Wherefore also God gave them up unto vile affections; for even their women did change the natural use into that which is against nature." What, however, the natural use is, according to them, we shall afterwards declare. "And likewise also the men, leaving the natural use of the woman, burned in their lust one toward another; men with men working that which is unseemly"—now the expression that which is unseemly signifies, according to these (Naasseni), the first and blessed substance, figureless, the cause of all figures to those things that are molded into shapes,—"and receiving in themselves that recompense of their error which was meet." For in these words which Paul has spoken they say the entire secret of theirs, and a hidden mystery of blessed pleasure, are comprised. For the promise of washing is not any other, according to them, than the introduction of him that is washed in, according to them, life-giving water, and anointed with ineffable ointment (than his introduction) into unfading bliss.

But they assert that not only is there in favor of their doctrine, testimony to be drawn from the mysteries of the Assyrians, but also from those of the Phrygians concerning the happy nature—concealed, and yet at the same time disclosed—of things that have been, and are coming into existence, and moreover will be,—(a happy nature) which, (the Naassene) says, is the kingdom of heaven to be sought for within a man. And concerning this (nature) they hand down an explicit passage, occurring in the Gospel inscribed according to Thomas, expressing themselves thus: "He who seeks me, will find me in children from seven years old; for there concealed, I shall in the fourteenth age be made manifest." This, however, is not (the teaching) of Christ, but of Hippocrates, who uses these words: "A child of seven years is half of a father." And so it is that these (heretics), placing the originative nature of the universe in causative seed, (and) having ascertained the (aphorism) of Hippocrates, that a child of seven years old is half of a father, say that in fourteen years, according to Thomas, he is manifested. This, with them, is the ineffable and mystical Logos. They assert, then, that the Egyptians, who after the Phrygians, it is established, are of greater antiquity than all mankind, and who confessedly were the first to proclaim to all the rest of men the rites and orgies of, at the same time, all the gods, as well as the species and energies (of things), have the sacred and august, and for those who are not initiated, unspeakable mysteries of Isis. These, however, are not anything else than what by her of the seven dresses and sable robe was sought and snatched away, namely, the pudendum of Osiris. And they say that Osiris is water. But the seven-robed nature, encircled and arrayed with seven mantles of ethereal texture—for so they call the planetary stars, allegorizing and denominating them ethereal robes, —is as it were the changeable generation, and is exhibited as the creature transformed by the ineffable and unportrayable, and inconceivable and figureless one. And this, (the Naassene) says, is what is declared in Scripture, "The just will fall seven times, and rise again." For these falls, he says, are the changes of the stars, moved by Him who puts all things in motion.

They affirm, then, concerning the substance of the seed which is a cause of all existent things, that it is none of these, but that it produces and forms all things that are made, expressing themselves thus: "I become what I wish, and I am what I am: on account of this I say, that what puts all things in motion is itself unmoved. For what exists remains forming all things, and naught of existing things is made." He says that this (one) alone is good, and that what is spoken by the Savior is declared concerning this (one): "Why do you say that am good? One is good, my Father which is in the heavens, who causes His sun to rise upon the just and unjust, and sends rain upon saints and sinners." But who the saintly ones are on whom He sends the rain, and the sinners on whom the same sends the rain, this likewise we shall afterwards declare with the rest. And this is the great and secret and unknown mystery of the universe, concealed and revealed among the Egyptians. For Osiris, (the Naassene) says, is in temples in front of Isis; and his pudendum stands exposed, looking downwards, and crowned with all its own fruits of things that are made. And (he affirms) that such stands not only in the most hallowed temples chief of idols, but that also, for the information of all, it is as it were a light not set under a bushel, but upon a candlestick, proclaiming its message upon the housetops, in all byways, and all streets, and near the actual dwellings, placed in front as a certain appointed limit and termination of the dwelling, and that this is denominated the good (entity) by all. For they style this good producing, not knowing what they say. And the Greeks, deriving this mystical (expression) from the Egyptians, preserve it until this day. For we behold, says (the Naassene), statues of Mercury, of such a figure honored among them.

Worshipping, however, Cyllenius with especial distinction, they style him Logios. For Mercury is Logos, who being interpreter and fabricator of the things that have been made simultaneously, and that are being produced, and that will exist, stands honored among them, fashioned into some such figure as is the pudendum of a man, having an impulsive power from the parts below towards those above. And that this (deity)—that is, a Mercury of this description—is, (the Naassene) says, a conjurer of the dead, and a guide of departed spirits, and an originator of souls; nor does this escape the notice of the poets, who express themselves thus: —

"Cyllenian Hermes also called
The souls of mortal suitors."

Not Penelope's suitors, says he, O wretches! but (souls) awakened and brought to recollection of themselves,
"From honor so great, and from bliss so long."
That is, from the blessed man from above, or the primal man or Adam, as it seems to them, souls have been conveyed down here into a creation of clay, that they may serve the Demiurge of this creation, Ialdabaoth, a fiery God, a fourth number; for so they call the Demiurge and father of the formal world:—

"And in hand he held a lovely
Wand of gold that human eyes enchants,

Of whom he will, and those again who slumber rouses."

This, he says, is he who alone has power of life and death. Concerning this, he says, it has been written, "Thou shalt rule them with a rod of iron." The poet, however, he says, being desirous of adorning the incomprehensible (potency) of the blessed nature of the Logos, invested him with not an iron, but golden wand. And he enchants the eyes of the dead, as he says, and raises up again those that are slumbering, after having been roused from sleep, and after having been suitors. And concerning these, he says, the Scripture speaks: "Awake thou that sleeps, and arise, and Christ will give thee light."

This is the Christ who, he says, in all that have been generated, is the portrayed Son of Man from the unportrayable Logos. This, he says, is the great and unspeakable mystery of the Eleusinian rites, Hye, Cye. And he affirms that all things have been subjected unto him, and this is that which has been spoken, "Their sound is gone forth unto all the earth," just as it agrees with the expressions, "Mercury waving his wand, guides the souls, but they twittering follow." I mean the disembodied spirits follow continuously in such a way as the poet by his imagery delineates, using these words: —

"And as when in the magic cave's recess
Bats humming fly, and when one drops
From ridge of rock, and each to other closely clings."

The expression "rock," he says, he uses of Adam. This, he affirms, is Adam: "The chief corner-stone become the head of the corner." For that in the head the substance is the formative brain from which the entire family is fashioned. "Whom," he says, "I place as a rock at the foundations of Zion." Allegorizing, he says, he speaks of the creation of the man. The rock is interposed (within) the teeth, as Homer says, "enclosure of teeth," that is, a wall and fortress, in which exists the inner man, who thither has fallen from Adam, the primal man above. And he has been "severed without hands to effect the division," and has been borne down into the image of oblivion, being earthly and clayish. And he asserts that the twittering spirits follow him, that is, the Logos: —

> "Thus these, twittering, came together; and then the souls
> That is, he guides them;
> Gentle Hermes led through wide-extended paths."

That is, he says, into the eternal places separated from all wickedness. For whither, he says, did they come: —

> "O'er ocean's streams they came, and Leuca's cliff,
> And by the portals of the sun and land of dreams."

This, he says, is ocean, "generation of gods and generation of men" ever whirled round by the eddies of water, at one time upwards, at another time downwards. But he says there ensues a generation of men when the ocean flows downwards; but when upwards to the wall and fortress and the cliff of Luecas, a generation of gods takes place. This, he asserts, is that which has been written: "I said, Ye are gods, and all children of the highest;" "If ye hasten to fly out of Egypt, and repair beyond the Red Sea into the wilderness," that is, from earthly intercourse to the Jerusalem above, which is the mother of the living; "If, moreover, again you return into Egypt," that is, into earthly intercourse, "ye shall die as men." For mortal, he says, is every generation below, but immortal that which is begotten above, for it is born of water only, and of spirit, being spiritual, not carnal. But what (is born) below is carnal, that is, he says, what is written. "That which is born of the flesh is flesh, and that which is born of the spirit is spirit." This, according to them, is the spiritual generation. This, he says, is the great Jordan which, flowing on (here) below, and preventing the children of Israel from departing out of Egypt—I mean from terrestrial intercourse, for Egypt is with them the body, —Jesus drove back, and made it flow upwards.

Chapter III.—Further Exposition of the Heresy of the Naasseni; Profess to Follow Homer; Acknowledge a Triad of Principles; Their Technical Names of the Triad; Support These on the Authority of Greek Poets; Allegorize Our Savior's Miracles; The Mystery of the Samothracians; Why the Lord Chose Twelve Disciples; The Name Corybas, Used by Thracians and Phrygians, Explained; Naasseni Profess to Find Their System in Scripture; Their Interpretation of Jacob's Vision; Their Idea of the "Perfect Man;" The "Perfect Man" Called "Papa" By the Phrygians; The Naasseni and Phrygians on the Resurrection; The Ecstasis of St. Paul; The Mysteries of Religion as Alluded to by Christ; Interpretation of the

Parable of the Sower; Allegory of the Promised Land; Comparison of the System of the Phrygians with the Statements of Scripture; Exposition of the Meaning of the Higher and Lower Eleusinian Mysteries; The Incarnation Discoverable Here According to the Naasseni.

Adopting these and such like (opinions), these most marvelous Gnostics, inventors of a novel grammatical art, magnify Homer as their prophet—as one, (according to them,) who, after the mode adopted in the mysteries, announces these truths; and they mock those who are not indoctrinated into the holy Scriptures, by betraying them into such notions. They make, however, the following assertion: he who says that all things derive consistence from one, is in error; but he who says that they are of three, is in possession of the truth, and will furnish a solution of the (phenomena of the) universe. For there is, says (the Naassene), one blessed nature of the Blessed Man, of him who is above, (namely) Adam; and there is one mortal nature, that which is below; and there is one kingless generation, which is begotten above, where, he says, is Mariam the sought-for one, and Iothor the mighty sage, and Sephora the gazing one, and Moses whose generation is not in Egypt, for children were born unto him in Madian; and not even this, he says, has escaped the notice of the poets.

> "Threefold was our partition; each obtained
> His meed of honor due."

For, says he, it is necessary that the magnitudes be declared, and that they thus be declared by all everywhere, "in order that hearing they may not hear, and seeing they may not see." For if, he says, the magnitudes were not declared, the world could not have obtained consistence. These are the three tumid expressions (of these heretics), Caulacau, Saulasau, Zeesar, i.e., Adam, who is farthest above; Saulasau, that is, the mortal one below; Zeesar, that is, Jordan that flows upwards. This, he says, is the hermaphrodite man (present) in all. But those who are ignorant of him, call him Geryon with the threefold body—Geryon, i.e., as if (in the sense of) flowing from earth—but (whom) the Greeks by common consent (style) "celestial horn of the moon," because he mixed and blended all things in all. "For all things," he says, "were made by him, and not even one thing was made without him, and what was made in him is life." This, says he, is the life, the ineffable generation of perfect men, which was not known by preceding generations. But the passage, "nothing was made without him," refers to the formal world, for it was created without his instrumentality by the third and fourth (of the quaternion named above). For says he, this is the cup "Condy, out of which the king, while he quaffs, draws his omens." This, he says, has been discovered hid in the beauteous seeds of Benjamin. And the Greeks likewise, he says, speak of this in the following terms:—

"Water to the raging mouth bring; thou slave, bring wine;
Intoxicate and plunge me into stupor.
My tankard tells me
The sort I must become."

This, says he, was alone sufficient for its being understood by men; (I mean) the cup of Anacreon declaring, (albeit) mutely, an ineffable mystery. For dumb, says he, is Anacreon's cup; and (yet) Anacreon affirms that it speaks to himself, in language mute, as to what sort he must become—that is spiritual, not carnal—if he shall listen in silence to the concealed mystery. And this is the water in those fair nuptials which Jesus changing made into wine. This, he says, is the mighty and true beginning of miracles which Jesus performed in Cana of Galilee, and (thus) manifested the kingdom of heaven. This, says he, is the kingdom of heaven that reposes within us as a treasure, as leaven hid in the three measures of meal. This is, he says, the great and ineffable mystery of the Samothracians, which it is allowable, he says, for us only who are initiated to know. For the Samothracians expressly hand down, in the mysteries that are celebrated among them, that (same) Adam as the primal man. And habitually there stand in the temple of the Samothracians two images of naked men, having both hands stretched aloft towards heaven, and their pudenda erecta, as with the statue of Mercury on Mount Cyllene. And the aforesaid images are figures of the primal man, and of that spiritual one that is born again, in every respect of the same substance with that man. This, he says, is what is spoken by the Savior: "If ye do not drink my blood, and eat my flesh, ye will not enter into the kingdom of heaven; but even though," He says, "ye drink of the cup which I drink of, whither I go, ye cannot enter there." For He says He was aware of what sort of nature each of His disciples was, and that there was a necessity that each of them should attain unto His own peculiar nature. For He says He chose twelve disciples from the twelve tribes and spoke by them to each tribe. On this account, He says, the preaching of the twelve disciples neither did all hear, nor, if they heard, could they receive. For the things that are not according to nature, are with them contrary to nature.

This, he says, the Thracians who dwell around Hæmus, and the Phrygians similarly with the Thracians, denominate Corybas, because, (though) deriving the beginning of his descent from the head above and from the unportrayed brain, and (though) permeating all the principles of the existing state of things, (yet) we do not perceive how and in what manner he comes down. This, says he, is what is spoken: "We have heard his voice, no doubt, but we have not seen his shape." For the voice of him that is set apart and portrayed is heard; but (his) shape, which descends from above from the unportrayed one,—what sort it is, nobody knows. It resides, however, in an earthly mold, yet no one recognizes it.

This, he says, is "the god that inhabited the flood," according to the Psalter, "and who speaks and cries from many waters." The "many waters," he says, are the diversified generation of mortal men, from which (generation) he cries and vociferates to the unportrayed man, saying, "Preserve my only-begotten from the lions." In reply to him, it has, says he, been declared, "Israel, thou art my child: fear not; even though thou passes through rivers, they shall not drown thee; even though thou passes through fire, it shall not scorch thee." By rivers he means, says he, the moist substance of generation, and by fire the impulsive principle and desire for generation. "Thou art mine; fear not." And again, he says, "If a mother forgets her children, so as not to have pity on them and give them food, I also will forget you." Adam, he says, speaks to his own men: "But even though a woman forget these things, yet I will not forget you. I have painted you on my hands." In regard, however, of his ascension, that is his regeneration, that he may become spiritual, not carnal, the Scripture, he says, speaks (thus): "Open the gates, ye who are your rulers; and be ye lift up, ye everlasting doors, and the King of glory shall come in," that is a wonder of wonders. "For who," he says, "is this King of glory? A worm, and not a man; a reproach of man, and an outcast of the people; himself is the King of glory, and powerful in war."

And by war he means the war that is in the body, because its frame has been made out of hostile elements; as it has been written, he says, "Remember the conflict that exists in the body." Jacob, he says, saw this entrance and this gate in his journey into Mesopotamia, that is, when from a child he was now becoming a youth and a man; that is, (the entrance and gate) were made known unto him as he journeyed into Mesopotamia. But Mesopotamia, he says, is the current of the great ocean flowing from the midst of the Perfect Man; and he was astonished at the celestial gate, exclaiming, "How terrible is this place! it is nought else than the house of God, and this (is) the gate of heaven." On account of this, he says, Jesus uses the words, "I am the true gate." Now he who makes these statements is, he says, the Perfect Man that is imaged from the unportrayable one from above. The Perfect Man therefore cannot, he says, be saved, unless, entering in through this gate, he be born again. But this very one the Phrygians, he says, call also Papa, because he tranquillized all things which, prior to his manifestation, were confusedly and dissonantly moved. For the name, he says, of Papa belongs simultaneously to all creatures—celestial, and terrestrial, and infernal—who exclaim, Cause to cease, cause to cease the discord of the world, and make "peace for those that are afar off," that is, for material and earthly beings; and "peace for those that are near," that is, for perfect men that are spiritual and endued with reason. But the Phrygians denominate this same also "corpse"—buried in the body, as it were, in a mausoleum and tomb. This, he says, is what has been declared, "Ye are whited sepulchers, full," he says, "of dead men's bones within," because there is not in you the living man. And again he exclaims, "The dead shall start forth from the graves," that is, from the earthly bodies, being born again spiritual, not carnal. For this, he says, is the Resurrection that takes place through the gate of heaven, through which, he says, all those that do not enter remain dead. These same Phrygians, however, he says, affirm again that this very (man), as a consequence of the change, (becomes) a god. For, he says, he becomes a god when, having risen from the dead, he will enter into heaven through a gate of this kind. Paul the apostle, he says, knew of this gate, partially opening it in a mystery, and stating "that he was caught up by an angel, and ascended as far as the second and third heaven into paradise itself; and that he beheld sights and heard unspeakable words which it would not be possible for man to declare."

These are, he says, what are by all called the secret mysteries, "which (also we speak), not in words taught of human wisdom, but in those taught of the Spirit, comparing spiritual things with spiritual. But the natural man receives not the things of the Spirit of God, for they are foolishness unto him." And these are, he says, the ineffable mysteries of the Spirit, which we alone are acquainted with. Concerning these, he says, the Savior has declared, "No one can come unto me, except my heavenly Father draw some one unto me." For it is very difficult, he says, to accept and receive this great and ineffable mystery. And again, it is said, the Savior has declared, "Not everyone that saith unto me, Lord, Lord, shall enter into the kingdom of heaven, but he that doeth the will of my Father which is in heaven." And it is necessary that they who perform this (will), not hear it merely, should enter into the kingdom of heaven. And again, he says, the Savior has declared, "The publicans and the harlots go into the kingdom of heaven before you." For "the publicans," he says, are those who receive the revenues of all things; but we, he says, are the publicans, "unto whom the ends of the ages have come." For "the ends," he says, are the seeds scattered from the unportrayable one upon the world, through which the whole cosmical system is completed; for through these also it began to exist. And this, he says, is what has been declared: "The Sower went forth to sow. And some fell by the wayside, and was trodden down; and some on the rocky places, and sprang up," he says, "and on account of its having no depth (of soil), it withered and died; and some," he says, "fell on fair and good ground, and brought forth fruit, some a hundred, some sixty, and some thirty fold. Who hath ears," he says, "to hear, let him hear." The meaning of this, he says, is as follows, that none becomes a hearer of these mysteries, unless only the perfect Gnostics. This, he says, is the fair and good land which Moses speaks of: "I will bring you into a fair and good land, into a land flowing with milk and honey." This, he says, is the honey and the milk, by tasting which those that are perfect become kingless, and share in the Pleroma. This, he says, is the Pleroma, through which all existent things that are produced have from the ingenerable one been both produced and completed.

And this same (one) is styled also by the Phrygians "unfruitful." For he is unfruitful when he is carnal, and causes the desire of the flesh. This, he says, is what is spoken: "Every tree not producing good fruit, is cut down and cast into the fire." For these fruits, he says, are only rational living men, who enter in through the third gate. They say, forsooth, "Ye devour the dead, and make the living; (but) if ye eat the living, what will ye do?" They assert, however, that the living "are rational faculties and minds, and men—pearls of that unportrayable one cast before the creature below." This, he says, is what (Jesus) asserts: "Throw not that which is holy unto the dogs, nor pearls unto the swine." Now they allege that the work of swine and dogs is the intercourse of the woman with a man. And the Phrygians, he says, call this very one "goat-herd" (Aipolis), not because, he says, he is accustomed to feed the goats female and male, as the natural (men) use the name, but because, he says, he is "Aipolis"—that is, always ranging over,—who both revolves and carries around the entire cosmical system by his revolutionary motion. For the word "Polein" signifies to turn and change things; whence, he says, they all call the twos center of the heaven poles (Poloi). And the poet says:—

"What sea-born sinless sage comes hither, Undying Egyptian Proteus?"

He is not undone, he says, but revolves as it were, and goes round himself. Moreover, also, cities in which we dwell, because we turn and go round in them, are denominated "Poleis." In this manner, he says, the Phrygians call this one "Aipolis," inasmuch as he everywhere ceaselessly turns all things, and changes them into their own peculiar (functions). And the Phrygians style him, he says, "very fruitful" likewise, "because," says he, "more numerous are the children of the desolate one, than those of her which hath an husband;" that is, things by being born again become immortal and abide forever in great numbers, even though the things that are produced may be few; whereas things carnal, he says, are all corruptible, even though very many things (of this type) are produced. For this reason, he says, "Rachel wept for her children, and would not," says (the prophet), "be comforted; sorrowing for them, for she knew," says he, "that they are not." But Jeremiah likewise utters lamentation for Jerusalem below, not the city in Phoenicia, but the corruptible generation below. For Jeremiah likewise, he says, was aware of the Perfect Man, of him that is born again—of water and the Spirit not carnal. At least Jeremiah himself remarked: "He is a man, and who shall know him?" In this manner, (the Naassene) says, the knowledge of the Perfect Man is exceedingly profound, and difficult of comprehension. For, he says, the beginning of perfection is a knowledge of man, whereas knowledge of God is absolute perfection.

The Phrygians, however, assert, he says, that he is likewise "a green ear of corn reaped." And after the Phrygians, the Athenians, while initiating people into the Eleusinian rites, likewise display to those who are being admitted to the highest grade at these mysteries, the mighty, and marvelous, and most perfect secret suitable for one initiated into the highest mystic truths: (I allude to) an ear of corn in silence reaped. But this ear of corn is also (considered) among the Athenians to constitute the perfect enormous illumination (that has descended) from the unportrayable one, just as the Hierophant himself (declares); not, indeed, emasculated like Attis, but made a eunuch by means of hemlock, and despising all carnal generation. (Now) by night in Eleusis, beneath a huge fire, (the Celebrant) enacting the great and secret mysteries, vociferates and cries aloud, saying, "August Brimo has brought forth a consecrated son, Brimus;" that is, a potent (mother has been delivered of) a potent child. But revered, he says, is the generation that is spiritual, heavenly, from above, and potent is he that is so born. For the mystery is called "Eleusin" and "Anactorium." "Eleusin," because, he says, we who are spiritual come flowing down from Adam above; for the word "eleusesthai" is, he says, of the same import with the expression "to come." But "Anactorium" is of the same import with the expression "to ascend upwards." This, he says, is what they affirm who have been initiated in the mysteries of the Eleusinians. It is, however, a regulation of law, that those who have been admitted into the lesser should again be initiated into the Great Mysteries. For greater destinies obtain greater portions. But the inferior mysteries, he says, are those of Proserpine below; in regard of which mysteries, and the path which leads thither, which is wide and spacious, and conducts those that are perishing to Proserpine, the poet likewise says:—

"But under her a fearful path extends, Hollow, miry, yet best guide to Highly honored Aphrodite's lovely grove."

These, he says, are the inferior mysteries, those appertaining to carnal generation. Now, those men who are initiated into these inferior (mysteries) ought to pause, and (then) be admitted into the great (and) heavenly (ones). For they, he says, who obtain their shares (in this mystery), receive greater portions. For this, he says, is the gate of heaven; and this a house of God, where the Good Deity dwells alone. And into this (gate), he says, no unclean person shall enter, nor one that is natural or carnal; but it is reserved for the spiritual only. And those who come hither ought to cast off their garments, and become all of them bridegrooms, emasculated through the virginal spirit. For this is the virgin who carries in her womb and conceives and brings forth a son, not animal, not corporeal, but blessed for evermore. Concerning these, it is said, the Savior has expressly declared that "straight and narrow is the way that leadeth unto life, and few there are that enter upon it; whereas broad and spacious is the way that leadeth unto destruction, and many there are that pass through it."

Chapter IV.—Further Use Made of the System of the Phrygians; Mode of Celebrating the Mysteries; The Mystery of the "Great Mother;" These Mysteries Have a Joint Object of Worship with the Naasseni; The Naasseni Allegorize the Scriptural Account of the Garden of Eden; The Allegory Applied to the Life of Jesus.

The Phrygians, however, further assert that the father of the universe is "Amygdalus," not a tree, he says, but that he is "Amygdalus" who previously existed; and he having in himself the perfect fruit, as it were, throbbing and moving in the depth, rent his breasts, and produced his now invisible, and nameless, and ineffable child, respecting whom we shall speak. For the word "Amyxai" signifies, as it were, to burst and sever through, as he says (happens) in the case of inflamed bodies, and which have in themselves any tumor; and when doctors have cut this, they call it "Amychai." In this way, he says, the Phrygians call him "Amygdalus," from which proceeded and was born the Invisible (One), "by whom all things were made, and nothing was made without Him." And the Phrygians say that what has been thence produced is "Syrictas" (piper), because the Spirit that is born is harmonious. "For God," he says, "is Spirit; wherefore," he affirms, "neither in this mountain do the true worshippers worship, nor in Jerusalem, but in spirit. For the adoration of the perfect ones," he says, "is spiritual, not carnal." The Spirit, however, he says, is there where likewise the Father is named, and the Son is there born from this Father. This, he says, is the many-named, thousand-eyed Incomprehensible One, of whom every nature—each, however, differently—is desirous. This, he says, is the word of God, which, he says, is a word of revelation of the Great Power. Wherefore it will be sealed, and hid, and concealed, lying in the habitation where lies the basis of the root of the universe, viz. Æons, Powers, Intelligences, Gods, Angels, delegated Spirits, Entities, Nonentities, Generables, Ingenerables, Incomprehensibles, Comprehensibles, Years, Months, Days, Hours, (and) Invisible Point from which what is least begins to increase gradually. That which is, he says, nothing, and which consists of nothing, inasmuch as it is indivisible—(I mean) a point—will become through its own reflective power a certain incomprehensible magnitude. This, he says, is the kingdom of heaven, the grain of mustard seed, the point which is indivisible in the body; and, he says, no one knows this (point) save the spiritual only. This, he says, is what has been spoken: "There is no speech nor language where their voice is not heard."

They rashly assume in this manner, that whatsoever things have been said and done by all men, (may be made to harmonize) with their own particular mental view, alleging that all things become spiritual. Whence likewise they assert, that those exhibiting themselves in theatres,—not even these say or do anything without premeditation. Therefore, he says, when, on the people assembling in the theatres, any one enters clad in a remarkable robe, carrying a harp and playing a tune (upon it, accompanying it) with a song of the great mysteries, he speaks as follows, not knowing what he says: "Whether (thou art) the race of Saturn or happy Jupiter, or mighty Rhea, Hail, Attis, gloomy mutilation of Rhea. Assyrians style thee thrice-longed-for Adonis, and the whole of Egypt (calls thee) Osiris, celestial horn of the moon; Greeks denominate (thee) Wisdom; Samothracians, venerable Adam; Hæmonians, Corybas; and them Phrygians (name thee) at one time Papa, at another time Corpse, or God, or Fruitless, or Aipolos, or green Ear of Corn that has been reaped, or whom the very fertile Amygdalus produced—a man, a musician." This, he says, is multiform Attis, whom while they celebrate in a hymn, they utter these words: "I will hymn Attis, son of Rhea, not with the buzzing sounds of trumpets, or of Idæan pipers, which accord with (the voices of) the Curetes; but I will mingle (my song) with Apollo's music of harps, 'evoe, evan,' inasmuch as thou art Pan, as thou art Bacchus, as thou art shepherd of brilliant stars."

On account of these and such like reasons, these constantly attend the mysteries called those of the "Great Mother," supposing especially that they behold by means of the ceremonies performed there the entire mystery. For these have nothing more than the ceremonies that are performed there, except that they are not emasculated: they merely complete the work of the emasculated. For with the utmost severity and vigilance they enjoin (on their votaries) to abstain, as if they were emasculated, from intercourse with a woman. The rest, however, of the proceeding (observed in these mysteries), as we have declared at some length, (they follow) just as (if they were) emasculated persons. And they do not worship any other object but Naas, (from thence) being styled Naasseni. But Naas is the serpent from whom, i.e., from the word Naas, (the Naassene) says, are all that under heaven are denominated temples (Naous). And (he states) that to him alone—that is, Naas—is dedicated every shrine and every initiatory rite, and every mystery; and, in general, that a religious ceremony could not be discovered under heaven, in which a temple (Naos) has no existence; and in the temple itself is Naas, from whom it has received its denomination of temple (Naos). And these affirm that the serpent is a moist substance, just as Thales also, the Milesian, (spoke of water as an originating principle,) and that nothing of existing things, immortal or mortal, animate or inanimate, could consist at all without him. And that all things are subject unto him, and that he is good, and that he has all things in himself, as in the horn of the one horned bull; so as that he imparts beauty and bloom to all things that exist according to their own nature and peculiarity, as if passing through all, just as ("the river) proceeding forth from Edem, and dividing itself into four heads."

They assert, however, that Edem is the brain, as it were, bound and tightly fastened in encircling robes, as if (in) heaven. But they suppose that man, as far as the head only, is Paradise, therefore that "this river, which proceeds out of Edem," that is, from the brain, "is divided into four heads, and that the name of the first river is called Phison; this is that which encompasses all the land of Havilath: there is gold, and the gold of that land is excellent, and there is bdellium and the onyx stone." This, he says, is the eye, which, by its honor (among the rest of the bodily organs), and its colors, furnishes testimony to what is spoken. "But the name of the second river is Gihon: this is that which compasses the land of Ethiopia." This, he says, is hearing, since Gihon is (a tortuous stream), resembling a sort of labyrinth. "And the name of the third is Tigris. This is that which flowed over against (the country of) the Assyrians." This, he says, is smelling, employing the exceedingly rapid current of the stream (as an analogy of this sense). But it flows over against (the country of) the Assyrians, because in every act of respiration following upon expiration, the breath drawn in from the external atmosphere enters with swifter motion and greater force. For this, he says, is the nature of respiration. "But the fourth river is Euphrates." This, they assert, is the mouth, through which are the passage outwards of prayer, and the passage inwards of nourishment. (The mouth) makes glad, and nurtures and fashions the Spiritual Perfect Man. This, he says, is "the water that is above the firmament," concerning which, he says, the Savior has declared, "If thou knew who it is that asks, thou wouldst have asked from Him, and He would have given you to drink living, bubbling water." Into this water, he says, every nature enters, choosing its own substances; and its peculiar quality comes to each nature from this water, he says, more than iron does to the magnet, and the gold to the backbone of the sea falcon, and the chaff to the amber.

## St. Hippolytus

But if any one, he says, is blind from birth, and has never beheld the true light, "which lightened every man that cometh into the world," by us let him recover his sight, and behold, as it were, through some paradise planted with every description of tree, and supplied with abundance of fruits, water coursing its way through all the trees and fruits; and he will see that from one and the same water the olive chooses for itself and draws the oil, and the vine the wine; and (so is it with) the rest of plants, according to each genus. That Man, however, he says, is of no reputation in the world, but of illustrious fame in heaven, being betrayed by those who are ignorant (of his perfections) to those who know him not, being accounted as a drop from a cask. We, however, he says, are spiritual, who, from the life-giving water of Euphrates, which flows through the midst of Babylon, choose our own peculiar quality as we pass through the true gate, which is the blessed Jesus. And of all men, we Christians alone are those who in the third gate celebrate the mystery, and are anointed there with the unspeakable chrism from a horn, as David (was anointed), not from an earthen vessel, he says, as (was) Saul, who held converse with the evil demon of carnal concupiscence.

Chapter V.—Explanation of the System of the Naasseni Taken from One of Their Hymns.

The foregoing remarks, then, though few out of many, we have thought proper to bring forward. For innumerable are the silly and crazy attempts of folly. But since, to the best of our ability, we have explained the unknown Gnosis, it seemed expedient likewise to adduce the following point. This psalm of theirs has been composed, by which they seem to celebrate all the mysteries of the error (advanced by) them in a hymn, couched in the following terms:—

The world's producing law was Primal Mind,
And next was First-born's outpoured Chaos;
And third, the soul received its law of toil:
Encircl'd, therefore, with an aqueous form,
With care o'erpowered it succumbs to death.
Now holding sway, it eyes the light,
And now it weeps on misery flung;
Now it mourns, now it thrills with joy;
Now it wails, now it hears its doom;
Now it hears its doom, now it dies,
And now it leaves us, never to return.
It, hapless straying, treads the maze of ills.
But Jesus said, Father, behold,
A strife of ills across the earth
Wanders from thy breath (of wrath);
But bitter Chaos (man) seeks to shun,
And knows not how to pass it through.
On this account, O Father, send me;
Bearing seals, I shall descend;
Through ages whole I'll sweep,
All mysteries I'll unravel,
And forms of Gods I'll show;
And secrets of the saintly path,
Styled "Gnosis," I'll impart.

Chapter VI.—The Ophites the Grand Source of Heresy.

These doctrines, then, the Naasseni attempt to establish, calling themselves Gnostics. But since the error is many-headed and diversified, resembling, in truth, the hydra that we read of in history; when, at one blow, we have struck off the heads of this (delusion) by means of refutation, employing the wand of truth, we shall entirely exterminate the monster. For neither do the remaining heresies present much difference of aspect from this, having a mutual connection through (the same) spirit of error. But since, altering the words and the names of the serpent, they wish that there should be many heads of the serpent, neither thus shall we fail thoroughly to refute them as they desire.

Chapter VII.—The System of the Peratæ;

Their Tritheism; Explanation of the Incarnation. There is also unquestionably a certain other (head of the hydra, namely, the heresy) of the Peratæ, whose blasphemy against Christ has for many years escaped notice. And the present is a fitting opportunity for bringing to light the secret mysteries of such (heretics). These allege that the world is one, triply divided. And of the triple division with them, one portion is a certain single originating principle, just as it were a huge fountain, which can be divided mentally into infinite segments. Now the first segment, and that which, according to them, is (a segment) in preference (to others), is a triad, and it is called a Perfect Good, (and) a Paternal Magnitude. And the second portion of the triad of these is, as it were, a certain infinite crowd of potentialities that are generated from themselves, (while) the third is formal. And the first, which is good, is unbegotten, and the second is a self-producing good, and the third is created; and hence it is that they expressly declare that there are three Gods, three Logoi, three Minds, three Men. For to each portion of the world, after the division has been made, they assign both Gods, and Logoi, and Minds, and Men, and the rest; but that from unorigination and the first segment of the world, when afterwards the world had attained unto its completion, there came down from above, for causes that we shall afterwards declare, in the time of Herod a certain man called Christ, with a threefold nature, and a threefold body, and a threefold power, (and) having in himself all (species of) concretions and potentialities (derivable) from the three divisions of the world; and that this, says (the Peratic), is what is spoken: "It pleased him that in him should dwell all fulness bodily," and in Him the entire Divinity resides of the triad as thus divided. For, he says, that from the two superjacent worlds—namely, from that (portion of the triad) which is unbegotten, and from that which is self-producing—there have been conveyed down into this world in which we are, seeds of all sorts of potentialities. What, however, the mode of the descent is, we shall afterwards declare.

(The Peratic) then says that Christ descended from above from unorigination, that by His descent all things triply divided might be saved. For some things, he says, being borne down from above, will ascend through Him, whereas whatever (beings) form plots against those which are carried down from above are cast off, and being placed in a state of punishment, are renounced. This, he says, is what is spoken: "For the Son of man came not into the world to destroy the world, but that the world through Him might be saved." The world, he says, he denominates those two parts that are situated above, viz., both the unbegotten (portion of the triad), and the self-produced one. And when Scripture, he says, uses the words, "that we may not be condemned with the world," it alludes to the third portion of (the triad, that is) the formal world. For the third portion, which he styles the world (in which we are), must perish; but the two (remaining portions), which are situated above, must be rescued from corruption.

Chapter VIII.—The Peratæ Derive Their System from the Astrologers; This Proved by a Statement of the Astrological Theories of the Zodiac; Hence the Terminology of the Peratic Heretics.

Let us, then, in the first place, learn how (the Peratists), deriving this doctrine from astrologers, act despitefully towards Christ, working destruction for those who follow them in an error of this description. For the astrologers, alleging that there is one world, divide it into the twelve fixed portions of the zodiacal signs, and call the world of the fixed zodiacal signs one immoveable world; and the other they affirm to be a world of erratic (signs), both in power, and position, and number, and that it extends as far as the moon. And (they lay down), that (one) world derives from (the other) world a certain power, and mutual participation (in that power), and that the subjacent obtain this participation from the superjacent (portions). In order, however, that what is (here) asserted may be perspicuous, I shall one by one employ those very expressions of the astrologers; (and in doing so) I shall only be reminding my readers of statements previously made in the department of the work where we have explained the entire art of the astrologers.

What, then, the opinions are which those (speculators) entertain, are as follow:—

(Their doctrine is), that from an emanation of the stars the generations of the subjacent (parts) is consummated. For, as they wistfully gazed upward upon heaven, the Chaldeans asserted that (the seven stars) contain a reason for the efficient causes of the occurrence of all the events that happen unto us, and that the parts of the fixed zodiacal signs co-operate (in this influence). Into twelve (parts they divide the zodiacal circle), and each zodiacal sign into thirty portions, and each portion into sixty diminutive parts; for so they denominate the very smallest parts, and those that are indivisible. And of the zodiacal signs, they term some male, but others feminine; and some with two bodies, but others not so; and some tropical, whereas others firm. The male signs, then, are either feminine, which possess a cooperative nature for the procreation of males, (or are themselves productive of females.) For Aries is a male zodiacal sign, but Taurus female; and the rest (are denominated) according to the same analogy, some male, but others female. And I suppose that the Pythagoreans, being swayed from such (considerations), style the Monad male, and the Duad female; and, again, the Triad male, and analogically the remainder of the even and odd numbers. Some, however, dividing each zodiacal sign into twelve parts, employ almost the same method. For example, in Aries, they style the first of the twelve parts both Aries and a male, but the second both Taurus and a female, and the third both Gemini and a male; and the same plan is pursued in the case of the rest of the parts. And they assert that there are signs with two bodies, viz., Gemini and the signs diametrically opposite, namely Sagittarius, and Virgo, and

Pisces, and that the rest have not two bodies. And (they state) that some are likewise tropical, and when the sun stands in these, he causes great turnings of the surrounding (sign). Aries is a sign of this description, and that which is diametrically opposite to it, just as Libra, and Capricorn, and Cancer. For in Aries is the vernal turning, and in Capricorn that of winter, and in Cancer that of summer, and in Libra that of autumn.

The details, however, concerning this system we have minutely explained in the book preceding this; and from it anyone who wishes instruction (on the point), may learn how it is that the originators of this Peratic heresy, viz., Euphrates the Peratic, and Celbes the Carystian, have, in the transference (into their own system of opinions from these sources), made alterations in name only, while in reality they have put forward similar tenets. (Nay more), they have, with immoderate zeal, themselves devoted (their attention) to the art (of the astrologers). For also the astrologers speak of the limits of the stars, in which they assert that the dominant stars have greater influence; as, for instance, on some they act injuriously, while on others they act well. And of these they denominate some malicious, and some beneficent. And (stars) are said to look upon one another, and to harmonize with each other, so that they appear according to (the shape of) a triangle or square. The stars, looking on one another, are figured according to (the shape of) a triangle, having an intervening distance of the extent of three zodiacal signs; whereas (those that have an interval of) two zodiacal signs are figured according to (the shape of) a square. And (their doctrine is), that as in the same way as in a man, the subjacent parts sympathize with the head, and the head likewise sympathizes with the subjacent parts, so all terrestrial (sympathize) with superlunar objects. But (the astrologers go further than this); for there exists (according to them) a certain difference and incompatibility between these, so as that they do not involve one and the same union. This combination and divergence of the stars, which is a Chaldean (tenet), has been arrogated to themselves by those of whom we have previously spoken.

Now these, falsifying the name of truth, proclaim as a doctrine of Christ an insurrection of Æons and revolts of good into (the ranks of) evil powers; and they speak of the confederations of good powers with wicked ones. Denominating them, therefore, Toparchai and Proastioi, and (though thus) framing for themselves very many other names not suggested (to them from other sources), they have yet unskillfully systematized the entire imaginary doctrine of the astrologers concerning the stars. And since they have introduced a supposition pregnant with immense error, they shall be refuted through the instrumentality of our admirable arrangement. For I shall set down, in contrast with the previously mentioned Chaldaic art of the astrologers, some of the Peratic treatises, from which, by means of comparison, there will be an opportunity of perceiving how the Peratic doctrines are those confessedly of the astrologers, not of Christ.

Chapter IX.—System of the Peratæ Explained Out of One of Their Own Books.

It seems, then, expedient to set forth a certain one of the books held in repute amongst them, in which the following passage occurs: "I am a voice of arousal from slumber in the age of night. Henceforward I commence to strip the power which is from chaos. The power is that of the lowest depth of mud, which uprears the slime of the incorruptible (and) humid expanse of space. And it is the entire power of the convulsion, which, ever in motion, and presenting the color of water, whirls things on that are stationary, restrains things tremulous, sets things free as they proceed, lightens things as they abide, removes things on the increase, a faithful steward of the track of the breezes, enjoying the things disgorged from the twelve eyes of the law, (and) manifesting a seal to the power which along with itself distributes the down borne invisible waters, and has been called Thalassa. This power ignorance has been accustomed to denominating Cronus, guarded with chains because he tightly bound the fold of the dense and misty and obscure and murky Tartarus. According to the image of this were produced Cepheus, Prometheus, (and) Japetus. The Power to which has been entrusted Thalassa is hermaphrodite. And it fastens the hissing sound arising from the twelve mouths into twelve pipes, and pours it forth. And the power itself is subtle, and removes the controlling, boisterous, upward motion (of the sea), and seals the tracks of its paths, lest (any antagonistic power) should wage war or introduce any alteration. The tempestuous daughter of this one is a faithful protectress of all sorts of waters. Her name is Chorzar. Ignorance is in the habit of styling this (power) Neptune, according to whose image was produced Glaucus, Melicertes, Ino, Nebroë. He that is encircled with the pyramid of twelve angels, and darkens the gate into the pyramid with various colors, and completes the entire in the sable hues of Night: this one ignorance denominated Cronus. And his ministers were five,—first U, second Aoai, third Uo, fourth Uoab, fifth...Other trustworthy managers (there are) of his province of night and day, who repose in their own power. Ignorance denominated these the erratic stars, from whom depends a corruptible generation. Manager of the rising of the star is Carphacasemeocheir, (and) Eccabbacara (is the same). Ignorance is in the habit of denominating these Curetes chief of the winds; third in order is Ariel, according to whose image was generated Æolus, Briares. And chief of the twelve-houred nocturnal (power) is Soclan, whom ignorance is accustomed to style Osiris; (and) according to the image of this one was born Admetus, Medea, Helen, Æthusa. Chief of the twelve-houred diurnal power is Euno. This is manager of the rising of the star Protocamarus and of the ethereal (region), but ignorance has denominated him Isis. A sign of this one is the Dog-star, according to whose image were born Ptolemæus son of Arsinoe, Didyma, Cleopatra, and Olympias. God's right-hand power is that which ignorance has denominated Rhea, according to whose image were produced Attis, Mygdon, (and) Œnone. The left-hand power has lordship over sustenance, and ignorance is in the habit of styling this Ceres, (while) her name is Bena; and according to the image of this one were born Celeus, Triptolemus, Misyr, and Praxidica. The right-hand power has lordship over fruits. This one ignorance has denominated Mena, according to whose image were born Bumegas, Ostanes, Mercury Trismegistus, Curites, Petosiris, Zodarium, Berosus, Astrampsuchus, (and) Zoroaster. The left-hand power is (lord) of fire, (and) ignorance has denominated this one Vulcan, according to whose image were born Ericthonius, Achilles, Capaneus, Phaëthon, Meleager, Tydeus, Enceladus, Raphael, Suriel, (and) Omphale. There are three intermediate powers suspended from air, authors of generation. These ignorance has been in the habit of denominating Fates; and according to the image of these were produced the house of Priam, the house of Laius, Ino, Autonoe, Agave, Athamas, Procne, Danaides, and Peliades. A power (there is) hermaphrodite, always continuing in infancy, never waxing old, cause of beauty, pleasure, maturity, desire, and concupiscence; and ignorance has been accustomed to style this Eros, according to whose image were born Paris, Narcissus, Ganymede, Endymion, Tithonus, Icarius, Leda, Amymone, Thetis, Hesperides, Jason, Leander, (and) Hero." These are Proastioi up to Æther, for with this title also he inscribes the book.

Chapter X.—The Peratic Heresy Nominally Different from Astrology, But Really the Same System Allegorized.

It has been easily made evident to all, that the heresy of the Peratæ is altered in name only from the (art) of the astrologers. And the rest of the books of these (heretics) contain the same method, if it were agreeable to anyone to wade through them all. For, as I said, they suppose that the causes of the generation of all begotten things are things unbegotten and superjacent, and that the world with us has been produced after the mode of emanation, which (world) they denominate formal. And (they maintain) that all those stars together which are beheld in the firmament have been causes of the generation of this world. They have, however, altered the name of these, as one may perceive from the Proastioi by means of a comparison (of the two systems). And secondly, according to the same method as that whereby the world was made from a supernal emanation, they affirm that in this manner objects here derive from the emanation of the stars their generation, and corruption, and arrangement. Since, then, astrologers are acquainted with the horoscope, and meridian, and setting, and the point opposite the meridian; and since these stars occupy at different times different positions in space, on account of the perpetual revolution of the universe, there are (necessarily) at different periods different declinations towards a center, and (different) ascensions to centers. (Now the Peratic heretics), affixing an allegorical import to this arrangement of the astrologers, delineate the center, as it were, a god and monad and lord over universal generation, whereas the declination (is regarded by them as a power) on the left, and ascension on the right. When any one, therefore, falling in with the treatises of these (heretics), finds mention among them of right or left power, let him recur to the center, and the declination, and the ascension (of the Chaldean sages, and) he will clearly observe that the entire system of these (Peratæ) consists of the astrological doctrine.

Chapter XI.—Why They Call Themselves Peratæ; Their Theory of Generation Supported by an Appeal to Antiquity; Their Interpretation of the Exodus of Israel; Their System of "The Serpent;" Deduced by Them from Scripture; This the Real Import of the Doctrines of the Astrologers.

They denominate themselves, however, Peratæ, imagining that none of those things existing by generation can escape the determined lot for those things that derive their existence from generation. For if, says (the Peratic), anything be altogether begotten, it also perishes, as also is the opinion of the Sibyl. But we alone, he says, who are conversant with the necessity of generation, and the paths through which man has entered into the world, and who have been accurately instructed (in these matters), we alone are competent to proceed through and pass beyond destruction. But water, he says, is destruction; nor did the world, he says, perish by any other thing quicker than by water. Water, however, is that which rolls around among the Proastioi, (and) they assert (it to be) Cronus. For such a power, he says, is of the color of water; and this power, he says—that is, Cronus—none of those things existent by generation can escape. For Cronus is a cause to every generation, in regard of succumbing under destruction, and there could not exist (an instance of) generation in which Cronus does not interfere. This, he says, is what the poets also affirm, and what even appals the gods:—

"For know, he says, this earth and spacious heaven above,
And Styx' flooded water, which is the oath
That greatest is, and dreaded most by gods of happy life."

And not only, he says, do the poets make this statement, but already also the very wisest men among the Greeks. And Heraclitus is even one of these, employing the following words: "For to souls water becomes death." This death, (the Peratic) says, seizes the Egyptians in the Red Sea, along with their chariots. All, however, who are ignorant (of this fact), he says, are Egyptians. And this, they assert, is the departure from Egypt, (that is,) from the body. For they suppose little Egypt to be body, and that it crosses the Red Sea—that is, the water of corruption, which is Cronus—and that it reaches a place beyond the

Red Sea, that is, generation; and that it comes into the wilderness, that is, that it attains a condition independent of generation, where there exist promiscuously all the gods of destruction and the God of salvation.

Now, he says, the stars are the gods of destruction, which impose upon existent things the necessity of alterable generation. These, he says, Moses denominated serpents of the wilderness, which gnaw and utterly ruin those who imagined that they had crossed the Red Sea. To those, then, he says, who of the children of Israel were bitten in the wilderness, Moses exhibited the real and perfect serpent; and they who believed on this serpent were not bitten in the wilderness, that is, (were not assailed) by (evil) powers. No one therefore, he says, is there who is able to save and deliver those that come forth from Egypt, that is, from the body and from this world, unless alone the serpent that is perfect and replete with fulness. Upon this (serpent), he says, he who fixes his hope is not destroyed by the snakes of the wilderness, that is, by the gods of generation. (This statement) is written, he says, in a book of Moses. This serpent, he says, is the power that attended Moses, the rod that was turned into a serpent. The serpents, however, of the magicians—(that is,) the gods of destruction—withstood the power of Moses in Egypt, but the rod of Moses reduced them all to subjection and slew them. This universal serpent is, he says, the wise discourse of Eve. This, he says, is the mystery of Edem, this the river of Edem; this the mark that was set upon Cain, that anyone who finds him might not kill him. This, he says, is Cain, whose sacrifice the god of this world did not accept. The gory sacrifice, however, of Abel he approved of; for the ruler of this world rejoices in (offerings of) blood. This, he says, is he who appeared in the last days, in form of a man, in the times of Herod, being born after the likeness of Joseph, who was sold by the hand of his brethren, to whom alone belonged the coat of many colors. This, he says, is he who is according to the likeness of Esau, whose garment—he not being himself present—was blessed; who did not receive, he says, the benediction uttered by him of enfeebled vision. He acquired, however, wealth from a source independent of this, receiving nothing from him whose eyes were dim; and Jacob saw his countenance, as a man beholds the face of God. In regard of this, he says, it has been written that "Nebrod was a mighty hunter before the Lord." And there are, he says, many who closely imitate this (Nimrod): as numerous are they as the gnawing (serpents) which were seen in the wilderness by the children of Israel, from which that perfect serpent which Moses set up delivered those that were bitten. This, he says, is that which has been declared: "In the same manner as Moses lifted up the serpent in the wilderness, so also must the Son of man be lifted up." According to the likeness of this was made in the desert the brazen serpent which Moses set up. Of this alone, he says, the image is in heaven, always conspicuous in light.

This, he says, is the great beginning respecting which Scripture has spoken. Concerning this, he says it has been declared: "In the beginning was the Word, and the Word was with God, and the Word was God. This was in the beginning with God, all things were made by Him, and without Him was not one thing that was made. And what was formed in Him is life." And in Him, he says, has been formed Eve; (now) Eve is life. This, however, he says, is Eve, mother of all living,—a common nature, that is, of gods, angels, immortals, mortals, irrational creatures, (and) rational ones. For, he says, the expression "all" he uttered of all (existences). And if the eyes of any, he says, are blessed, this one, looking upward on the firmament, will behold at the mighty summit of heaven the beauteous image of the serpent, turning itself, and becoming an originating principle of every (species of) motion to all things that are being produced. He will (thereby) know that without him nothing consists, either of things in heaven, or things on earth. or things under the earth. Not night, not moon, not fruits, not generation, not wealth, not sustenance, not anything at all of existent things, is without his guidance. In regard of this, he says, is the great wonder which is beheld in the firmament by those who are able to observe it. For, he says, at this top of his head, a fact which is more incredible than all things to those who are ignorant, "are setting and rising mingled one with other." This it is in regard of which ignorance is in the habit of affirming: in heaven.

"Draco revolves, marvel mighty of monster dread."
And on both sides of him have been placed Corona and Lyra; and above, near the top itself of the head, is visible the piteous man "Engonasis,"

"Holding the right foot's end of Draco fierce."

And at the back of Engonasis is an imperfect serpent, with both hands tightly secured by Anguitenens, and being hindered from touching Corona that lies beside the perfect serpent.

## Chapter XII.—Compendious Statement of the Doctrines of the Peratæ.

This is the diversified wisdom of the Peratic heresy, which it is difficult to declare in its entirety, so intricate is it on account of its seeming to consist of the astrological art. As far forth, then, as this is possible, we shall briefly explain the whole force of this (heresy). In order, however, that we may by a compendious statement elucidate the entire doctrine of these persons, it appears expedient to subjoin the following observations. According to them, the universe is Father, Son, (and) Matter; (but) each of these three has endless capacities in itself. Intermediate, then, between the Matter and the Father sits the Son, the Word, the Serpent, always being in motion towards the unmoved Father, and (towards) Matter itself in motion. And at one time he is turned towards the Father and receives the powers into his own person; but at another time takes up these powers, and is turned towards Matter. And Matter, (though) devoid of attribute, and being unfashioned, molds (into itself) forms from the Son which the Son molded from the Father.

But the Son derives shape from the Father after a mode ineffable, and unspeakable, and unchangeable; (that is,) in such a manner as Moses says that the colors of the conceived (kine) flowed from the rods which were fixed in the drinking-troughs. And in like manner, again, that capacities flowed also from the Son into Matter, similarly to the power in reference to conception which came from the rods upon the conceived (kine). And the difference of colors, and the dissimilarity which flowed from the rods through the waters upon the sheep, is, he says, the difference of corruptible and incorruptible generation. As, however, one who paints from nature, though he takes nothing away from animals, transfers by his pencil all forms to the canvas; so the Son, by a power which belongs to himself, transfers paternal marks from the Father into Matter. All the paternal marks are here, and there are not anymore. For if any one, he says, of those (beings) which are here will have strength to perceive that he is a paternal mark transferred hither from above, (and that he is) incarnate—just as by the conception resulting from the rod a something white is produced,—he is of the same substance altogether with the Father in heaven, and returns thither. If, however, he may not happen upon this doctrine, neither will he understand the necessity of generation, just as an abortion born at night will perish at night. When, therefore, he says, the Savior observes, "your Father which is in heaven," he alludes to that one from whom the Son deriving his characteristics has transferred them hither. When, however, (Jesus) remarks, "Your father is a murderer from the beginning," he alludes to the Ruler and Demiurge of matter, who, appropriating the marks delivered from the Son, generated him here who from the beginning was a murderer, for his work causes corruption and death.

No one, then, he says, can be saved or return (into heaven) without the Son, and the Son is the Serpent. For as he brought down from above the paternal marks, so again he carries up from thence those marks roused from a dormant condition and rendered paternal characteristics, substantial ones from the unsubstantial Being, transferring them hither from thence. This, he says, is what is spoken: "I am the door." And he transfers (those marks), he says, to those who close the eyelid, as the naphtha drawing the fire in every direction towards itself; nay rather, as the magnet (attracting) the iron and not anything else, or just as the backbone of the sea falcon, the gold and nothing else, or as the chaff is led by the amber. In this manner, he says, is the portrayed, perfect, and consubstantial genus drawn again from the world by the Serpent; nor does he (attract) anything else, as it has been sent down by him. For a proof of this, they adduce the anatomy of the brain, assimilating, from the fact of its immobility, the brain itself to the Father, and the cerebellum to the Son, because of its being moved and being of the form of (the head of) a serpent. And they allege that this (cerebellum), by an ineffable and inscrutable process, attracts through the pineal gland the spiritual and life-giving substance emanating from the vaulted chamber (in which the brain is embedded). And on receiving this, the cerebellum in an ineffable manner imparts the ideas, just as the Son does, to matter; or, in other words, the seeds and the genera of the things produced according to the flesh flow along into the spinal marrow. Employing this exemplar, (the heretics) seem to adroitly introduce their secret mysteries, which are delivered in silence. Now it would be impious for us to declare these; yet it is easy to form an idea of them, by reason of the many statements that have been made.

Chapter XIII.—The Peratic Heresy Not Generally Known.

But since I consider that I have plainly explained the Peratic heresy, and by many (arguments) have rendered evident (a system that hitherto) has always escaped notice, and is altogether a tissue of fable, and one that disguises its own peculiar venom, it seems expedient to advance no further statement beyond those already put forward; for the opinions propounded by (the heretics) themselves are sufficient for their own condemnation.

Chapter XIV.—The System of the Sethians; Their Triad of Infinite Principles; Their Heresy Explained; Their Interpretation of the Incarnation.

Let us then see what the Sithians affirm. To these it appears that there are three definite principles of the universe, and that each of these principles possesses infinite powers. And when they speak of powers let him that heareth take into account that they make this statement. Everything whatsoever you discern by an act of intelligence, or also omit (to discern) as not being understood, this by nature is fitted to become each of the principles, as in the human soul every art whatsoever which is made the subject of instruction. Just for instance, he says, this child will be a musician, having waited the requisite time for (acquiring a knowledge of) the harp; or a geometrician, (having previously undergone the necessary study for acquiring a knowledge) of geometry; (or) a grammarian, (after having sufficiently studied) grammar; (or) a workman, (having acquired a practical acquaintance) with a handicraftsman's business; and to one brought into contact with the rest of the arts a similar occurrence will take place. Now of principles, he says, the substances are light and darkness; and of these, spirit is intermediate without admixture. The spirit, however, is that which has its appointed place in the midst of darkness, which is below, and light which is above. It is not spirit as a current of wind, or some gentle breeze that can be felt; but, as it were, some odor of ointment or of incense formed out of a compound. (It is) a subtle power, that insinuates itself by means of some impulsive quality in a fragrance, which is inconceivable and better than could be expressed by words. Since, however, light is above and darkness below, and spirit is intermediate in such a way as stated between these; and since light is so constituted, that, like a ray of the sun, it shines from above upon the underlying darkness; and again, since the fragrance of the spirit, holding an intermediate place, is extended and carried in every direction, as in the case of incense-offerings placed upon fire, we detect the fragrance that is being wafted in every direction: when, I say, there is a power of this description belonging unto the principles which are classified under three divisions, the power of spirit and light simultaneously exists in the darkness that is situated underneath them. But the darkness is a terrible water, into which light is absorbed and translated into a nature of the same description with spirit. The darkness, however, is not devoid of intelligence, but altogether reflective, and is conscious that, where the light has been abstracted from the darkness, the darkness remains isolated, invisible, obscure, impotent, inoperative, (and) feeble. Wherefore it is constrained, by all its reflection and understanding, to collect into itself the luster and scintillation of light with the fragrance of the spirit. And it is possible to behold an image of the nature of these in the human countenance; for instance, the pupil of the eye, dark from the subjacent humors, (but) illuminated with spirit. As, then, the darkness seeks after the splendor, that it may keep in bondage the spark, and may have perceptive power, so the light and spirit seek after the power that belongs to themselves, and strive to uprear, and towards each other to carry up their intermingled powers into the dark and formidable water lying underneath.

But all the powers of the three originating principles, which are as regards number indefinitely infinite, are each according to its own substance reflective and intelligent, unnumbered in multitude. And since what are reflective and intelligent are numberless in multitude, while they continue by themselves, they are all at rest. If, however, power approaches power, the dissimilarity of (what is set in) juxtaposition produces a certain motion and energy, which are formed from the motion resulting from the concourse effected by the juxtaposition of the coalescing powers. For the concourse of the powers ensues, just like any mark of a seal that is impressed by means of the concourse correspondingly with (the seal) which prints the figure on the substances that are brought up (into contact with it). Since, therefore, the powers of the three principles are infinite in number, and from infinite powers (arise) infinite concourses, images of infinite seals are necessarily produced. These images, therefore, are the forms of the different sorts of animals. From the first great concourse, then, of the three principles, ensues a certain great form, a seal of heaven and earth. The heaven and the earth have a figure similar to the womb, having a navel in the midst; and if, he says, any one is desirous of bringing this figure under the organ of vision, let him artfully scrutinize the pregnant womb of whatsoever animal he wishes, and he will discover an image of the heaven and the earth, and of the things which in the midst of all are unalterably situated underneath.

(And so it is, that the first great concourse of the three principles) has produced such a figure of heaven and earth as is similar to a womb after the first coition. But, again, in the midst of the heaven and the earth have been generated infinite concourses of powers. And each concourse did not effect and fashion anything else than a seal of heaven and earth similar to a womb. But, again, in the earth, from the infinite seals are produced infinite crowds of various animals. But into all this infinity of the different animals under heaven is diffused and distributed, along with the light, the fragrance of the Spirit from above. From the water, therefore, has been produced a first-begotten originating principle, viz., wind, (which is) violent and boisterous, and a cause of all generation. For producing a sort of ferment in the waters, (the wind) uplifts waves out of the waters; and the motion of the waves, just as when some impulsive power of pregnancy is the origin of the production of a man or mind, is caused when (the ocean), excited by the impulsive power of spirit, is propelled forward. When, however, this wave that has been raised out of the water by the wind, and rendered pregnant in its nature, has within itself obtained the power, possessed by the female, of generation, it holds together the light scattered from above along with the fragrance of the spirit—that is, mind molded in the different species. And this (light) is a perfect God, who from the unbegotten radiance above, and from the spirit, is borne down into human nature as into a temple, by the impulsive power of Nature, and by the motion of wind. And it is produced from water being commingled and blended with bodies as if it were a salt of existent things, and a light of darkness. And it struggles to be released from bodies, and is not able to find liberation and an egress for itself. For a very diminutive spark, a severed splinter from above like the ray of a star, has been mingled in the much compounded waters of many (existences), as, says he, (David) remarks in a psalm. Every thought, then, and solicitude actuating the supernal light is as to how and in what manner mind may be liberated, by the death of the depraved and dark body, from the Father that is below, which is the wind that with noise and tumult uplifted the waves, and who generated a perfect mind his own Son; not, however, being his peculiar (offspring) substantially. For he was a ray (sent down) from above, from that perfect light, (and) was overpowered in the dark, and formidable, and bitter, and defiled water; and he is a luminous spirit borne down over the water. When, therefore, the waves that have been upreared from the waters have received within themselves the power of generation possessed by females, they contain, as a certain womb, in different species, the infused radiance, so as that it is visible in the case of all animals. But the wind, at the same time fierce and formidable, whirling along, is, in respect of its hissing sound, like a serpent.

First, then, from the wind—that is, from the serpent—has resulted the originating principle of generation in the manner declared, all things having simultaneously received the principle of generation. After, then, the light and the spirit had been received, he says, into the polluted and baneful (and) disordered womb, the serpent—the wind of the darkness, the first-begotten of the waters—enters within and produces man, and the impure womb neither loves nor recognizes any other form. The perfect Word of supernal light being therefore assimilated (in form) to the beast, (that is,) the serpent, entered into the defiled womb, having deceived (the womb) through the similitude of the beast itself, in order that (the Word) may loose the chains that encircle the perfect mind which has been begotten amidst impurity of womb by the primal offspring of water, (namely,) serpent, wind, (and) beast. This, he says, is the form of the servant, and this the necessity of the Word of God coming down into the womb of a virgin. But he says it is not sufficient that the Perfect Man, the Word, has entered into the womb of a virgin, and loosed the pangs which were in that darkness. Nay, more than this was requisite; for after his entrance into the foul mysteries of the womb, he was washed, and drank of the cup of life-giving bubbling water. And it was altogether needful that he should drink who was about to strip off the servile form, and assume celestial raiment.

Chapter XV.—The Sethians Support Their Doctrines by an Allegorical Interpretation of Scripture; Their System Really Derived from Natural Philosophers and from the Orphic Rites; Adopt the Homeric Cosmogony.

These are the statements which the patrons of the Sethian doctrines make, as far as it is possible to declare in a few words. Their system, however, is made up (of tenets) from natural (philosophers), and of expressions uttered in reference to different other subjects; and transferring (the sense of) these to the Eternal Logos, they explain them as we have declared. But they assert likewise that Moses confirms their doctrine when he says, "Darkness, and mist, and tempest." These, (the Sethian) says, are the three principles (of our system); or when he states that three were born in paradise—Adam, Eve, the serpent; or when he speaks of three (persons, namely) Cain, Abel, Seth; and again of three (others)—Shem,

Ham, Japheth; or when he mentions three patriarchs—Abraham, Isaac, Jacob; or when he speaks of the existence of three days before sun and moon; or when he mentions three laws—prohibitory, permissive, and adjudicatory of punishment. Now, a prohibitory law is as follows: "Of every tree that is in paradise thou mayest freely eat; but of the tree of the knowledge of good and evil thou mayest not eat." But in the passage, "Come forth from thy land and from thy kindred, and hither into a land which I shall show thee," this law, he says, is permissive; for one who is so disposed may depart, and one who is not so disposed may remain. But a law adjudicatory of punishment is that which makes the following declaration: "Thou shalt not commit adultery, thou shalt not kill, thou shalt not steal;" for a penalty is awarded to each of these acts of wickedness.

The entire system of their doctrine, however, is (derived) from the ancient theologians Musæus, and Linus, and Orpheus, who elucidates especially the ceremonies of initiation, as well as the mysteries themselves. For their doctrine concerning the womb is also the tenet of Orpheus; and the (idea of the) navel, which is harmony, is (to be found) with the same symbolism attached to it in the Bacchanalian orgies of Orpheus. But prior to the observance of the mystic rite of Celeus, and Triptolemus, and Ceres, and Proserpine, and Bacchus in Eleusis, these orgies have been celebrated and handed down to men in Phlium of Attica. For antecedent to the Eleusinian mysteries, there are (enacted) in Phlium the orgies of her denominated the "Great (Mother)." There is, however, a portico in this (city), and on the portico is inscribed a representation, (visible) up to the present day, of all the words which are spoken (on such occasions). Many, then, of the words inscribed upon that portico are those respecting which Plutarch institutes discussions in his ten books against Empedocles. And in the greater number of these books is also drawn the representation of a certain aged man, grey-haired, winged, having his pudendum erectum, pursuing a retreating woman of azure color. And over the aged man is the inscription "phaos ruentes," and over the woman "pereëphicola." But "phaos ruentes" appears to be the light (which exists), according to the doctrine of the Sethians, and "phicola" the darkish water; while the space in the midst of these seems to be a harmony constituted from the spirit that is placed between. The name, however, of "phaos ruentes" manifests, as they allege, the flow from above of the light downwards. Wherefore one may reasonably assert that the Sethians celebrate rites among themselves, very closely bordering upon those orgies of the "Great (Mother" which are observed among) the Phliasians. And the poet likewise seems to bear his testimony to this triple division, when he remarks, "And all things have been triply divided, and everything obtains its (proper) distinction;" that is, each member of the threefold division has obtained (a particular) capacity. But now, as regards the tenet that the subjacent water below, which is dark, ought, because the light has set (over it), to convey upwards and receive the spark borne down from (the light) itself; in the assertion of this tenet, I say, the all-wise Sethians appear to derive (their opinion) from Homer:—

"By earth I sware, and yon broad Heaven above,
And Stygian stream beneath, the weightiest oath
Of solemn power, to bind the blessed gods."

That is, according to Homer, the gods suppose water to be loathsome and horrible. Now, similar to this is the doctrine of the Sethians, which affirms (water) to be formidable to the mind.

Chapter XVI.—The Sethian Theory Concerning "Mixture" And "Composition;" Application of It to Christ; Illustration from the Well of Ampa.

These, and other assertions similar to these, are made (by the Sethians) in their interminable commentaries. They, however, persuade their disciples to become conversant with the theory respecting composition and mixture. But this theory has formed a subject of meditation to many, but (among others) also to Andronicus the Peripatetic. The Sethians, then, affirm that the theory concerning composition and mixture is constituted according to the following method: The luminous ray from above is intermingled, and the very diminutive spark is delicately blended in the dark waters beneath; and (both of these) become united, and are formed into one compound mass, just as a single savor (results) from the mixture of many incense-offerings in the fire, and (just as) an adept, by having a test in an acute sense of smell, ought to be able from the single odor of the incense to distinguish accurately each (ingredient) of the incense-offerings that have been mingled in the fire,— whether, for example, storax, and myrrh, and frankincense, or whatever other (ingredient) may be mixed (in the incense). They, however, employ also other examples, saying both that brass is mixed with gold, and that some art has been discovered which separates the brass from the gold. And, in like manner, if tin or brass, or any substance homogeneous with it, be discovered mixed with silver, these likewise, by some art superior to that of mixing, are distinguished. But already someone also distinguishes water mingled with wine. So, say they, though all things are commingled, they are capable of being separated. Nay, but, he says, derive the same lesson from the case of animals. For when the animal is dead, each of its parts is separated; and when dissolution takes place, the animal in this way vanishes. This is, he says, what has been spoken: "I came not to send peace on the earth, but a sword,"—that is, the division and separation of the things that have been commingled. For each of the things that have been commingled is separated and divided when it reaches its proper place. For as there is one place of mixture for all animals, so also has there been established one (locality) of separation. And, he says, no one is aware of this (place), save we alone that have been born again, spiritual, not carnal, whose citizenship is in heaven above.

In this manner insinuating themselves, they corrupt their pupils, partly by misusing the words spoken (by themselves), while they wickedly pervert, to serve any purpose they wish, what has been admirably said (in Scripture); and partly by concealing their nefarious conduct, by means of whatever comparisons they please. All these things, then, he says, that have been commingled, possess, as has been declared, their own particular place, and hurry towards their own peculiar (substances), as iron towards the magnet, and the chaff to the vicinity of amber, and the gold to the spur of the sea falcon. In like manner, the ray of light which has been commingled with the water, having obtained from discipline and instruction its own proper locality, hastens towards the Logos that comes from above in servile form; and along with the Logos exists as a logos in that place where the Logos is still: (the light, I say, hastens to the Logos with greater speed) than the iron towards the magnet.

And that these things, he says, are so, and that all things that have been commingled are separated in their proper places, learn. There is among the Persians in a city Ampa, near the river Tigris, a well; and near the well, at the top, has been constructed a certain reservoir, supplied with three outlets; and when one pumps from this well, and draws off some of its contents in a vessel, what is thus pumped out of the well, whatever it is at all, he pours into the reservoir hard by. And when what is thus infused reaches the outlets, and when what is taken up (out of each outlet) in a single vessel is examined, a separation is observed to have taken place. And in the first of the outlets is exhibited a concretion of salt, and in the second of asphalt, and in the third of oil; and the oil is black, just as, he says, Herodotus also narrates, and it yields a heavy smell, and the Persians call this "rhadinace." The similitude of the well is, say the Sethians, more sufficient for the demonstration of their proposition than all the statements that have been previously made.

Chapter XVII.—The Sethian Doctrines to Be Learned from the "Paraphrase of Seth."

The opinion of the Sethians appears to us to have been sufficiently elucidated. If, however, any one is desirous of learning the entire doctrine according to them, let him read a book inscribed Paraphrase of Seth; for all their secret tenets he will find deposited there. But since we have explained the opinions entertained by the Sethians, let us see also what are the doctrines advanced by Justinus.

Chapter XVIII.—The System of Justinus Antiscriptural and Essentially Pagan.

Justinus was entirely opposed to the teaching of the holy Scriptures, and moreover to the written or oral teaching of the blessed evangelists, according as the Logos was accustomed to instruct His disciples, saying, "Go not into the way of the Gentiles;" and this signifies that they should not attend to the futile doctrine of the Gentiles. This (heretic) endeavors to lead on his hearers into an acknowledgment of prodigies detailed by the Gentiles, and of doctrines inculcated by them. And he narrates, word for word, legendary accounts prevalent among the Greeks, and does not previously teach or deliver his perfect mystery, unless he has bound his dupe by an oath. Then he brings forward (these) fables for the purpose of persuasion, in order that they who are conversant with the incalculable trifling of these books may have some consolation in the details of these legends. Thus it happens as when in like manner one making a long journey deems it expedient, on having fallen in with an inn, to take repose. And so it is that, when once more they are induced to turn towards studying the diffuse doctrine of these lectures, they may not abhor them while they, undergoing instruction unnecessarily prolix, rush stupefied into the transgression devised by (Justinus); and previously he binds his followers with horrible oaths, neither to publish nor abjure these doctrines, and forces upon them an acknowledgment (of their truth). And in this manner he delivers the mysteries impiously discovered by himself, partly, according to the statements previously made, availing himself of the Hellenic legends, and partly of those pretended books which, to some extent, bear a resemblance to the foresaid heresies. For all, forced together by one spirit, are drawn into one profound abyss of pollution, inculcating the same tenets, and detailing the same legends, each after a different method. All those, however, style themselves Gnostics in this peculiar sense, that they alone themselves have imbibed the marvelous knowledge of the Perfect and Good (Being).

Chapter XIX.—The Justinian Heresy Unfolded in the "Book of Baruch."

But swear, says Justinus, if you wish to know "what eye hath not seen, and ear hath not heard, and the things which have not entered into the heart;" that is, if you wish to know Him who is good above all, Him who is more exalted, (swear) that you will preserve the secrets (of the Justinian) discipline, as intended to be kept silent. For also our Father, on beholding the Good One, and on being initiated with Him, preserved the mysteries respecting which silence is enjoined, and swore, as it has been written, "The Lord swore, and will not repent." Having, then, in this way set the seal to these tenets, he seeks to inveigle (his followers) with more legends, (which are detailed) through a greater number of books; and so he conducts (his readers) to the Good One, consummating the initiated (by admitting them into) the unspeakable Mysteries. In order, however, that we may not wade through more of their volumes, we shall illustrate the ineffable Mysteries (of Justinus) from one book of his, inasmuch as, according to his supposition, it is (a work) of high repute. Now this volume is inscribed Baruch; and one fabulous account out of many which is explained by (Justinus) in this (volume), we shall point out, inasmuch as it is to be found in Herodotus. But after imparting a different shape to this (account), he explains it to his pupils as if it were something novel, being under the impression that the entire arrangement of his doctrine (springs) out of it.

Chapter XX.—The Cosmogony of Justinus an Allegorical Explanation of Herodotus' Legend of Hercules.

Herodotus, then, asserts that Hercules, when driving the oxen of Geryon from Erytheia, came into Scythia, and that, being wearied with travelling, he retired into some desert spot and slept for a short time. But while he slumbered his horse disappeared, seated on which he had performed his lengthened journey. On being aroused from repose, he, however, instituted a diligent search through the desert, endeavoring to discover his horse. And though he is unsuccessful in his search after the horse, he yet finds in the desert a certain damsel, half of whose form was that of woman, and proceeded to question her if she had seen the horse anywhere. The girl, however, replies that she had seen (the animal), but that 70 she would not show him unless Hercules previously would come along with her for the purpose of sexual intercourse. Now Herodotus informs us that her upper parts as far as the groin were those of a virgin, but that everything below the body after the groin presented some horrible appearance of a snake. In anxiety, however, for the discovery of his horse, Hercules complies with the monster's request; for he knew her (carnally), and made her pregnant. And he foretold, after coition, that she had by him in her womb three children at the same time, who were destined to become illustrious. And he ordered that she, on bringing forth, should impose on the children as soon as born the following names: Agathyrsus, Gelonus, and Scytha. And as the reward of this (favor) receiving his horse from the beast-like damsel, he went on his way, taking with him the cattle also. But after these (details), Herodotus has a protracted account; adieu, however, to it for the present. But what the opinions are of Justinus, who transfers this legend into (his account of) the generation of the universe, we shall explain.

Chapter XXI.—Justinus' Triad of Principles; His Angelography Founded on This Triad; His Explanation of the Birth, Life, and Death of Our Lord.

This (heresiarch) makes the following statement. There are three unbegotten principles of the universe, two male (and) one female. Of the male (principles), however, a certain one, is denominated good, and it alone is called after this manner, and possesses a power of prescience concerning the universe. But the other is father of all begotten things, devoid of prescience, and invisible. And the female (principle) is devoid of prescience, passionate, two-minded, two-bodied, in every respect answering (the description of) the girl in the legend of Herodotus, as far as the groin a virgin, and (in) the parts below (resembling) a snake, as Justinus says. But this girl is styled Edem and

Israel. And these principles of the universe are, he says, roots and fountains from which existing things have been produced, but that there was not anything else. The Father, then, who is devoid of prescience, beholding that half-woman Edem, passed into a concupiscent desire for her. But this Father, he says, is called Elohim. Not less did Edem also long for Elohim, and the mutual passion brought them together into the one nuptial couch of love. And from such an intercourse the Father generates out of Edem unto himself twelve angels. And the names of the angels begotten by the Father are these: Michaël, Amen, Baruch, Gabriel, Esaddæus....And of the maternal angels which Edem brought forth, the names in like manner have been subjoined, and they are as follows: Babel, Achamoth, Naas, Bel, Belias, Satan, Saël, Adonæus, Leviathan, Pharao, Carcamenos, (and) Lathen.

Of these twenty-four angels the paternal ones are associated with the Father, and do all things according to His will; and the maternal (angels are associated with) Edem the Mother. And the multitude of all these angels together is Paradise, he says, concerning which Moses speaks: "God planted a garden in Eden towards the east," that is, towards the face of Edem, that Edem might behold the garden—that is, the angels—continually. Allegorically the angels are styled trees of this garden, and the tree of life is the third of the paternal angels—Baruch. And the tree of the knowledge of good and evil is the third of the maternal angels—Naas. For so, says (Justinus), one ought to interpret the words of Moses, observing, "Moses said these things disguisedly, from the fact that all do not attain the truth." And, he says, Paradise being formed from the conjugal joy of Elohim and Edem, the angels of Elohim receiving from the most beauteous earth, that is, not from the portion of Edem resembling a monster, but from the parts above the groin of human shape, and gentle—in aspect,—make man out of the earth. But out of the parts resembling a monster are produced wild beasts, and the rest of the animal creation. They made man, therefore, as a symbol of the unity and love (subsisting) between them; and they depute their own powers unto him, Edem the soul, but Elohim the spirit. And the man Adam is produced as some actual seal and memento of love, and as an everlasting emblem of the marriage of Edem and Elohim. And in like manner also Eve was produced, he says, as Moses has described, an image and emblem (as well as) a seal, to be preserved for ever, of Edem. And in like manner also a soul was deposited in Eve,—an image—from Edem, but a spirit from Elohim. And there were given to them commandments, "Be fruitful, and multiply, and replenish the earth," that is, Edem; for so he wishes that it had been written. For the entire of the power belonging unto herself, Edem conferred upon Elohim as a sort of nuptial dowry. Whence, he says, from imitation of that primary marriage up to this day, women bring a dowry to their husbands, complying with a certain divine and paternal law that came into existence on the part of Edem towards Elohim.

And when all things were created as has been described by Moses—both heaven and earth, and the things therein—the twelve angels of the Mother were divided into four principles, and each fourth part of them is called a river—Phison, and Gehon, and Tigris, and Euphrates, as, he says, Moses states. These twelve angels, being mutually connected, go about into four parts, and manage the world, holding from Edem a sort of viceregal authority over the world. But they do not always continue in the same places, but move around as if in a circular dance, changing place after place, and at set times and intervals retiring to the localities subject to themselves. And when Phison holds sway over places, famine, distress, and affliction prevail in that part of the earth, for the battalion of these angels is niggardly. In like manner also there belong to each part of the four, according to the power and nature of each, evil times and hosts of diseases. And continually, according to the dominion of each fourth part, this stream of evil, just (like a current) of rivers, careers, according to the will of Edem, uninterruptedly around the world. And from some cause of this description has arisen the necessity of evil.

When Elohim had prepared and created the world as a result from joint pleasure, He wished to ascend up to the elevated parts of heaven, and to see that not anything of what pertained to the creation labored under deficiency. And He took His Own angels with Him, for His nature was to mount aloft, leaving Edem below: for inasmuch as she was earth, she was not disposed to follow upward her spouse. Elohim, then, coming to the highest part of heaven above, and beholding a light superior to that which He Himself had created, exclaimed, "Open me the gates, that entering in I may acknowledge the Lord; for I considered Myself to be Lord." A voice was returned to Him from the light, saying, "This is the gate of the Lord: through this the righteous enter in." And immediately the gate was opened, and the Father, without the angels, entered, (advancing) towards the Good One, and beheld "what eye hath not seen, and ear hath not heard, and what hath not entered into the heart of man to (conceive)." Then the Good One says to him, "Sit thou on my right hand." And the Father says to the Good One, "Permit me, Lord, to overturn the world which I have made, for my spirit is bound to men. And I wish to receive it back (from them." Then the Good One replies to him, "No evil canst thou do while thou art with me, for both thou and Edem made the world as a result of conjugal joy. Permit Edem, then, to hold possession of the world as long as she wishes; but do you remain with me." Then Edem, knowing that she had been deserted by Elohim, was seized with grief, and placed beside herself her own angels. And she adorned herself after a comely fashion, if by any means Elohim, passing into concupiscent desire, might descend (from heaven) to her.

When, however, Elohim, overpowered by the Good One, no longer descended to Edem, Edem commanded Babel, which is Venus, to cause adulteries and dissolutions of marriages among men. (And she adopted this expedient) in order that, as she had been divorced from Elohim, so also the spirit of Elohim, which is in men, being wrong with sorrow, might be punished by such separations, and might undergo precisely the sufferings which (were being endured by) the deserted Edem. And Edem gives great power to her third angel, Naas, that by every species of punishment she might chasten the spirit of Elohim which is in men, in order that Elohim, through the spirit, might be punished for having deserted his spouse, in violation of the agreements entered into between them. Elohim the father, seeing these things, sends forth Baruch, the third angel among his own, to succor the spirit that is in all men. Baruch then coming, stood in the midst of the angels of Edem, that is, in the midst of paradise—for paradise is the angels, in the midst of whom he stood,—and issued to the man the following injunction: "Of every tree that is in paradise thou mayest freely eat, but thou mayest not eat of the tree of the knowledge of good and evil," which is Naas. Now the meaning is, that he should obey the rest of the eleven angels of Edem, for the eleven possess passions, but are not guilty of transgression. Naas, however, has committed sin, for he went in unto Eve, deceiving her, and debauched her; and (such an act as) this is a violation of law. He, however, likewise went in unto Adam, and had unnatural intercourse with him; and this is itself also a piece of turpitude, whence have arisen adultery and sodomy.

Henceforward vice and virtue were prevalent among men, arising from a single source—that of the Father. For the Father having ascended to the Good One, points out from time to time the way to those desirous of ascending (to him likewise). After having, however, departed from Edem, he caused an originating principle of evil for the spirit of the Father that is in men. Baruch therefore was dispatched to Moses, and through him spoke to the children of Israel, that they might be converted unto the Good One. But the third angel (Naas), by the soul which came from Edem upon Moses, as also upon all men, obscured the precepts of Baruch, and caused his own peculiar injunctions to be hearkened unto. For this reason the soul is arrayed against the spirit, and the spirit against the soul. For the soul is Edem, but the spirit Elohim, and each of these exists in all men, both females and males. Again, after these (occurrences), Baruch was sent to the Prophets, that through the Prophets the spirit that dwelleth in men might hear (words of warning), and might avoid Edem and the wicked fiction, just as the Father had fled from Elohim. In like manner also—by the prophets—Naas, by a similar device, through the soul that dwells in man, along with the spirit of the Father, enticed away the prophets, and all (of them) were allured after him, and did not follow the words of Baruch, which Elohim enjoined.

Ultimately Elohim selected Hercules, an uncircumcised prophet, and sent him to quell the twelve angels of Edem, and release the Father from the twelve angels, those wicked ones of the creation. These are the twelve conflicts of Hercules which Hercules underwent, in order, from first to last, viz., Lion, and Hydra, and Boar, and the others successively. For they say that these are the names (of them) among the Gentiles, and they have been derived with altered denominations from the energy of the maternal angels. When he seemed to have vanquished his antagonists, Omphale—now she is Babel or Venus—clings to him and entices away Hercules, and divests him of his power, viz., the commands of Baruch which Elohim issued. And in place (of this power, Babel) envelopes him in her own peculiar robe, that is, in the power of Edem, who is the power below; and in this way the prophecy of Hercules remained unfulfilled, and his works.

Finally, however, in the days of Herod the king, Baruch is dispatched, being sent down once more by Elohim; and coming to Nazareth, he found Jesus, son of Joseph and Mary, a child of twelve years, feeding sheep. And he announces to him all things from the beginning, whatsoever had been done by Edem and Elohim, and whatsoever would be likely to take place hereafter, and spoke the following words: "All the prophets anterior to you have been enticed. Put forth an effort, therefore, Jesus, Son of man, not to be allured, but preach this word unto men, and carry back tidings to them of things pertaining to the Father, and things pertaining to the Good One, and ascend to the Good One, and sit there with Elohim, Father of us all." And Jesus was obedient unto the angel, saying that, "I shall do all things, Lord," and proceeded to preach. Naas therefore wished to entice this one also. (Jesus, however, was not disposed to listen to his overtures), for he remained faithful to Baruch. Therefore Naas, being inflamed with anger because he was not able to seduce him, caused him to be crucified. He, however, leaving the body of Edem on the (accursed) tree, ascended to the Good One; saying, however, to Edem, "Woman, thou retains thy son," that is, the natural and the earthly man. But (Jesus) himself commending his spirit into the hands of the Father, ascended to the Good One. Now the Good One is Priapus, (and) he it is who antecedently caused the production of everything that exists. On this account he is styled Priapus, because he previously fashioned all things (according to his own design). For this reason, he says, in every temple is placed his statue, which is revered by every creature; and (there are images of him) in the highways, carrying over his head ripened fruits, that is, the produce of the creation, of which he is the cause, having in the first instance formed, (according to His own design), the creation, when as yet it had no existence. When, therefore, he says, you hear men asserting that the swan went in unto Leda, and begat a child from her, (learn that) the swan is Elohim, and Leda Edem. And when people allege that an eagle went in unto Ganymede, (know that) the eagle is Naas, and Ganymede Adam. And when they assert that gold (in a shower) went in unto Danaë and begat a child from her, (recollect that) the gold is Elohim, and Danaë is Edem. And similarly, in the same manner adducing all accounts of this description, which correspond with (the nature of) legends, they pursue the work of instruction. When, therefore, the prophet says, "Hearken, O heaven, and give ear, O earth; the Lord hath spoken," he means by heaven, (Justinus) says, the spirit which is in man from Elohim; and by earth, the soul which is in man along with the spirit; and by Lord, Baruch; and by Israel, Edem, for Israel as well as Edem is called the spouse of Elohim. "Israel," he says, "did not know me (Elohim); for had he known me, that I am with the Good One, he would not have punished through paternal ignorance the spirit which is in men."

Chapter XXII.—Oath Used by the Justinian Heretics; The Book of Baruch; The Repertory of Their System.

Hence also, in the first book inscribed "Baruch," has been written the oath which they compel those to swear who are about to hear these mysteries, and be initiated with the Good One. And this oath, (Justinus) says, our Father Elohim swore when He was beside the Good One, and having sworn He did not repent (of the oath), respecting which, he says, it has been written, "The Lord swore, and will not repent." Now the oath is couched in these terms: "I swear by that Good One who is above all, to guard these mysteries, and to divulge them to no one, and not to relapse from the Good One to the creature." And when he has sworn this oath, he goes on to the Good One, and beholds "whatever things eye hath not seen, and ear hath not heard, and which have not entered into the heart of man;" and he drinks from life-giving water, which is to them, as they suppose, a bath, a fountain of life-giving, bubbling water. For there has been a separation made between water and water; and there is water, that below the firmament of the wicked creation, in which earthly and animal men are washed; and there is life-giving water, (that) above the firmament, of the Good One, in which spiritual (and) living men are washed; and in this Elohim washed Himself. and having washed did not repent. And when, he says, the prophet affirms, "Take unto yourself a wife of whoredom, since the earth has abandoned itself to fornication, (departing) from (following) after the Lord;" that is, Edem (departs) from Elohim. (Now) in these words, he says, the prophet clearly declares the entire mystery, and is not hearkened unto by reason of the wicked machinations of Naas. According to that same manner, they deliver other prophetical passages in a similar spirit of interpretation throughout numerous books. The volume, however, inscribed "Baruch," is pre-eminently to them the one in which the reader will ascertain the entire explanation of their legendary system (to be contained). Beloved, though I have encountered many heresies, yet with no wicked (heresiarch) worse than this (Justinus) has it been my lot to meet. But, in truth, (the followers of Justinus) ought to imitate the example of his Hercules, and to cleanse, as the saying is, the cattle-shed of Augias, or rather I should say, a ditch, into which, as soon as the adherents of this (heresiarch) have fallen, they can never be cleansed; nay, they will not be able even to raise their heads.

## Chapter XXIII.—Subsequent Heresies Deducible from the System of Justinus.

Since, then, we have explained the attempts (at a system) of the pseudo-gnostic Justinus, it appears likewise expedient in the following books to elucidate the opinions put forward in heresies following (in the way of consequence upon the doctrines of Justinus), and to leave not a single one of these (speculators) unrefuted. Our refutation will be accomplished by adducing the assertions made by them; such (at least of their statements) as are sufficient for making a public example (of these heretics). (And we shall attain our purpose), even though there should only be condemned606 the secret and ineffable (mysteries) practiced amongst them, into which, silly mortals that they are, scarcely (even) with considerable labor are they initiated. Let us then see what also Simon affirms.

## Book VI.

Contents. The following are the contents of the sixth book of the Refutation of all Heresies:—

What the opinions are that are attempted (to be established) by Simon, and that his doctrine derives its force from the (lucubrations) of magicians and poets.

What are the opinions propounded by Valentinus, and that his system is not constructed out of the Scriptures, but out of the Platonic and Pythagorean tenets.

And what are the opinions of Secundus, and Ptolemæus, and Heracleon, as persons also who themselves advanced the same doctrines as the philosophers among the Greeks but enunciated them in different phraseology.

And what are the suppositions put forward by Marcus and Colarbasus, and that some of them devoted their attention to magical arts and the Pythagorean numbers.

Chapter I.—The Ophites the Progenitors of Subsequent Heresies.

Whatever opinions, then, were entertained by those who derived the first principles (of their doctrine) from the serpent, and in process of time deliberately brought forward into public notice their tenets, we have explained in the book preceding this, (and) which is the fifth of the Refutation of Heresies. But now also I shall not be silent as regards the opinions of (heresiarchs) who follow these (Ophites in succession); nay, not one (speculation) will I leave unrefuted, if it is possible to remember all (their tenets), and the secret orgies of these (heretics) which one may fairly style orgies,—for they who propagate such audacious opinions are not far distant from the anger (of God),—that I may avail myself of the assistance of etymology.

Chapter II.—Simon Magus.

It seems, then, expedient likewise to explain now the opinions of Simon, a native of Gitta, a village of Samaria; and we shall also prove that his successors, taking a starting point from him, have endeavored (to establish) similar opinions under a change of name. This Simon being an adept in sorceries, both making a mockery of many, partly according to the art of Thrasymedes, in the manner in which we have explained above, and partly also by the assistance of demons perpetrating his villainy, attempted to deify himself. (But) the man was a (mere) cheat, and full of folly, and the Apostles reproved him in the Acts. With much greater wisdom and moderation than Simon, did Apsethus the Libyan, inflamed with a similar wish, endeavor to have himself considered a god in Libya. And inasmuch as his legendary system does not present any wide divergence from the inordinate desire of that silly Simon, it seems expedient to furnish an explanation of it, as one worthy of the attempt made by this man.

Chapter III.—Story of Apsethus the Libyan.

Apsethus the Libyan inordinately longed to become a god; but when, after repeated intrigues, he altogether failed to accomplish his desire, he nevertheless wished to appear to have become a god; and he did at all events appear, as time wore on, to have in reality become a god. For the foolish Libyans were accustomed to sacrifice unto him as to some divine power, supposing that they were yielding credence to a voice that came down from above, from heaven. For, collecting into one and the same cage a great number of birds,—parrots,—he shut them up. Now there are very many parrots throughout Libya, and very distinctly these imitate the human voice. This man, having for a time nourished the birds, was in the habit of teaching them to say, "Apsethus is a god." After, however, the birds had practiced this for a long period, and were accustomed to the utterance of that which he thought, when said, would make it supposed that Apsethus was a god, then, opening the habitation (of the birds), he let forth the parrots, each in a different direction. While the birds, however, were on the wing, their sound went out into all Libya, and the expressions of these reached as far as the Hellenic country. And thus the Libyans, being astonished at the voice of the birds, and not perceiving the knavery perpetrated by Apsethus, held Apsethus to be a god. Someone, however, of the Greeks, by accurate examination, perceiving the trick of the supposed god, by means of those same parrots not only refutes, but also utterly destroys, that boastful and tiresome fellow. Now the Greek, by confining many of the parrots, taught them anew to say, "Apsethus, having caged us, compelled us to say, Apsethus is a god." But having heard of the recantation of the parrots, the Libyans, coming together, all unanimously decided on burning Apsethus.

Chapter IV.—Simon's Forced Interpretation of Scripture; Plagiarizes from Heraclitus and Aristotle; Simon's System of Sensible and Intelligible Existences.

In this way we must think concerning Simon the magician, so that we may compare him unto the Libyan, far sooner than unto Him who, though made man, was in reality God. If, however, the assertion of this likeness is in itself accurate, and the sorcerer was the subject of a passion similar to Apsethus, let us endeavor to teach anew the parrots of Simon, that Christ, who stood, stands, and will stand, (that is, was, is, and is to come,) was not Simon. But (Jesus) was man, offspring of the seed of a woman, born of blood and the will of the flesh, as also the rest (of humanity). And that these things are so, we shall easily prove as the discussion proceeds.

Now Simon, both foolishly and knavishly paraphrasing the law of Moses, makes his statements (in the manner following): For when Moses asserts that "God is a burning and consuming fire," taking what is said by Moses not in its correct sense, he affirms that fire is the originating principle of the universe. (But Simon) does not consider what the statement is which is made, namely, that it is not that God is a fire, but a burning and consuming fire, (thereby) not only putting a violent sense upon the actual law of Moses, but even plagiarizing from Heraclitus the Obscure. And Simon denominates the originating principle of the universe an indefinite power, expressing himself thus: "This is the treatise of a revelation of (the) voice and name (recognizable) by means of intellectual apprehension of the Great Indefinite Power. Wherefore it will be sealed, (and) kept secret, (and) hid, (and) will repose in the habitation, at the foundation of which lies the root of all things." And he asserts that this man who is born of blood is (the aforesaid) habitation, and that in him resides an indefinite power, which he affirms to be the root of the universe. Now the indefinite power which is fire, constitutes, according to Simon, not any uncompounded (essence, in conformity with the opinion of those who) assert that the four elements are simple, and who have (therefore) likewise imagined that fire, (which is one of the four,) is simple. But (this is far from being the case): for there is, (he maintains,) a certain twofold nature of fire; and of this twofold (nature) he denominates one part a something secret, and another a something manifest, and that the secret are hidden in the manifest portions of the fire, and that the manifest portions of the fire derive their being from its secret (portions). This, however, is what Aristotle denominates by (the expressions) "potentiality" and "energy," or (what) Plato (styles) "intelligible" and "sensible." And the manifest portion of the fire comprises all things in itself, whatsoever any one might discern, or even whatever objects of the visible creation he may happen to overlook. But the entire secret (portion of the fire) which one may discern is cognized by intellect and evades the power of the senses; or one fails to observe it, from want of a capacity for that particular sort of perception. In general, however, inasmuch as all existing things fall under the categories, namely, of what are objects of Sense, and what are objects of Intellect, and as for the denomination of these (Simon) employs the terms secret and manifest; it may, (I say, in general,) be affirmed that the fire, (I mean) the super-celestial (fire), is a treasure, as it were a large tree, just such a one as in a dream was seen by Nabuchodonosor, out of which all flesh is nourished. And the manifest portion of the fire he regards as the stem, the branches, the leaves, (and) the external rind which overlaps them. All these (appendages), he says, of the Great Tree being kindled, are made to disappear by reason of the blaze of the all-devouring fire. The fruit, however, of the tree, when it is fully grown, and has received its own form, is deposited in a granary, not (flung) into the fire. For, he says, the fruit has been produced for the purpose of being laid in the storehouse, whereas the chaff that it may be delivered over to the fire. (Now the chaff) is stem, (and is) generated not for its own sake, but for that of the fruit.

## Chapter V.—Simon Appeals to Scripture in Support of His System.

And this, he says, is what has been written in Scripture: "For the vineyard of the Lord of Sabaoth is the house of Israel, and the man of Judah is His beloved plant." If, however, the man of Judah (is) the beloved plant, it has been proved, he says, that there is not any other tree but that man. But concerning the secretion and dissolution of this (tree), Scripture, he says, has spoken sufficiently. And as regards instruction for those who have been fashioned after the image (of him), that statement is enough which is made (in Scripture), that "all flesh is grass, and all the glory of flesh, as it were, a flower of grass. The grass withered, and its flower falls; but the word of the Lord abides forever." The word of the Lord, he says, is that word which is produced in the mouth, and (is) a Logos, but nowhere else exists there a place of generation.

## Chapter VI.—Simon's System Expounded in the Work, Great Announcement; Follows Empedocles.

Now, to express myself briefly, inasmuch as the fire is of this description, according to Simon, and since all things are visible and invisible, (and) in like manner resonant and not resonant, numerable and not subjects of numeration; he denominates in the Great Announcement a perfect intelligible (entity), after such a mode, that each of those things which, existing indefinitely, may be infinitely comprehended, both speaks, and understands, and acts in such a manner as Empedocles speaks of:—

"For earth, indeed, by earth we see, and water by water,
And air divine by air, and fire fierce by fire,
And love by love, and also strife by gloomy strife."

Chapter VII.—Simon's System of a Threefold Emanation by Pairs.

For, he says, he is in the habit of considering that all these portions of the fire, both visible and invisible, are possessed of perception and a share of intelligence. The world, therefore, that which is generated, was produced from the unbegotten fire. It began, however, to exist, he says, according to the following manner. He who was begotten from the principle of that fire took six roots, and those primary ones, of the originating principle of generation. And, he says that the roots were made from the fire in pairs, which roots he terms "Mind" and "Intelligence," "Voice" and "Name," "Ratiocination" and "Reflection." And that in these six roots resides simultaneously the entire indefinite power potentially, (however) not actually. And this indefinite power, he says, is he who stood, stands, and will stand. Wherefore, whensoever he may be made into an image, inasmuch as he exists in the six powers, he will exist (there) substantially, potentially, quantitively, (and) completely. (And he will be a power) one and the same with the unbegotten and indefinite power, and not laboring under any greater deficiency than that unbegotten and unalterable (and) indefinite power. If, however, he may continue only potentially in the six powers, and has not been formed into an image, he vanishes, he says, and is destroyed in such a way as the grammatical or geometrical capacity in man's soul. For when the capacity takes unto itself an art, a light of existent things is produced; but when (the capacity) does not take unto itself (an art), unskillfulness and ignorance are the results; and just as when (the power) was non-existent, it perishes along with the expiring man.

Chapter VIII.—Further Progression of This Threefold Emanation; Co-Existence with the Double Triad of a Seventh Existence.

And of those six powers, and of the seventh which co-exists with them, the first pair, Mind and Intelligence, he calls Heaven and Earth. And that one of these, being of male sex, beholds from above and takes care of his partner, but that the earth receives below the rational fruits, akin to the earth, which are borne down from the heaven. On this account, he says, the Logos, frequently looking towards the things that are being generated from Mind and Intelligence, that is, from Heaven and Earth, exclaims, "Hear, O heaven, and give ear, O earth, because the Lord has spoken. I have brought forth children, and exalted them; and these have rejected me." Now, he who utters these words, he says, is the seventh power—he who stood, stands, and will stand; for he himself is cause of those beauteous objects of creation which Moses commended, and said that they were very good. But Voice and Name (the second of the three pairs) are Sun and Moon; and Ratiocination and Reflection (the third of the three pairs) are Air and Water. And in all these is intermingled and blended, as I have declared, the great, the indefinite, the (self-) existing power.

Chapter IX.—Simon's Interpretation of the Mosaic Hexaëmeron; His Allegorical Representation of Paradise.

When, therefore, Moses has spoken of "the six days in which God made heaven and earth, and rested on the seventh from all His works," Simon, in a manner already specified, giving (these and other passages of Scripture) a different application (from the one intended by the holy writers), deifies himself. When, therefore, (the followers of Simon) affirm that there are three days begotten before sun and moon, they speak enigmatically of Mind and Intelligence, that is, Heaven and Earth, and of the seventh power, (I mean) the indefinite one. For these three powers are produced antecedent to all the rest. But when they say, "He begot me prior to all the Ages," such statements, he says, are alleged to hold good concerning the seventh power. Now this seventh power, which was a power existing in the indefinite power, which was produced prior to all the Ages, this is, he says, the seventh power, respecting which Moses utters the following words: "And the Spirit of God was wafted over the water;" that is, says (the Simonian), the Spirit which contains all things in itself, and is an image of the indefinite power about which Simon speaks,—"an image from an incorruptible form, that alone reduces all things into order." For this power that is wafted over the water, being begotten, he says, from an incorruptible form alone, reduces all things into order. When, therefore, according to these (heretics), there ensued some such arrangement, and (one) similar (to it) of the world, the Deity, he says, proceeded to form man, taking clay from the earth. And He formed him not uncompounded, but twofold, according to (His own) image and likeness. Now the image is the Spirit that is wafted over the water; and whosoever is not fashioned into a figure of this, will perish with the world, inasmuch as he continues only potentially, and does exist actually. This, he says, is what has been spoken, "that we should not be condemned with the world." If one, however, be made into the figure of (the Spirit), and be generated from an indivisible point, as it has been written in the Announcement, (such a one, albeit) small, will become great. But what is great will continue unto infinite and unalterable duration, as being that which no longer is subject to the conditions of a generated entity.

How then, he says, and in what manner, does God form man? In Paradise; for so it seems to him. Grant Paradise, he says, to be the womb; and that this is a true (assumption) the Scripture will teach, when it utters the words, "I am He who forms thee in thy mother's womb." For this also he wishes to have been written so. Moses, he says, resorting to allegory, has declared Paradise to be the womb, if we ought to rely on his statement. If, however, God forms man in his mother's womb—that is, in Paradise—as I have affirmed, let Paradise be the womb, and Edem the after-birth, "a river flowing forth from Edem, for the purpose of irrigating Paradise," (meaning by this) the navel. This navel, he says, is separated into four principles; for on either side of the navel are situated two arteries, channels of spirit, and two veins, channels of blood. But when, he says, the umbilical vessels proceed forth from Edem, that is, the caul in which the fetus is enveloped grows into the (fetus) that is being formed in the vicinity of the epigastrium,—(now) all in common denominate this a navel,—these two veins through which the blood flows, and is conveyed from Edem, the afterbirth, to what are styled the gates of the liver; (these veins, I say,) nourish the fetus. But the arteries which we have spoken of as being channels of spirit, embrace the bladder on both sides, around the pelvis, and connect it with the great artery, called the aorta, in the vicinity of the dorsal ridge. And in this way the spirit, making its way through the ventricles to the heart, produces a movement of the fetus. For the infant that was formed in Paradise neither receives nourishment through the mouth, nor breathes through the nostrils: for as it lay in the midst of moisture, at its feet was death, if it attempted to breathe; for it would (thus) have been drawn away from moisture, and perished (accordingly). But (one may go further than this); for the entire (fetus) is bound tightly round by a covering styled the caul, and is nourished by a navel, and it receives through the (aorta), in the vicinity of the dorsal ridge, as I have stated, the substance of the spirit.

Chapter X.—Simon's Explanation of the First Two Books of Moses.

The river, therefore, he says, which proceeds out of Edem is divided into four principles, four channels—that is, into four senses, belonging to the creature that is being born, viz., seeing, smelling, taste, and touch; for the child formed in Paradise has these senses only. This, he says, is the law which Moses appointed; and in reference to this very law, each of his books has been written, as the inscriptions evince. The first book is Genesis. The inscription of the book is, he says, sufficient for a knowledge of the universe. For this is (equivalent in meaning with) generation, (that is,) vision, into which one section of the river is divided. For the world was seen by the power of vision. Again, the inscription of the second book is Exodus. For what has been produced, passing through the Red Sea, must come into the wilderness,—now they say he calls the Red (Sea) blood,—and taste bitter water. For bitter, he says, is the water which is (drunk) after (crossing) the Red Sea, which (water) is a path to be trodden, that leads (us) to a knowledge in (this) life of (our) toilsome and bitter lot. Altered, however, by Moses—that is, by the Logos—that bitter (water) becomes sweet. And that this is so we may hear in common from all who express themselves according to the (sentiments of the) poets:—

> "Dark at the root, like milk, the flower,
> Gods call it 'Moly,' and hard for mortal men
> To dig, but power divine is boundless."

Chapter XI.—Simon's Explanation of the Three Last Books of the Pentateuch.

What is spoken by the Gentiles is sufficient for a knowledge of the universe to those who have ears (capable) of hearing. For whosoever, he says, has tasted this fruit, is not the only one that is changed by Circe into a beast; but also, employing the power of such a fruit, he forms anew and molds afresh, and re-entices into that primary peculiar character of theirs, those that already have been altered into beasts. But a faithful man, and beloved by that sorceress, is, he says, discovered through that milk-like and divine fruit. In like manner, the third book is Leviticus, which is smelling, or respiration. For the entire of that book is (an account) of sacrifices and offerings. Where, however, there is a sacrifice, a certain savor of the fragrance arises from the sacrifice through the incense-offerings; and in regard of this fragrance (the sense of) smelling is a test. Numbers, the fourth of the books, signifies taste, where the discourse is operative. For, from the fact of its speaking all things, it is denominated by numerical arrangement. But Deuteronomy, he says, is written in reference to the (sense of) touch possessed by the child that is being formed. For as touch, by seizing the things that are seen by the other senses, sums them up and ratifies them, testing what is rough, or warm, or clammy, (or cold); so the fifth book of the law constitutes a summary of the four books preceding this.

All things, therefore, he says, when unbegotten, are in us potentially, not actually, as the grammatical or geometrical (art). If, then, one receives proper instruction and teaching, and (where consequently) what is bitter will be altered into what is sweet,—that is, the spears into pruning-hooks, and the swords into plough-shares,—there will not be chaff and wood begotten for fire, but mature fruit, fully formed, as I said, equal and similar to the unbegotten and indefinite power. If, however, a tree continues alone, not producing fruit fully formed, it is utterly destroyed. For somewhere near, he says, is the axe (which is laid) at the roots of the tree. Every tree, he says, which does not produce good fruit, is hewn down and cast into fire.

## Chapter XII.—Fire a Primal Principle, According to Simon.

According to Simon, therefore, there exists that which is blessed and incorruptible in a latent condition in every one—(that is,) potentially, not actually; and that this is He who stood, stands, and is to stand. He has stood above in unbegotten power. He stands below, when in the stream of waters, He was begotten in a likeness. He is to stand above, beside the blessed indefinite power, if He be fashioned into an image. For, he says, there are three who have stood; and except there were three Æons who have stood, the unbegotten one is not adorned. (Now the unbegotten one) is, according to them, wafted over the water, and is re-made, according to the similitude (of an eternal nature), a perfect celestial (being), in no (quality of) intelligence formed inferior to the unbegotten power: that is what they say—I and you, one; you, before me; I, that which is after you. This, he says, is one power divided above (and) below, generating itself, making itself grow, seeking itself, finding itself, being mother of itself, father of itself, sister of itself, spouse of itself, daughter of itself, son of itself, mother, father, a unit, being a root of the entire circle of existence.

And that, he says, the originating principle of the generation of things begotten is from fire, he discerns after some such method as the following. Of all things, (i.e.) of whatsoever there is a generation, the beginning of the desire of the generation is from fire. Wherefore the desire after mutable generation is denominated "to be inflamed." For when the fire is one, it admits of two conversions. For, he says, blood in the man being both warm and yellow, is converted as a figured flame into seed; but in the woman this same blood is converted into milk. And the conversion of the male becomes generation, but the conversion of the female nourishment for the fetus. This, he says, is "the flaming sword, which turned to guard the way of the tree of life." For the blood is converted into seed and milk, and this power becomes mother and father—father of those things that are in process of generation, and the augmentation of those things that are being nourished; (and this power is) without further want, (and) self-sufficient. And, he says, the tree of life is guarded, as we have stated, by the brandished flaming sword. And it is the seventh power, that which (is produced) from itself, (and) which contains all (powers, and) which reposes in the six powers. For if the flaming sword be not brandished, that good tree will be destroyed, and perish. If, however, these be converted into seed and milk, the principle that resides in these potentially, and is in possession of a proper position, in which is evolved a principle of souls, (such a principle,) beginning, as it were, from a very small spark, will be altogether magnified, and will increase and become a power indefinite (and) unalterable, (equal and similar) to an unalterable age, which no longer passes into the indefinite age.

Chapter XIII.—His Doctrine of Emanation Further Expanded.

Therefore, according to this reasoning, Simon became confessedly a god to his silly followers, as that Libyan, namely, Apsethus—begotten, no doubt, and subject to passion, when he may exist potentially, but devoid of propensions. (And this too, though born from one having propensions, and uncreated though born) from one that is begotten, when He may be fashioned into a figure, and, becoming perfect, may come forth from two of the primary powers, that is, Heaven and Earth. For Simon expressly speaks of this in the "Revelation" after this manner: "To you, then, I address the things which I speak, and (to you) I write what I write. The writing is this: there are two offshoots from all the Æons, having neither beginning nor end, from one root. And this is a power, viz., Sige, (who is) invisible (and) incomprehensible. And one of these (offshoots) appears from above, which constitutes a great power, (the creative) Mind of the universe, which manages all things, (and is) a male. The other (offshoot), however, is from below, (and constitutes) a great Intelligence, and is a female which produces all things. From whence, ranged in pairs opposite each other, they undergo conjugal union, and manifest an intermediate interval, namely, an incomprehensible air, which has neither beginning nor end. But in this is a father who sustains all things, and nourishes things that have beginning and end. This is he who stood, stands, and will stand, being an hermaphrodite power according to the pre-existent indefinite power, which has neither beginning nor end. Now this (power) exists in isolation. For Intelligence, (that subsists) in unity, proceeded forth from this (power), (and) became two. And that (father) was one, for having in himself this (power) he was isolated, and, however, He was not primal though pre-existent; but being rendered manifest to himself from himself, he passed into a state of duality. But neither was he denominated father before this (power) would style him father. As, therefore, he himself, bringing forward himself by means of himself, manifested unto himself his own peculiar intelligence, so also the intelligence, when it was manifested, did not exercise the function of creation. But beholding him, she concealed the Father within herself, that is, the power; and it is an hermaphrodite power, and an intelligence. And hence it is that they are ranged in pairs, one opposite the other; for power is in no wise different from intelligence, inasmuch as they are one. For from those things that are above is discovered power; and from those below, intelligence. So it is, therefore, that likewise what is manifested from these, being unity, is discovered (to be) duality, an hermaphrodite having the female in itself. This, (therefore,) is Mind (subsisting) in Intelligence; and these are separable one from the other, (though both taken together) are one, (and) are discovered in a state of duality."

Chapter XIV.—Simon Interprets His System by the Mythological Representation of Helen of Troy; Gives an Account of Himself in Connection with the Trojan Heroine; Immorality of His Followers; Simon's View of Christ; The Simonists' Apology for Their Vice.

Simon then, after inventing these (tenets), not only by evil devices interpreted the writings of Moses in whatever way he wished, but even the (works) of the poets. For also he fastens an allegorical meaning on (the story of) the wooden horse and Helen with the torch, and on very many other (accounts), which he transfers to what relates to himself and to Intelligence, and (thus) furnishes a fictitious explanation of them. He said, however, that this (Helen) was the lost sheep. And she, always abiding among women, confounded the powers in the world by reason of her surpassing beauty. Whence, likewise, the Trojan war arose on her account. For in the Helen born at that time resided this Intelligence; and thus, when all the powers were for claiming her (for themselves), sedition and war arose, during which (this chief power) was manifested to nations. And from this circumstance, without doubt, we may believe that Stesichorus, who had through (some) verses reviled her, was deprived of the use of his eyes; and that, again, when he repented and composed recantations, in which he sung (Helen's) praises, he recovered the power of vision. But the angels and the powers below—who, he says, created the world—caused the transference from one body to another of (Helen's soul); and subsequently she stood on the roof of a house in Tyre, a city of Phœnicia, and ongoing down thither (Simon professed to have) found her. For he stated that, principally for the purpose of searching after this (woman), he had arrived (in Tyre), in order that he might rescue her from bondage. And after having thus redeemed her, he was in the habit of conducting her about with himself, alleging that this (girl) was the lost sheep, and affirming himself to be the Power above all things. But the filthy fellow, becoming enamored of this miserable woman called Helen, purchased her (as his slave), and enjoyed her person. He, (however,) was likewise moved with shame towards his disciples, and concocted this figment.

But, again, those who become followers of this impostor—I mean Simon the sorcerer—indulge in similar practices, and irrationally allege the necessity of promiscuous intercourse. They express themselves in the manner following: "All earth is earth, and there is no difference where any one sows, provided he does sow."

But even they congratulate themselves on account of this indiscriminate intercourse, asserting that this is perfect love, and employing the expressions, "holy of holies," and "sanctify one another." For (they would have us believe) that they are not overcome by the supposed vice, for that they have been redeemed. "And (Jesus), by having redeemed Helen in this way," (Simon says,) "has afforded salvation to men through his own peculiar intelligence. For inasmuch as the angels, by reason of their lust for pre-eminence, improperly managed the world, (Jesus Christ) being transformed, and being assimilated to the rulers and powers and angels, came for the restoration (of things). And so (it was that Jesus) appeared as man, when in reality he was not a man. And (so it was) that likewise he suffered—though not actually undergoing suffering, but appearing to the Jews to do so—in Judea as 'Son,' and in Samaria as 'Father,' and among the rest of the Gentiles as 'Holy Spirit.'" And (Simon alleges) that Jesus tolerated being styled by whichever name (of the three just mentioned) men might wish to call him. "And that the prophets, deriving their inspiration from the world-making angels, uttered predictions (concerning him)." Wherefore, (Simon said,) that towards these (prophets) those felt no concern up to the present, who believe on Simon and Helen, and that they do whatsoever they please, as persons free; for they allege that they are saved by grace. For that there is no reason for punishment, even though one shall act wickedly; for such a one is not wicked by nature, but by enactment. "For the angels who created the world made," he says, "whatever enactments they pleased," thinking by such (legislative) words to enslave those who listened to them. But, again, they speak of a dissolution of the world, for the redemption of his own particular adherents.

Chapter XV.—Simon's Disciples Adopt the Mysteries; Simon Meets St. Peter at Rome; Account of Simon's Closing Years.

The disciples, then, of this (Magus), celebrate magical rites, and resort to incantations. And (they profess to) transmit both love-spells and charms, and the demons said to be senders of dreams, for the purpose of distracting whomsoever they please. But they also employ those denominated Paredroi. "And they have an image of Simon (fashioned) into the figure of Jupiter, and (an image) of Helen in the form of Minerva; and they pay adoration to these." But they call the one Lord and the other Lady. And if any one amongst them, on seeing the images of either Simon or Helen, would call them by name, he is cast off, as being ignorant of the mysteries. This Simon, deceiving many in Samaria by his sorceries, was reproved by the Apostles, and was laid under a curse, as it has been written in the Acts. But he afterwards abjured the faith, and attempted these (aforesaid practices). And journeying as far as Rome, he fell in with the Apostles; and to him, deceiving many by his sorceries, Peter offered repeated opposition. This man, ultimately repairing to…(and) sitting under a plane tree, continued to give instruction (in his doctrines). And in truth at last, when conviction was imminent, in case he delayed longer, he stated that, if he were buried alive, he would rise the third day. And accordingly, having ordered a trench to be dug by his disciples, he directed himself to be interred there. They, then, executed the injunction given; whereas he remained (in that grave) until this day, for he was not the Christ. This constitutes the legendary system advanced by Simon, and from this Valentinus derived a starting point (for his own doctrine. This doctrine, in point of fact, was the same with the Simonian, though Valentinus) denominated it under different titles: for "Nous," and "Aletheia," and "Logos," and "Zoe," and "Anthropos," and "Ecclesia," and Æons of Valentinus, are confessedly the six roots of Simon, viz., "Mind" and "Intelligence," "Voice" and "Name," "Ratiocination" and "Reflection." But since it seems to us that we have sufficiently explained Simon's tissue of legends, let us see what also Valentinus asserts.

Chapter XVI.—Heresy of Valentinus; Derived from Plato and Pythagoras.

The heresy of Valentinus is certainly, then, connected with the Pythagorean and Platonic theory. For Plato, in the Timæus, altogether derives his impressions from Pythagoras, and therefore Timæus himself is his Pythagorean stranger. Wherefore, it appears expedient that we should commence by reminding (the reader) of a few points of the Pythagorean and Platonic theory, and that (then we should proceed) to declare the opinions of Valentinus. For even although in the books previously finished by us with so much pains, are contained the opinions advanced by both Pythagoras and Plato, yet at all events I shall not be acting unreasonably, in now also calling to the recollection of the reader, by means of an epitome, the principal heads of the favorite tenets of these (speculators). And this (recapitulation) will facilitate our knowledge of the doctrines of Valentinus, by means of a nearer comparison, and by similarity of composition (of the two systems). For (Pythagoras and Plato) derived these tenets originally from the Egyptians and introduced their novel opinions among the Greeks. But (Valentinus took his opinions) from these, because, although he has suppressed the truth regarding his obligations to (the Greek philosophers), and in this way has endeavored to construct a doctrine, (as it were,) peculiarly his own, yet, in point of fact, he has altered the doctrines of those (thinkers) in names only, and numbers, and has adopted a peculiar terminology (of his own). Valentinus has formed his definitions by measures, in order that he may establish a Hellenic heresy, diversified no doubt, but unstable, and not connected with Christ.

Chapter XVII.—Origin of the Greek Philosophy.

The origin, then, from which Plato derived his theory in the Timæus, is (the) wisdom of the Egyptians. For from this source, by some ancient and prophetical tradition, Solon taught his entire system concerning the generation and destruction of the world, as Plato says, to the Greeks, who were (in knowledge) young children, and were acquainted with no theological doctrine of greater antiquity. In order, therefore, that we may trace accurately the arguments by which Valentinus established his tenets, I shall now explain what are the principles of the philosophy of Pythagoras of Samos,—a philosophy (coupled) with that Silence so celebrated by the Greeks. And next in this manner (I shall elucidate) those (opinions) which Valentinus derives from Pythagoras and Plato, but refers with all solemnity of speech to Christ, and before Christ to the Father of the universe, and to Silence conjoined with the Father.

Chapter XVIII.—Pythagoras' System of Numbers.

Pythagoras, then, declared the originating principle of the universe to be the unbegotten monad, and the generated duad, and the rest of the numbers. And he says that the monad is the father of the duad, and the duad the mother of all things that are being begotten—the begotten one (being mother) of the things that are begotten. And Zaratas, the pupil of Pythagoras, was in the habit of denominating unity a father, and duality a mother. For the duad has been generated from the monad, according to Pythagoras; and the monad is male and primary, but the duad female (and secondary). And from the duad, again, as Pythagoras states, (are generated) the triad and the succeeding numbers up to ten. For Pythagoras is aware that this is the only perfect number—I mean the decade—for that eleven and twelve are an addition and repetition of the decade; not, however, that what is added constitutes the generation of another number. And all solid bodies he generates from incorporeal (essences). For he asserts that an element and principle of both corporeal and incorporeal entities is the point which is indivisible. And from a point, he says, is generated a line, and from a line a surface; and a surface flowing out into a height becomes, he says, a solid body. Whence also the Pythagoreans have a certain object of adjuration, viz., the concord of the four elements. And they swear in these words:—

"By him who to our head quaternion gives,
A font that has the roots of everlasting nature."

Now the quaternion is the originating principle of natural and solid bodies, as the monad of intelligible ones. And that likewise the quaternion generates, he says, the perfect number, as in the case of intelligibles (the monad) does the decade, they teach thus. If any, beginning to number, says one, and adds two, then in like manner three, these (together) will be six, and to these (add) moreover four, the entire (sum), in like manner, will be ten. For one, two, three, four, become ten, the perfect number. Thus, he says, the quaternion in every respect imitated the intelligible monad, which was able to generate a perfect number.

Chapter XIX.—Pythagoras' Duality of Substances; His "Categories."

There are, then, according to Pythagoras, two worlds: one intelligible, which has the monad for an originating principle; and the other sensible. But of this (latter) is the quaternion having the iota, the one tittle, a perfect number. And there likewise is, according to the Pythagoreans, the i, the one tittle, which is chief and most dominant, and enables us to apprehend the substance of those intelligible entities which are capable of being understood through the medium of intellect and of sense. (And in this substance inhere) the nine incorporeal accidents which cannot exist without substance, viz., "quality," and "quantity," and "relation," and "where," and "when," and "position," and "possession," and "action," and "passion." These, then, are the nine accidents (inhering in) substance, and when reckoned with these (substances), contains the perfect number, the i. Wherefore, the universe being divided, as we said, into the intelligible and sensible world, we have also reason from the intelligible (world), in order that by reason we may behold the substance of things that are cognized by intellect, and are incorporeal and divine. But we have, he says, five senses—smelling, seeing, hearing, taste, and touch. Now, by these we arrive at a knowledge of things that are discerned by sense; and so, he says, the sensible is divided from the intelligible world. And that we have for each of these an instrument for attaining knowledge, we perceive from the following consideration. Nothing, he says, of intelligibles can be known to us from sense. For he says neither eye has seen, nor ear heard, nor any whatsoever of the other senses known that (which is cognized by mind). Neither, again, by reason is it possible to arrive at a knowledge of any of the things discernible by sense. But one must see that a thing is white, and taste that it is sweet, and know by hearing that it is musical or out of tune. And whether any odor is fragrant or disagreeable, is the function of smell, not of reason. It is the same with objects of touch; for anything rough, or soft, or warm, or cold, it is not possible to know by hearing, but (far from it), for touch is the judge of such (sensations). Things being thus constituted, the arrangement of things that have been made and are being made is observed to happen in conformity with numerical (combinations). For in the same manner as, commencing from monad, by an addition of monads or triads, and a collection of the succeeding numbers, we make some one very large complex whole of number; (and) then, again, from an amassed number thus formed by addition, we accomplish, by means of a certain subtraction and re-calculation, a solution of the totality of the aggregate numbers; so likewise he asserts that the world, bound by a certain arithmetical and musical chain, was, by its tension and relaxation, and by addition and subtraction, always and forever preserved incorrupt.

Chapter XX.—Pythagoras' Cosmogony; Similar to that of Empedocles.

The Pythagoreans therefore declare their opinion concerning the continuance of the world in some such manner as this:—

"For heretofore it was and will be; never, I ween,
Of both of these will void the age eternal be."

"Of these;" but what are they? Discord and Love. Now, in their system, Love forms the world incorruptible (and) eternal, as they suppose. For substance and the world are one. Discord, however, separates and puts asunder, and evinces numerous attempts by subdividing to form the world. It is just as if one severs into small parts, and divides arithmetically, the myriad into thousands, and hundreds, and tens; and drachma into oboli and small farthings. In this manner, he says, Discord severs the substance of the world into animals, plants, metals and things similar to these. And the fabricator of the generation of all things produced is, according to them, Discord; whereas Love, on the other hand, manages and provides for the universe in such a manner that it enjoys permanence. And conducting together into unity the divided and scattered parts of the universe, and leading them forth from their (separate) mode of existence, (Love) unites and adds to the universe, in order that it may enjoy permanence; and it thus constitutes one system. They will not therefore cease,—neither Discord dividing the world, nor Love attaching to the world the divided parts. Of some such description as this, so it appears, is the distribution of the world according to Pythagoras. But Pythagoras says that the stars are fragments from the sun, and that the souls of animals are conveyed from the stars; and that these are mortal when they are in the body, just as if buried, as it were, in a tomb: whereas that they rise (out of this world) and become immortal, when we are separated from our bodies. Whence Plato, being asked by someone, "What is philosophy?" replied, "It is a separation of soul from body."

Chapter XXI.—Other Opinions of Pythagoras.

Pythagoras, then, became a student of these doctrines likewise, in which he speaks both by enigmas and some such expressions as these: "When you depart from your own (tabernacle), return not; if, however, (you act) not (thus), the Furies, auxiliaries to justice, will overtake you,"—denominating the body one's own (tabernacle), and its passions the Furies. When, therefore, he says, you depart, that is, when you go forth from the body, do not earnestly crave for this; but if you are eagerly desirous (for departure), the passions will once more confine you within the body. For these suppose that there is a transition of souls from one body to another, as also Empedocles, adopting the principles of Pythagoras, affirms. For, says he, souls that are lovers of pleasure, as

Plato states, if, when they are in the condition of suffering incidental to man, they do not evolve theories of philosophy, must pass through all animals and plants (back) again into a human body. And when (the soul) may form a system of speculation thrice in the same body, (he maintains) that it ascends up to the nature of some kindred star. If, however, (the soul) does not philosophize, (it must pass) through the same (succession of changes once more). He affirms, then, that the soul sometimes may become even mortal, if it is overcome by the Furies, that is, the passions (of the body); and immortal, if it succeeds in escaping the Furies, which are the passions.

Chapter XXII.—The "Sayings" Of Pythagoras.

But since also we have chosen to mention the sayings darkly expressed by Pythagoras to his disciples by means of symbols, it seems likewise expedient to remind (the reader) of the rest (of his doctrines. And we touch on this subject) on account also of the heresiarchs, who attempt by some method of this description to converse by means of symbols; and these are not their own, but they have, (in propounding them,) taken advantage of expressions employed by the Pythagoreans. Pythagoras then instructs his disciples, addressing them as follows: "Bind up the sack that carries the bedding." (Now,) inasmuch as they who intend going upon a journey tie their clothes into a wallet, to be ready for the road; so, (in like manner,) he wishes his disciples to be prepared, since every moment death is likely to come upon them by surprise. (In this way Pythagoras sought to effect) that (his followers) should labor under no deficiency in the qualifications required in his pupils. Wherefore of necessity he was in the habit, with the dawn of day, of instructing the Pythagoreans to encourage one another to bind up the sack that carries the bedding, that is, to be ready for death. "Do not stir fire with a sword;" (meaning,) do not, by addressing him, quarrel with an enraged man; for a person in a passion is like fire, whereas the sword is the uttered expression. "Do not trample on a besom;" (meaning,) despise not a small matter. "Plant not a palm tree in a house;" (meaning,) foment not discord in a family, for the palm tree is a symbol of battle and slaughter. "Eat not from a stool;" (meaning,) do not undertake an ignoble art, in order that you may not be a slave to the body, which is corruptible, but make a livelihood from literature. For it lies within your reach both to nourish the body, and make the soul better. "Don't take a bite out of an uncut loaf;" (meaning,) diminish not thy possessions, but live on the profit (of them), and guard thy substance as an entire loaf. "Feed not on beans; (meaning,) accept not the government of a city, for with beans they at that time were accustomed to ballot for their magistrates.

Chapter XXIII.—Pythagoras' Astronomic System.

These, then, and such like assertions, the Pythagoreans put forward; and the heretics, imitating these, are supposed by some to utter important truths. The Pythagorean system, however, lays down that the Creator of all alleged existences is the Great Geometrician and Calculator—a sun; and that this one has been fixed in the whole world, just as in the bodies a soul, according to the statement of Plato. For the sun (being of the nature of) fire, resembles the soul, but the earth (resembles the) body. And, separated from fire, there would be nothing visible, nor would there be any object of touch without something solid; but not any solid body exists without earth. Whence the Deity, locating air in the midst, fashioned the body of the universe out of fire and earth. And the Sun, he says, calculates and geometrically measures the world in some such manner as the following: The world is a unity cognizable by sense; and concerning this (world) we now make these assertions. But one who is an adept in the science of numbers, and a geometrician, has divided it into twelve parts. And the names of these parts are as follow: Aries, Taurus, Gemini, Cancer, Leo, Virgo, Libra, Scorpio, Sagittarius, Capricorn, Aquarius, Pisces. Again, he divides each of the twelve parts into thirty parts, and these are days of the month. Again, he divides each part of the thirty parts into sixty small divisions, and (each) of these small (divisions) he subdivides into minute portions, and (these again) into portions still more minute. And always doing this, and not intermitting, but collecting from these divided portions (an aggregate), and constituting it a year; and again resolving and dividing the compound, (the sun) completely finishes the great and everlasting world.

Chapter XXIV.—Valentinus Convicted of Plagiarisms from the Platonic and Pythagoric Philosophy; The Valentinian Theory of Emanation by Duads.

Of some such nature, as I who have accurately examined their systems (have attempted) to state compendiously, is the opinion of Pythagoras and Plato. And from this (system), not from the Gospels, Valentinus, as we have proved, has collected the (materials of) heresy—I mean his own (heresy)—and may (therefore) justly be reckoned a Pythagorean and Platonist, not a Christian. Valentinus, therefore, and Heracleon, and Ptolemæus, and the entire school of these (heretics), as disciples of Pythagoras and Plato, (and) following these guides, have laid down as a fundamental principle of their doctrine the arithmetical system. For, likewise, according to these (Valentinians), the originating cause of the universe is a Monad, unbegotten, imperishable, incomprehensible, inconceivable, productive, and a cause of the generation of all existent things. And the aforesaid Monad is styled by them Father. There is, however, discoverable among them some considerable diversity of opinion. For some of them, in order that the Pythagorean doctrine of Valentinus may be altogether free from admixture (with other tenets), suppose that the Father is unfeminine, and unwedded, and solitary. But others, imagining it to be impossible that from a male only there could proceed a generation at all of any of those things that have been made to exist, necessarily reckon along with the Father of the universe, in order that he may be a father, Sige as a spouse. But as to Sige, whether at any time she is united in marriage (to the Father) or not, this is a point which we leave them to wrangle about among themselves. We at present, keeping to the Pythagorean principle, which is one, and unwedded, unfeminine, (and) deficient in nothing, shall proceed to give an account of their doctrines, as they themselves inculcate them. There is, says (Valentinus), not anything at all begotten, but the Father is alone unbegotten, not subject to the condition of place, not (subject to the condition of) time, having no counsellor, (and) not being any other substance that could be realized according to the ordinary methods of perception. (The Father,) however, was solitary, subsisting, as they say, in a state of quietude, and Himself reposing in isolation within Himself. When, however, He became productive, it seemed to Him expedient at one time to generate and lead forth the most beautiful and perfect (of those germs of existence) which He possessed within Himself, for (the Father) was not fond of solitariness. For, says he, He was all love, but love is not love except there may be some object of affection. The Father Himself, then, as He was solitary, projected and produced Nous and Aletheia, that is, a duad which became mistress, and origin, and mother of all the Æons computed by them (as existing) within the Pleroma. Nous and Aletheia being projected from the Father, one capable of continuing generation, deriving existence from a productive being, (Nous) himself likewise, in imitation of the Father, projected Logos and Zoe; and Logos and Zoe project Anthropos and Ecclesia. But Nous and Aletheia, when they beheld that their own offspring had been born productive, returned thanks to the Father of the universe, and offer unto Him a perfect number, viz., ten Æons. For, he says, Nous and Aletheia could not offer unto the Father a more perfect (one) than this number. For the Father, who is perfect, ought to be celebrated by a perfect number, and ten is a perfect number, because this is first of those (numbers) that are formed by plurality, (and therefore) perfect. The Father, however, being more perfect, because being alone unbegotten, by means of the one primary conjugal union of Nous and Aletheia, found means of projecting all the roots of existent things.

Chapter XXV.—The Tenet of the Duad Made the Foundation of Valentinus' System of the Emanation of Æons.

Logos himself also, and Zoe, then saw that Nous and Aletheia had celebrated the Father of the universe by a perfect number; and Logos himself likewise with Zoe wished to magnify their own father and mother, Nous and Aletheia. Since, however, Nous and Aletheia were begotten, and did not possess paternal (and) perfect uncreatedness, Logos and Zoe do not glorify Nous their father with a perfect number, but far from it, with an imperfect one. For Logos and Zoe offer twelve Æons unto Nous and Aletheia. For, according to Valentinus, these—namely, Nous and Aletheia, Logos and Zoe, Anthropos and Ecclesia—have been the primary roots of the Æons. But there are ten Æons proceeding from Nous and Aletheia, and twelve from Logos and Zoe—twenty and eight in all. And to these (ten) they give these following denominations: Bythus and Mixis, Ageratus and Henosis, Autophyes and Hedone, Acinetus and Syncrasis, Monogenes and Macaria. These are ten Æons whom some say (have been projected) by Nous and Aletheia, but some by Logos and Zoe. Others, however, affirm that the twelve (Æons have been projected) by Anthropos and Ecclesia, while others by Logos and Zoe. And upon these they bestow these following names: Paracletus and Pistis, Patricus and Elpis, Metricus and Agape, Æinous and Synesis, Ecclesiasticus and Macariotes, Theletus and Sophia. But of the twelve, the twelfth and youngest of all the twenty-eight Æons, being a female, and called Sophia, observed the multitude and power of the begetting Æons, and hurried back into the depth of the Father. And she perceived that all the rest of the Æons, as being begotten, generate by conjugal intercourse. The Father, on the other hand, alone, without copulation, has produced (an offspring). She wished to emulate the Father, and to produce (offspring) of herself without a marital partner, that she might achieve a work in no wise inferior to (that of) the Father. (Sophia, however,) was ignorant that the Unbegotten One, being an originating principle of the universe, as well as root and depth and abyss, alone possesses the power of self-generation. But Sophia, being begotten, and born after many more (Æons), is not able to acquire pos☐session of the power inherent in the Unbegotten One. For in the Unbegotten One, he says, all things exist simultaneously, but in the begotten (Æons) the female is projective of substance, and the male is formative of the substance which is projected by the female. Sophia, therefore, prepared to project that only which she was capable (of projecting), viz., a formless and undigested substance. And this, he says, is what Moses asserts: "The earth was invisible, and unfashioned." This (substance) is, he says, the good (and) the heavenly Jerusalem, into which God has promised to conduct the children of Israel, saying, "I will bring you into a land flowing with milk and honey."

Chapter XXVI.—Valentinus' Explanation of the Existence of Christ and the Spirit.

Ignorance, therefore, having arisen within the Pleroma in consequence of Sophia, and shapelessness in consequence of the offspring of Sophia, confusion arose in the Pleroma. (For all) the Æons that were begotten (became overwhelmed with apprehension, imagining) that in like manner formless and incomplete progenies of the Æons should be generated; and that some destruction, at no distant period, should at length seize upon the Æons. All the Æons, then, betook themselves to supplication of the Father, that he would tranquillize the sorrowing Sophia; for she continued weeping and bewailing on account of the abortion produced by her,—for so they term it. The Father, then, compassionating the tears of Sophia, and accepting the supplication of the Æons, orders a further projection. For he did not, (Valentinus) says, himself project, but Nous and Aletheia (projected) Christ and the Holy Spirit for the restoration of Form, and the destruction of the abortion, and (for) the consolation and cessation of the groans of Sophia. And thirty Æons came into existence along with Christ and the Holy Spirit. Some of these (Valentinians) wish that this should be a triacontad of Æons, whereas others desire that Sige should exist along with the Father, and that the Æons should be reckoned along with them.

Christ, therefore, being additionally projected, and the Holy Spirit, by Nous and Aletheia, immediately this abortion of Sophia, (which was) shapeless, (and) born of herself only, and generated without conjugal intercourse, separates from the entire of the Æons, lest the perfect Æons, beholding this (abortion), should be disturbed by reason of its shapelessness. In order, then, that the shapelessness of the abortion might not at all manifest itself to the perfect Æons, the Father also again projects additionally one Æon, viz., Staurus. And he being begotten great, as from a mighty and perfect father, and being projected for the guardianship and defense of the Æons, becomes a limit of the Pleroma, having within itself all the thirty Æons together, for these are they that had been projected. Now this (Æon) is styled Horos, because he separates from the Pleroma the Hysterema that is outside. And (he is called) Metocheus, because he shares also in the Hysterema. And (he is denominated) Staurus, because he is fixed inflexibly and inexorably, so that nothing of the Hysterema can come near the Æons who are within the Pleroma. Outside, then, Horos, (or) Metocheus, (or) Staurus, is the Ogdoad, as it is called, according to them, and is that Sophia which is outside the Pleroma, which (Sophia) Christ, who was additionally projected by Nous and Aletheia, formed and made a perfect Æon so that in no respect she should be inferior in power to any of the Æons within the Pleroma. Since, however, Sophia was formed outside, and it was not possible and equitable that Christ and the Holy Spirit, who were projected from Nous and Aletheia, should remain outside the Pleroma, Christ hurried away, and the Holy Spirit, from her who had had shape imparted to her, unto Nous and Aletheia within the Limit, in order that with the rest of the Æons they might glorify the Father.

Chapter XXVII.—Valentinus' Explanation of the Existence of Jesus; Power of Jesus Over Humanity.

After, then, there ensued someone (treaty of) peace and harmony between all the Æons within the Pleroma, it appeared expedient to them not only by a conjugal union to have magnified the Son, but also that by an offering of ripe fruits they should glorify the Father. Then all the thirty Æons consented to project one Æon, joint fruit of the Pleroma, that he might be (an earnest) of their union, and unanimity, and peace. And he alone was projected by all the Æons in honor of the Father. This (one) is styled among them "Joint Fruit of the Pleroma." These (matters), then, took place within the Pleroma in this way. And the "Joint Fruit of the Pleroma" was projected, (that is,) Jesus,—for this is his name,—the great High Priest. Sophia, however, who was outside the Pleroma in search of Christ, who had given her form, and of the Holy Spirit, became involved in great terror that she would perish, if he should separate from her, who had given her form and consistency. And she was seized with grief, and fell into a state of considerable perplexity, (while) reflecting who was he who had given her form, what the Holy Spirit was, whither he had departed, who it was that had hindered them from being present, who it was that had been envious of that glorious and blessed spectacle. While involved in sufferings such as these, she turns herself to prayer and supplication of him who had deserted her. During the utterance of her entreaties, Christ, who is within the Pleroma, had mercy upon (her), and all the rest of the Æons (were similarly affected); and they send forth beyond the Pleroma "the Joint Fruit of the Pleroma" as a spouse for Sophia, who was outside, and as a rectifier of those sufferings which she underwent in searching after Christ.

"The Fruit," then, arriving outside the Pleroma, and discovering (Sophia) in the midst of those four primary passions, both fear and sorrow, and perplexity and entreaty, he rectified her affections. While, however, correcting them, he observed that it would not be proper to destroy these, inasmuch as they are (in their nature) eternal, and peculiar to Sophia; and yet that neither was it seemly that Sophia should exist in the midst of such passions, in fear and sorrow, supplication (and) perplexity. He therefore, as an Æon so great, and (as) offspring of the entire Pleroma, caused the passions to depart from her, and he made these substantially-existent essences. He altered fear into animal desire, and (made) grief material, and (rendered) perplexity (the passion) of demons. But conversion, and entreaty, and supplication, he constituted as a path to repentance and power over the animal essence, which is denominated right.690 The Creator691 (acted) from fear; (and) that is what, he says, Scripture affirms: "The fear of the Lord is the beginning of wisdom." For this is the beginning of the affections of Sophia, for she was seized with fear, next with grief, then with perplexity, and so she sought refuge in entreaty and supplication. And the animal essence is, he says, of a fiery nature, and is also termed by them the super-celestial Topos, and Hebdomad, and "Ancient of Days." And whatever other such statements they advance respecting this (Æon), these they allege to hold good of the animalish (one), whom they assert to be creator of the world. Now he is of the appearance of fire. Moses also, he says, expresses himself thus: "The Lord thy God is a burning and consuming fire." For he, likewise, wishes (to think) that it has been so written. There is, however, he says, a twofold power of the fire; for fire is all-consuming, (and) cannot be quenched. According, therefore, to this division, there exists, subject to death, a certain soul which is a sort of mediator, for it is a Hebdomad and Cessation. For underneath the Ogdoad, where Sophia is, but above Matter, which is the Creator, a day has been formed, and the "Joint Fruit of the Pleroma." If the soul has been fashioned in the image of those above, that is, the Ogdoad, it became immortal and repaired to the Ogdoad, which is, he says, heavenly Jerusalem. If, however, it has been fashioned in the image of Matter, that is, the corporeal passions, the soul is of a perishable nature, and is (accordingly) destroyed.

## Chapter XXVIII.—The Valentinian Origin of the Creation.

As, therefore, the primary and greatest power of the animal essence came into existence, an image (of the only begotten Son); so also the devil, who is the ruler of this world, constitutes the power of the material essence, as Beelzebub is of the essence of demons which emanates from anxiety. (In consequence of this,) Sophia from above exerted her energy from the Ogdoad to the Hebdomad. For the Demiurge, they say, knows nothing at all, but is, according to them, devoid of understanding, and silly, and is not conscious of what he is doing or working at. But in him, while thus in a state of ignorance that even he is producing, Sophia wrought all sorts of energy, and infused vigor (into him). And (although Sophia) was really the operating cause, he himself imagines that he evolves the creation of the world out of himself: whence he commenced, saying, "I am God, and beside me there is no other."

## Chapter XXIX.—The Other Valentinian Emanations in Conformity with the Pythagorean System of Numbers.

The quaternion, then, advocated by Valentinus, is "a source of the everlasting nature having roots;" and Sophia (is the power) from whom the animal and material creation has derived its present condition. But Sophia is called "Spirit," and the Demiurge "Soul," and the Devil "the ruler of this world," and Beelzebub "the (ruler) of demons." These are the statements which they put forward. But further, in addition to these, rendering, as I have previously mentioned, their entire system of doctrine (akin to the) arithmetical (art), (they determine) that the thirty Æons within the Pleroma have again, in addition to these, projected other Æons, according to the (numerical) proportion (adopted by the Pythagoreans), in order that the Pleroma might be formed into an aggregate, according to a perfect number. For how the Pythagoreans divided (the celestial sphere) into twelve and thirty and sixty parts, and how they have minute parts of diminutive portions, has been made evident.

In this manner these (followers of Valentinus) subdivide the parts within the Pleroma. Now likewise the parts in the Ogdoad have been subdivided, and there has been projected Sophia, which is, according to them, mother of all living creatures, and the "Joint Fruit of the Pleroma," (who is) the Logos, (and other Æons,) who are celestial angels that have their citizenship in Jerusalem which is above, which is in heaven. For this Jerusalem is Sophia, she (that is) outside (the Pleroma), and her spouse is the "Joint Fruit of the Pleroma." And the Demiurge projected souls; for this (Sophia) is the essence of souls. This (Demiurge), according to them, is Abraham, and these (souls) the children of Abraham. From the material and devilish essence the Demiurge fashioned bodies for the souls. This is what has been declared: "And God formed man, taking clay from the earth, and breathed upon his face the breath of life, and man was made into a living soul." This, according to them, is the inner man, the natural (man), residing in the material body: Now a material (man) is perishable, incomplete, (and) formed out of the devilish essence. And this is the material man, as it were, according to them an inn, or domicile, at one time of soul only, at another time of soul and demons, at another time of soul and Logoi. And these are the Logoi that have been dispersed from above, from the "Joint Fruit of the Pleroma" and (from) Sophia, into this world. And they dwell in an earthly body, with a soul, when demons do not take up their abode with that soul. This, he says, is what has been written in Scripture: "On this account I bend my knees to the God and Father and Lord of our Lord Jesus Christ, that God would grant you to have Christ dwelling in the inner man,"—that is, the natural (man), not the corporeal (one),—"that you may be able to understand what is the depth," which is the Father of the universe, "and what is the breadth," which is Staurus, the limit of the Pleroma, "or what is the length," that is, the Pleroma of the Æons. Wherefore, he says, "the natural man receives not the things of the Spirit of God, for they are foolishness unto him;" but folly, he says, is the power of the Demiurge, for he was foolish and devoid of understanding, and imagined himself to be fabricating the world. He was, however, ignorant that Sophia, the Mother, the Ogdoad, was really the cause of all the operations performed by him who had no consciousness in reference to the creation of the world.

Chapter XXX.—Valentinus' Explanation of the Birth of Jesus; Twofold Doctrine on the Nature of Jesus' Body; Opinion of the Italians, that Is, Heracleon and Ptolemæus; Opinion of the Orientals, that Is, Axionicus and Bardesanes.

All the prophets, therefore, and the law, spoke by means of the Demiurge,—a silly god, he says, (and themselves) fools, who knew nothing. On account of this, he says, the Savior observes: "All that came before me are thieves and robbers." And the apostle (uses these words): "The mystery which was not made known to former generations." For none of the prophets, he says, said anything concerning the things of which we speak; for (a prophet) could not but be ignorant of all (these) things, inasmuch as they certainly had been uttered by the Demiurge only. When, therefore, the creation received completion, and when after (this) there ought to have been the revelation of the sons of God—that is, of the Demiurge, which up to this had been concealed, and in which obscurity the natural man was hid, and had a veil upon the heart;—when (it was time), then, that the veil should be taken away, and that these mysteries should be seen, Jesus was born of Mary the virgin, according to the declaration (in Scripture), "The Holy Ghost will come upon thee"—Sophia is the Spirit—"and the power of the Highest will overshadow thee"—the Highest is the Demiurge,—"wherefore that which shall be born of thee shall be called holy." For he has been generated not from the highest alone, as those created in (the likeness of) Adam have been created from the highest alone—that is, (from) Sophia and the Demiurge. Jesus, however, the new man, (has been generated) from the Holy Spirit—that is, Sophia and the Demiurge—in order that the Demiurge may complete the conformation and constitution of his body, and that the Holy Spirit may supply his essence, and that a celestial Logos may proceed from the Ogdoad being born of Mary.

Concerning this (Logos) they have a great question amongst them—an occasion both of divisions and dissension. And hence the doctrine of these has become divided: and one doctrine, according to them, is termed Oriental, and the other Italian. They from Italy, of whom is Heracleon and Ptolemæus, say that the body of Jesus was (an) animal (one). And on account of this, (they maintain) that at his baptism the Holy Spirit as a dove came down—that is, the Logos of the mother above, (I mean Sophia)—and became (a voice) to the animal (man), and raised him from the dead. This, he says, is what has been declared: "He who raised Christ from the dead will also quicken your mortal and natural bodies." For loam has come under a curse; "for," says he, "dust thou art, and unto dust shalt thou return." The Orientals, on the other hand, of whom is Axionicus and Bardesianes, assert that the body of the Savior was spiritual; for there came upon Mary the Holy Spirit—that is, Sophia and the power of the highest. This is the creative art, (and was vouchsafed) in order that what was given to Mary by the Spirit might be fashioned.

Chapter XXXI.—Further Doctrines of Valentinus Respecting the Æons; Reasons for the Incarnation.

Let, then, those (heretics) pursue these inquiries among themselves, (and let others do 90 so likewise,) if it should prove agreeable to anybody else to investigate (such points. Valentinus) subjoins, however, the following statement: That the trespasses appertaining to the Æons within (the Pleroma) had been corrected; and likewise had been rectified the trespasses appertaining to the Ogdoad, (that is,) Sophia, outside (the Pleroma); and also (the trespasses) appertaining to the Hebdomad (had been rectified). For the Demiurge had been taught by Sophia that He is not Himself God alone, as He imagined, and that except Himself there is not another (Deity). But when taught by Sophia, He was made to recognize the superior (Deity). For He was instructed by her, and initiated and indoctrinated into the great mystery of the Father and of the Æons, and divulged this to none. This is, as he says, what (God) declares to Moses: "I am the God of Abraham, and the God of Isaac, and the God of Jacob; and my name I have not announced to them;" that is, I have not declared the mystery, nor explained who is God, but I have preserved the mystery which I have heard from Sophia in secrecy with myself. When, then, the trespasses of those above had been rectified, it was necessary, according to the same consequence, that the (transgressions) here likewise should obtain rectification. On this account Jesus the Savior was born of Mary that he might rectify (the trespasses committed) here; as the Christ who, having been projected additionally from above by Nous and Aletheia, had corrected the passions of Sophia—that is, the abortion (who was) outside (the Pleroma). And, again, the Savior who was born of Mary came to rectify the passions of the soul. There are therefore, according to these (heretics), three Christs: (the first the) one additionally projected by Nous and Aletheia, along with the Holy Spirit; and (the second) the "Joint Fruit of the Pleroma," spouse of Sophia, who was outside (the Pleroma). And she herself is likewise styled Holy Spirit, but one inferior to the first (projection). And the third (Christ is) He who was born of Mary for the restoration of this world of ours.

following names: first, Proarche; next, Anennœtus; third, Arrhetus; and fourth, Aoratus. And that from the first, Proarche, was projected by a first and fifth place, Arche; and from Anennœtus, by a second and sixth place, Acataleptus; and from Arrhetus, by a third and seventh place, Anonomastus; and from Aoratus, Agennetus, a complement of the first Ogdoad. They wish that these powers should exist before Bythus and Sige. Concerning, however, Bythus himself, there are many different opinions. Some affirm him to be unwedded, neither male nor female; but others (maintain) that Sige, who is a female, is present with him, and that this constitutes the first conjugal union.

But the followers of Ptolemæus assert that (Bythus) has two spouses, which they call likewise dispositions, viz., Ennoia and Thelesis (conception and volition). For first the notion was conceived of projecting anything; next followed, as they say, the will to do so. Wherefore also these two dispositions and powers—namely, Ennoia and Thelesis—being, as it were, mingled one with the other, there ensued a projection of Monogenes and Aletheia by means of a conjugal union. And the consequence was, that visible types and images of those two dispositions of the Father came forth from the invisible (Æons), viz., from Thelema, Nous, and from Ennoia, Aletheia. And on this account the image of the subsequently generated Thelema is (that of a) male; but (the image) of the unbegotten Ennoia is (that of a) female, since volition is, as it were, a power of conception. For conception always cherished the idea of a projection, yet was not of itself at least able to project itself, but cherished the idea (of doing so). When, however, the

Chapter XXXII.—Valentinus Convicted of Plagiarisms from Plato.

I think that the heresy of Valentinus which is of Pythagorean (origin), has been sufficiently, indeed more than sufficiently, delineated. It therefore seems also expedient, that having explained his opinions, we should desist from (further) refutation (of his system). Plato, then, in expounding mysteries concerning the universe, writes to Dionysius expressing himself after some such manner as this: "I must speak to you by riddles, in order that if the letter may meet with any accident in its leaves by either sea or land, he who reads (what falls into his hands) may not understand it. For so it is. All things are about the King of all, and on his account are all things, and he is cause of all the glorious (objects of creation). The second is about the second, and the third about the third. But pertaining to the King there is none of those things of which I have spoken. But after this the soul earnestly desires to learn what sort these are, looking upon those things that are akin to itself, and not one of these is (in itself) sufficient. This is, O son of Dionysius and Doris, the question (of yours) which is a cause of all evil things. Nay, but rather the solicitude concerning this is innate in the soul; and if one does not remove this, he will never really attain truth. But what is astonishing in this matter, listen. For there are men who have heard these things—(men) furnished with capacities for learning, and furnished with capacities of memory, and persons who altogether in every way are endued with an aptitude for investigation with a view to inference. (These are) at present aged speculators. And they assert that opinions which at one time were credible are now incredible, and that things once incredible are now the contrary. While, therefore, turning the eye of examination towards these (inquiries), exercise caution, lest at any time you should have reason to repent in regard of those things should they happen in a manner unbecoming to your dignity. On this account I have written nothing concerning these (points); nor is there any treatise of Plato's (upon them), nor ever shall there be. The observations, however, now made are those of Socrates, conspicuous for virtue even while he was a young man."

Valentinus, falling in with these (remarks), has made a fundamental principle in his system "the King of all," whom Plato mentioned, and whom this heretic styles Pater, and Bythos, and Proarche over the rest of the Æons. And when Plato uses the words, "what is second about things that are second," Valentinus supposes to be second all the Æons that are within the limit (of the Pleroma, as well as) the limit (itself). And when Plato uses the words, "what is third about what is third," he has (constituted as third) the entire of the arrangement (existing) outside the limit and the Pleroma. And Valentinus has elucidated this (arrangement) very succinctly, in a psalm commencing from below, not as Plato does, from above, expressing himself thus: "I behold all things suspended in air by spirit, and I perceive all things wafted by spirit; the flesh (I see) suspended from soul, but the soul shining out from air, and air depending from Æther, and fruits produced from Bythus, and the fetus borne from the womb." Thus (Valentinus) formed his opinion on such (points). Flesh, according to these (heretics), is matter which is suspended from the soul of the Demiurge. And soul shines out from air; that is, the Demiurge emerges from the spirit, (which is) outside the Pleroma. But air springs forth from Æther;

that is, Sophia, which is outside (the Pleroma, is from the Pleroma) which is within the limit, an the entire Pleroma (generally). And from Bythus produced; (that is,) the entire projection of the made from the Father. The opinions, then, adv Valentinus have been sufficiently declared. It re us to explain the tenets of those who have eman his school, though each adherent (of V entertains different opinions.

Chapter XXXIII.—Secundus' System Epiphanes; Ptolemæus.

A certain (heretic) Secundus, born abo time with Ptolemæus, expresses himself thus that there is a right tetrad and a left tetrad,—n and darkness. And he affirms that the po withdrew and labored under deficiency, was n from the thirty Æons, but from the fruits of other (heretic), however—Epiphanes, a tea them—expresses himself thus: "The earlies principle was inconceivable, ineffable, and u and he calls this Monotes. And (he maintair co-exists with this (principle) a power denominates Henotes. This Henotes and this by projection (from themselves), sent fort (that should preside) over all intelligibles; ( both unbegotten and invisible, and he style "With this power co-exists a power of the which very (power) I call Unity. These fou forth the remainder of the projections of th others, again, denominate the chief an Ogdoad, (which is) fourth (and) invi

## Chapter XXXII.—Valentinus Convicted of Plagiarisms from Plato.

I think that the heresy of Valentinus which is of Pythagorean (origin), has been sufficiently, indeed more than sufficiently, delineated. It therefore seems also expedient, that having explained his opinions, we should desist from (further) refutation (of his system). Plato, then, in expounding mysteries concerning the universe, writes to Dionysius expressing himself after some such manner as this: "I must speak to you by riddles, in order that if the letter may meet with any accident in its leaves by either sea or land, he who reads (what falls into his hands) may not understand it. For so it is. All things are about the King of all, and on his account are all things, and he is cause of all the glorious (objects of creation). The second is about the second, and the third about the third. But pertaining to the King there is none of those things of which I have spoken. But after this the soul earnestly desires to learn what sort these are, looking upon those things that are akin to itself, and not one of these is (in itself) sufficient. This is, O son of Dionysius and Doris, the question (of yours) which is a cause of all evil things. Nay, but rather the solicitude concerning this is innate in the soul; and if one does not remove this, he will never really attain truth. But what is astonishing in this matter, listen. For there are men who have heard these things—(men) furnished with capacities for learning, and furnished with capacities of memory, and persons who altogether in every way are endued with an aptitude for investigation with a view to inference. (These are) at present aged speculators. And they assert that opinions which at one time were credible are now incredible, and that things once incredible are now the contrary. While, therefore, turning the eye of examination towards these (inquiries), exercise caution, lest at any time you should have reason to repent in regard of those things should they happen in a manner unbecoming to your dignity. On this account I have written nothing concerning these (points); nor is there any treatise of Plato's (upon them), nor ever shall there be. The observations, however, now made are those of Socrates, conspicuous for virtue even while he was a young man."

Valentinus, falling in with these (remarks), has made a fundamental principle in his system "the King of all," whom Plato mentioned, and whom this heretic styles Pater, and Bythos, and Proarche over the rest of the Æons. And when Plato uses the words, "what is second about things that are second," Valentinus supposes to be second all the Æons that are within the limit (of the Pleroma, as well as) the limit (itself). And when Plato uses the words, "what is third about what is third," he has (constituted as third) the entire of the arrangement (existing) outside the limit and the Pleroma. And Valentinus has elucidated this (arrangement) very succinctly, in a psalm commencing from below, not as Plato does, from above, expressing himself thus: "I behold all things suspended in air by spirit, and I perceive all things wafted by spirit; the flesh (I see) suspended from soul, but the soul shining out from air, and air depending from Æther, and fruits produced from Bythus, and the fetus borne from the womb." Thus (Valentinus) formed his opinion on such (points). Flesh, according to these (heretics), is matter which is suspended from the soul of the Demiurge. And soul shines out from air; that is, the Demiurge emerges from the spirit, (which is) outside the Pleroma. But air springs forth from Æther;

that is, Sophia, which is outside (the Pleroma, is projected from the Pleroma) which is within the limit, and (from) the entire Pleroma (generally). And from Bythus fruits are produced; (that is,) the entire projection of the Æons is made from the Father. The opinions, then, advanced by Valentinus have been sufficiently declared. It remains for us to explain the tenets of those who have emanated from his school, though each adherent (of Valentinus) entertains different opinions.

Chapter XXXIII.—Secundus' System of Æons; Epiphanes; Ptolemæus.

A certain (heretic) Secundus, born about the same time with Ptolemæus, expresses himself thus: (he says) that there is a right tetrad and a left tetrad,—namely, light and darkness. And he affirms that the power which withdrew and labored under deficiency, was not produced from the thirty Æons, but from the fruits of these. Some other (heretic), however—Epiphanes, a teacher among them—expresses himself thus: "The earliest originating principle was inconceivable, ineffable, and unnameable;" and he calls this Monotes. And (he maintains) that there co-exists with this (principle) a power which he denominates Henotes. This Henotes and this Monotes, not by projection (from themselves), sent forth a principle (that should preside) over all intelligibles; (and this was) both unbegotten and invisible, and he styles it a Monad. "With this power co-exists a power of the same essence, which very (power) I call Unity. These four powers sent forth the remainder of the projections of the Æons." But others, again, denominate the chief and originating Ogdoad, (which is) fourth (and) invisible, by the following names: first, Proarche; next, Anennœtus; third, Arrhetus; and fourth, Aoratus. And that from the first, Proarche, was projected by a first and fifth place, Arche; and from Anennœtus, by a second and sixth place, Acataleptus; and from Arrhetus, by a third and seventh place, Anonomastus; and from Aoratus, Agennetus, a complement of the first Ogdoad. They wish that these powers should exist before Bythus and Sige. Concerning, however, Bythus himself, there are many different opinions. Some affirm him to be unwedded, neither male nor female; but others (maintain) that Sige, who is a female, is present with him, and that this constitutes the first conjugal union.

But the followers of Ptolemæus assert that (Bythus) has two spouses, which they call likewise dispositions, viz., Ennoia and Thelesis (conception and volition). For first the notion was conceived of projecting anything; next followed, as they say, the will to do so. Wherefore also these two dispositions and powers—namely, Ennoia and Thelesis—being, as it were, mingled one with the other, there ensued a projection of Monogenes and Aletheia by means of a conjugal union. And the consequence was, that visible types and images of those two dispositions of the Father came forth from the invisible (Æons), viz., from Thelema, Nous, and from Ennoia, Aletheia. And on this account the image of the subsequently generated Thelema is (that of a) male; but (the image) of the unbegotten Ennoia is (that of a) female, since volition is, as it were, a power of conception. For conception always cherished the idea of a projection, yet was not of itself at least able to project itself, but cherished the idea (of doing so). When, however, the power of volition (would be present), then it projects the idea which had been conceived.

Chapter XXXIV.—System of Marcus; A Mere Impostor; His Wicked Devices Upon the Eucharistic Cup.

A certain other teacher among them, Marcus, an adept in sorcery, carrying on operations partly by sleight of hand and partly by demons, deceived many from time to time. This (heretic) alleged that there resided in him the mightiest power from invisible and unnameable places. And very often, taking the Cup, as if offering up the Eucharistic prayer, and prolonging to a greater length than usual the word of invocation, he would cause the appearance of a purple, and sometimes of a red mixture, so that his dupes imagined that a certain Grace descended and communicated to the potion a blood-red potency. The knave, however, at that time succeeded in escaping detection from many; but now, being convicted (of the imposture), he will be forced to desist from it. For, infusing secretly into the mixture some drug that possessed the power of imparting such a color (as that alluded to above), uttering for a considerable time nonsensical expressions, he was in the habit of waiting, (in expectation) that the (drug), obtaining a supply of moisture, might be dissolved, and, being intermingled with the potion, might impart its color to it. The drugs, however, that possess the quality of furnishing this effect we have previously mentioned in the book on magicians. And here we have taken occasion to explain how they make dupes of many, and thoroughly ruin them. And if it should prove agreeable to them to apply their attention with greater accuracy to the statement made by us, they will become aware of the deceit of Marcus.

Chapter XXXV.—Further Acts of Jugglery on the Part of Marcus.

And this (Marcus), infusing (the aforesaid) mixture into a smaller cup, was in the habit of delivering it to a woman to offer up the Eucharistic prayer, while he himself stood by, and held (in his hand) another empty (chalice) larger than that. And after his female dupe had pronounced the sentence of Consecration, having received (the cup from her), he proceeded to infuse (its contents) into the larger (chalice), and, pouring them frequently from one cup to the other, was accustomed at the same time to utter the following invocation: "Grant that the inconceivable and ineffable Grace which existed prior to the universe, may fill thine inner man, and make to abound in thee the knowledge of this (grace), as She disseminates the seed of the mustard-tree upon the good soil." And simultaneously pronouncing some such words as these, and astonishing both his female dupe and those that are present, he was regarded as one performing a miracle; while the larger was being filled from the smaller chalice, in such a way as that (the contents), being superabundant, flowed over. And the contrivance of this (juggler) we have likewise explained in the aforesaid (fourth) book, where we have proved that very many drugs, when mingled in this way with liquid substances, are endued with the quality of yielding augmentation, more particularly when diluted in wine. Now, when (one of these impostors) previously smears, in a clandestine manner, an empty cup with any one of these drugs, and shows it (to the spectators) as if it contained nothing, by infusing into it (the contents) from the other cup, and pouring them back again, the drug, as it is of a flatulent nature, is dissolved by being blended with the moist substance. And the effect of this was, that a superabundance of the mixture ensued, and was so far augmented, that what was infused was put in motion, such being the nature of the drug. And if one stow away (the chalice) when it has been filled, (what has been poured into it) will after no long time return to its natural dimensions, inasmuch as the potency of the drug becomes extinct by reason of the continuance of moisture. Wherefore he was in the habit of hurriedly presenting the cup to those present, to drink; but they, horrified at the same time, and eager (to taste the contents of the cup), proceeded to drink (the mixture), as if it were something divine, and devised by the Deity.

Chapter XXXVI.—The Heretical Practices of the Marcites in Regard of Baptism.

Such and other (tricks) this impostor attempted to perform. And so it was that he was magnified by his dupes, and sometimes he was supposed to utter predictions. But sometimes he tried to make others (prophesy), partly by demons carrying on these operations, and partly by practicing sleight of hand, as we have previously stated. Hoodwinking therefore multitudes, he led on (into enormities) many (dupes) of this description who had become his disciples, by teaching them that they were prone, no doubt, to sin, but beyond the reach of danger, from the fact of their belonging to the perfect power, and of their being participators in the inconceivable potency. And subsequent to the (first) baptism, to these they promise another, which they call Redemption. And by this (other baptism) they wickedly subvert those that remain with them in expectation of redemption, as if persons, after they had once been baptized, could again obtain remission. Now, it is by means of such knavery as this that they seem to retain their hearers. And when they consider that these have been tested, and are able to keep (secret the mysteries) committed unto them, they then admit them to this (baptism). They, however, do not rest satisfied with this alone, but promise (their votaries) some other (boon) for the purpose of confirming them in hope, in order that they may be inseparable (adherents of their sect). For they utter something in an inexpressible (tone of) voice, after having laid hands on him who is receiving the redemption. And they allege that they could not easily declare (to another) what is thus spoken unless one were highly tested, or one were at the hour of death, (when) the bishop comes and whispers (it) into the (expiring one's) ear. And this knavish device (is undertaken) for the purpose of securing the constant attendance upon the bishop of (Marcus') disciples, as individuals eagerly panting to learn what that may be which is spoken at the last, by (the knowledge of) which the learner will be advanced to the rank of those admitted into the higher mysteries. And in regard of these I have maintained a silence for this reason, lest at any time one should suppose that I was guilty of disparaging these (heretics). For this does not come within the scope of our present work, only so far as it may contribute to prove from what source (the heretics) have derived the standing-point from which they have taken occasion to introduce the opinions advanced by them.

Chapter XXXVII.—Marcus' System Explained by Irenaeus; Marcus' Vision; The Vision of Valentinus Revealing to Him His System.

For also the blessed presbyter Irenaeus, having approached the subject of a refutation in a more unconstrained spirit, has explained such washings and redemptions, stating more in the way of a rough digest what are their practices. (And it appears that some of the Marcosians,) on meeting with (Irenaeus' work), deny that they have so received (the secret word just alluded to), but they have learned that always they should deny. Wherefore our anxiety has been more accurately to investigate, and to discover minutely what are the (instructions) which they deliver in the case of the first bath, styling it by some such name; and in the case of the second, which they denominate Redemption. But not even has this secret of theirs escaped (our scrutiny). For these opinions, however, we consent to pardon Valentinus and his school.

But Marcus, imitating his teacher, himself also feigns a vision, imagining that in this way he would be magnified. For Valentinus likewise alleges that he had seen an infant child lately born; and questioning (this child), he proceeded to inquire who it might be. And (the child) replied, saying that he himself is the Logos, and then subjoined a sort of tragic legend; and out of this (Valentinus) wishes the heresy attempted by him to consist. Marcus, making a similar attempt with this (heretic), asserts that the Tetrad came to him in the form of a woman,—since the world could not bear, he says, the male (form) of this Tetrad, and that she revealed herself who she was, and explained to this (Marcus) alone the generation of the universe, which she never had revealed to any, either of gods or of men, expressing herself after this mode: When first the self-existent Father, He who is inconceivable and without substance, He who is neither male nor female, willed that His own ineffability should become realized in something spoken, and that His invisibility should become realized in form, He opened His mouth, and sent forth similar to Himself a Logos. And this (Logos) stood by Him, and showed unto Him who he was, viz., that he himself had been manifested as a (realization in) form of the Invisible One. And the pronunciation of the name was of the following description. He was accustomed to utter the first word of the name itself, which was Arche, and the syllable of this was (composed) of four letters. Then he subjoined the second (syllable), and this was also (composed) of four letters. Next he uttered the third (syllable), which was (composed) of ten letters; and he uttered the fourth (syllable), and this was (composed) of twelve letters. Then ensued the pronunciation of the entire name, (composed) of thirty letters, but of four syllables. And each of the elements had its own peculiar letters, and its own peculiar form, and its own peculiar pronunciation, as well as figures and images. And not one of these was there that beholds the form of that (letter) of which this was an element. And of course, none of them could know the pronunciation of the (letter) next to this, but (only) as he himself pronounces it, (and that in such a way) as that, 94 in pronouncing the whole (word), he supposed that he was uttering the entire (name). For each of these (elements), being part of the entire (name), he denominates (according to) its own peculiar sound, as if the whole (of the word). And he does not intermit sounding until he arrived at the last letter of the last element and uttered it in a single articulation. Then he said that the restoration of the entire ensued when all the (elements), coming down into the one letter, sounded one and the same pronunciation, and an image of the pronunciation he supposed to exist when we simultaneously utter the word Amen. And that these sounds are those which gave form to the insubstantial and unbegotten Æon, and that those forms are what the Lord declared to be angels—the (forms) that uninterruptedly behold the face of the Father.

Chapter XXXVIII.—Marcus' System of Letters.

But the generic and expressed names of the elements he called Æons, and Logoi, and Roots, and Seeds, and Pleromas, and Fruits. (And he maintains) that every one of these, and what was peculiar to each, is perceived as being contained in the name of "Ecclesia." And the final letter of the last element sent forth its own peculiar articulation. And the sound of this (letter) came forth and produced, in accordance with images of the elements, its own peculiar elements. And from these he says that things existing here were garnished, and the things antecedent to these were produced. The letter itself certainly, of which the sound was concomitant with the sound below, he says, was received up by its own syllable into the complement of the entire (name); but that the sound, as if cast outside, remained below. And that the element itself, from which the letter along with its own pronunciation descended below, he says, is (composed) of thirty letters, and that each one of the thirty letters contains in itself other letters, by means of which the title of the letter is named. And again, that the other (letters) are named by different letters, and the rest by different (ones still). So that by writing down the letters individually, the number would eventuate in infinity. In this way one may more clearly understand what is spoken. The element Delta, (he says,) has five letters in itself, (viz.), Delta, and Epsilon, and Lambda, and Tau, and Alpha; and these very letters are (written) by means of other letters. If, therefore, the entire substance of the Delta eventuates in infinity, (and if) different letters invariably produce different letters, and succeed one another, by how much greater than that element is the more enormous sea of the letters? And if one letter is thus infinite, behold the entire name's depth of the letters out of which the patient industry, nay, rather (I should say,) the vain toil of Marcus wishes that the Progenitor (of things) should consist! Wherefore also (he maintains) that the Father, who knew that He was inseparable from Himself, gave (this depth) to the elements, which he likewise denominates Æons. And he uttered aloud to each one of them its own peculiar pronunciation, from the fact that one could not pronounce the entire.

## Chapter XXXIX.—The Quaternion Exhibits "Truth."

And (Marcus alleged) that the Quaternion, after having explained these things, spoke as follows: "Now, I wish also to exhibit to you Truth herself, for I have brought her down from the mansions above, in order that you may behold her naked, and become acquainted with her beauty; nay, also that you may hear her speak, and may marvel at her wisdom. Observe," says the Quaternion, "then, first, the head above, Alpha (and long) O; the neck, B and P[si]; shoulders, along with hands, G and C[hi]; breasts, Delta and P[hi]; diaphragm, Eu; belly, Z and T; pudenda, Eta and S; thighs, T[h] and R; knees, Ip; calves, Ko; ankles, Lx[si]; feet, M and N." This is in the body of Truth, according to Marcus. This is the figure of the element; this the character of the letter. And he styles this element Man and affirms it to be the source of every word, and the originating principle of every sound, and the realization in speech of everything that is ineffable, and a mouth of taciturn silence. And this is the body of (Truth) herself. But do you, raising aloft the conceiving power of the understanding, hear from the mouths of Truth (of) the Logos, who is Self-generator and Progenitor.

Chapter XL.—The Name of Christ Jesus.

But, after uttering these words, (Marcus details) that Truth, gazing upon him, and opening her mouth, spoke the discourse (just alluded to). And (he tells us) that the discourse became a name, and that the name was that which we know and utter, viz., Christ Jesus, and that as soon as she had named this (name) she remained silent. While Marcus, however, was expecting that she was about to say more, the Quaternion, again advancing into the midst, speaks as follows: "Thou didst regard as contemptible this discourse which you have heard from the mouth of Truth. And yet this which you know and seem long since to possess is not the name; for you have merely the sound of it but are ignorant of the power. For Jesus is a remarkable name, having six letters, invoked by all belonging to the called (of Christ); whereas the other (name, that is, Christ,) consists of many parts, and is among the (five) Æons of the Pleroma. (This name) is of another form and a different type and is recognized by those existences who are connate with him, and whose magnitudes subsist with him continually.

Chapter XLI.—Marcus' Mystic Interpretation of the Alphabet.

Know, (therefore,) that these letters which with you are (reckoned at) twenty-four, are emanations from the three powers, and are representative of those (powers) which embrace even the entire number of the elements. For suppose that there are some letters that are mute—nine of them—of Pater and Aletheia, from the fact that these are mute—that is, ineffable and unutterable. And (again, assume) that there are other (letters that are) semi-vowels—eight of them—of the Logos and of Zoe, from the fact that these are intermediate between consonants and vowels, and receive the emanation of the (letters) above them, but the reflux of those below them. And (likewise take for granted) that there are vowels—and these are seven—of Anthropos and Ecclesia, inasmuch as the voice of Anthropos proceeded forth, and imparted form to the (objects of the) universe. For the sound of the voice produced figure and invested them with it. From this it follows that there are Logos and Zoe, which have eight (semi-vowels); and Anthropos and Ecclesia, which have seven (vowels); and Pater and Aletheia, which have nine (mutes). But from the fact that Logos wanted (one of being an ogdoad), he who is in the Father was removed (from his seat on God's right hand) and came down (to earth). And he was sent forth (by the Father) to him from whom he was separated, for the rectification of actions that had been committed. (And his descent took place) in order that the unifying process, which is inherent in Agathos, of the Pleromas might produce in all the single power that emanates from all. And thus, he who is of the seven (vowels) acquired the power of the eight (semi-vowels); and there were produced three topoi, corresponding with the (three) numbers (nine, seven, and eight),—(these topoi) being ogdoads. And these three being added one to the other, exhibited the number of the twenty-four (letters). And (he maintains), of course, that the three elements,—(which he himself affirms to be (allied) with the three powers by conjugal union, and which (by this state of duality) become six, and from which have emanated the twenty☐four elements,—being rendered fourfold by the Quaternion's ineffable word, produce the same number (twenty-four) with these. And these, he says, belong to Anonomastus. And (he asserts) that these are conveyed by the six powers into a similarity with Aoratus. And (he says) that there are six double letters of these elements, images of images, which, being reckoned along with the twenty-four letters, produce, by an analogical power, the number thirty.

Chapter XLII.—His System Applied to Explain Our Lord's Life and Death.

And he says, as the result of this computation and that proportion, that in the similitude of an image He appeared who after the six days Himself ascended the mountain a fourth person and became the sixth. And (he asserts) that He (likewise) descended and was detained by the Hebdomad, and thus became an illustrious Ogdoad. And He contains in Himself of the elements the entire number which He manifested, as He came to His baptism. (And the symbol of manifestation was) the descent of the dove, which is O[mega] and Alpha, and which by the number manifested (by these is) 801. And for this reason (he maintains) that Moses says that man was created on the sixth day. And (he asserts) that the dispensation of suffering (took place) on the sixth day, which is the preparation; (and so it was) that on this (day) appeared the last man for the regeneration of the first man. And that the beginning and end of this dispensation is the sixth hour, at which He was nailed to the (accursed) tree. For (he says) that perfect Nous, knowing the sixfold number to be possessed of the power of production and regeneration, manifested to the sons of light the regeneration that had been introduced into this number by that illustrious one who had appeared. Whence also he says that the double letters involve the remarkable number. For the illustrious number, being intermingled with the twenty-four elements, produced the name (consisting) of the thirty letters.

Chapter XLIII—Letters, Symbols of the Heavens.

He has, however, employed the instrumentality of the aggregate of the seven numbers, in order that the result of the self-devised (counsel) might be manifested. Understand, he says, for the present, that remarkable number to be Him who was formed by the illustrious one, and who was, as it were, divided, and remained outside.

And He, through both His Own power and wisdom, by means of the projection of Himself, imparted, in imitation of the seven powers, animation to this world, so as to make it consist of seven powers, and constituted (this world) the soul of the visible universe. And therefore, this one has resorted to such all operation as what was spontaneously undertaken by Himself; and these minister, inasmuch as they are imitations of things inimitable, unto the intelligence of the Mother. And the first heaven sounds Alpha, and the one after that E[psilon], and the third Eta, and the fourth, even that in the midst of the seven (vowels, enunciates) the power of Iota, and the fifth of O[micron], and the sixth of U[psilon], and the seventh and fourth from the central one, O[mega]. And all the powers, when they are connected together in one, emit a sound, and glorify that (Being) from whom they have been projected. And the glory of that sound is transmitted upwards to the Progenitor. And furthermore, he says that the sound of this ascription of glory being conveyed to the earth, became a creator and producer of terrestrial objects. And (he maintains) that the proof of this (may be drawn) from the case of infants recently born, whose soul, simultaneously with exit from the womb utters similarly this sound of each one of the elements. As, then, he says, the seven powers glorify the Logos, so also does the sorrowing soul in babes (magnify Him).And on account of this, he says, David likewise has declared, "Out of the mouths of babes and sucklings Thou hast perfected praise." And again, "The heavens declare the glory of God." When, however, the soul is involved in hardships, it utters no other exclamation than the O[mega], inasmuch as it is afflicted in order that the soul above, becoming aware of what is akin to herself (below), may send down one to help this (earthly soul).

## Chapter XLIV.—Respecting the Generation of the Twenty-Four Letters.

And so far for these points. Respecting, however, the generation of the twenty-four elements, he expresses himself thus: that Henotes coexists with Monotes, and that from these issue two projections, viz., Monas and Hen, and that these being added together become four, for twice two are four. And again, the two and four (projections) being added together, manifested the number six; and these six made fourfold, produce the twenty-four forms. And these are the names of the first tetrad, and they are understood as Holy of Holies, and cannot be expressed and they are recognized by the Son alone. These the Father knows which they are. Those names which with Him are pronounced in silence and with faith, are Arrhetus and Sige, Pater and Aletheia. And of this tetrad the entire number is (that) of twenty-four letters. For Arrhetus has seven elements, Sige five, and Pater five, and Aletheia seven. And in like manner also (is it with) the second tetrad; (for) Logos and Zoe, Anthropos and Ecclesia, exhibited the same number of elements. And (he says) that the expressed name—(that is, Jesus)—of the Savior consists of six letters, but that His ineffable name, according to the number of the letters, one by one, consists of twenty-four elements, but Christ a Son of twelve. And (he says) that the ineffable (name) in Christ consists of thirty letters, and this exists, according to the letters which are in Him, the elements being counted one by one. For the (name) Christ consists of eight elements;

for Chi consists of three, and R[ho] of two, and EI of two, and I[ota], of four, S[igma] of five, and T[au] of three, and OU of two, and San of three. Thus the ineffable name in Christ consists, they allege, of thirty letters. And they assert that for this reason He utters the words, "I am Alpha and Omega," displaying the dove, which (symbolically) has this number, which is eight hundred and one.

Chapter XLV.—Why Jesus is Called Alpha.

Now Jesus possesses this ineffable generation. For from the mother of the universe, I mean the first tetrad, proceeded forth, in the manner of a daughter, the second tetrad. And it became an ogdoad, from which proceeded forth the decade; and thus was produced ten, and next eighteen. The decade, therefore, coming in along with the ogdoad, and rendering it tenfold, produced the number eighty; and again making eighty tenfold, generated the number eight hundred. And so it is that the entire number of letters that proceeded forth from ogdoad into decade is eight hundred and eighty-eight, which is Jesus; for the name Jesus, according to the number in letters, is eight hundred and eighty-eight. Now likewise the Greek alphabet has eight monads and eight decades, and eight hecatontads; and these exhibit the calculated sum of eight hundred and eighty-eight, that is, Jesus, who consists of all numbers. And that on this account He is called Alpha (and Omega), indicating His generation (to be) from all.

Chapter XLVI.—Marcus' Account of the Birth and Life of Our Lord.

But concerning the creation of this (Jesus), he expresses himself thus: That powers emanating from the second tetrad fashioned Jesus, who appeared on earth, and that the angel Gabriel filled the place of the Logos, and the Holy Spirit that of Zoe, and the "Power of the Highest" that of Anthropos, and the Virgin that of Ecclesia. And so it was, in Marcus' system, that the man (who appeared) in accordance with the dispensation was born through Mary. And when He came to the water, (he says) that He descended like a dove upon him who had ascended above and filled the twelfth number. And in Him resides the seed of these, that is, such as are sown along with Him, and that descend with (Him), and ascend with (Him). And that this power which descended upon Him, he says, is the seed of the Pleroma, which contains in itself both the Father and the Son, and the unnameable power of Sige, which is recognized through these and all the Æons. And that this (seed) is the spirit which is in Him and spoke in Him through the mouth of the Son, the confession of Himself as Son of man, and of His being one who would manifest the Father; (and that) when this spirit came down upon Jesus, He was united with Him. The Savior, who was of the dispensation, he says, destroyed death, whereas He made known (as) the Father Christ (Jesus). He says that Jesus, therefore, is the name of the man of the dispensation, and that it has been set forth for the assimilation and formation of Anthropos, who was about to descend upon Him; and that when He had received Him unto Himself, He retained possession of Him. And (he says) that He was Anthropos, (that) He (was) Logos, (that) He (was) Pater, and Arrhetus, and Sige, and Aletheia, and Ecclesia, and Zoe.

Chapter XLVII.—The System of Marcus Shown to Be that of Pythagoras, by Quotations from the Writings of Marcus' Followers.

I trust, therefore, that as regards these doctrines it is obvious to all possessed of a sound mind, that (these tenets) are unauthoritative, and far removed from the knowledge that is in accordance with Religion, and are mere portions of astrological discovery, and the arithmetical art of the Pythagoreans. And this assertion, ye who are desirous of learning shall ascertain (to be true, by a reference to the previous books, where,) amongst other opinions elucidated by us, we have explained these doctrines likewise. In order, however, that we may prove it a more clear statement, viz., that these (Marcosians) are disciples not of Christ but of Pythagoras, I shall proceed to explain those opinions that have been derived (by these heretics) from Pythagoras concerning the meteoric (phenomena) of the stars as far as it is possible (to do so) by an epitome.

Now the Pythagoreans make the following statements: that the universe consists of a Monad and Duad, and that by reckoning from a monad as far as four they thus generate a decade. And again, a duad coming forth as far as the remarkable (letter),—for instance, two and four and six,—exhibited the (number) twelve. And again, if we reckon from the duad to the decade, thirty is produced; and in this are comprised the ogdoad, and decade, and dodecade. And therefore, on account of its having the remarkable (letter), the dodecade has concomitant with it a remarkable passion. And for this reason (they maintain) that when an error had arisen respecting the twelfth number, the sheep skipped from the flock and wandered away; for that the apostasy took place, they say, in like manner from the decade. And with a similar reference to the dodecade, they speak of the piece of money which, on losing, a woman, having lit a candle, searched for diligently. (And they make a similar application) of the loss (sustained) in the case of the one sheep out of the ninety and nine; and adding these one into the other, they give a fabulous account of numbers. And in this way, they affirm, when the eleven is multiplied into nine, that it produces the number ninety and nine; and on this account that it is said that the word Amen embraces the number ninety-nine. And in regard of another number they express themselves in this manner: that the letter Eta along with the remarkable one constitutes an ogdoad, as it is situated in the eighth place from Alpha. Then, again, computing the number of these elements without the remarkable (letter), and adding them together up to Eta, they exhibit the number thirty. For any one beginning from the Alpha to the Eta will, after subtracting the remarkable (letter), discover the number of the elements to be the number thirty. Since, therefore, the number thirty is unified from the three powers; when multiplied thrice into itself it produced ninety, for thrice thirty is ninety, (and this triad when multiplied into itself produced nine). In this way the Ogdoad brought forth the number ninety-nine from the first Ogdoad, and Decade, and Dodecade. And at one time they collect the number of this (trio) into an entire sum, and produce a triacontad; whereas at another time they subtract twelve, and reckon it at eleven. And in like manner, (they subtract) ten and make it nine. And connecting these one into the other, and multiplying them tenfold, they complete the number ninety-nine. Since, however, the twelfth Æon, having left the eleven (Æons above), and departing downwards, withdrew, they allege that even this is correlative (with the letters). For the figure of the letters teaches (us as much). For L is placed eleventh of the letters, and this L is the number thirty. And (they say) that this is placed according to an image of the dispensation above; since from Alpha, irrespective of the remarkable (letter), the number of the letters themselves, added together up to L, according to the augmentation of the letters with the L itself, produces the number ninety-nine. But that the L, situated in the eleventh (of the alphabet), came down to search after the number similar to itself, in order that it might fill up the twelfth number, and that when it was discovered it was filled up, is manifest from the shape itself of the letter. For Lambda, when it attained unto, as it were, the investigation of what is similar to itself, and when it found such and snatched it away, filled up the place of the twelfth, the letter M, which is composed of two Lambdas. And for this reason (it was) that these (adherents of Marcus), through their knowledge, avoid the place of the ninety-nine, that is, the Hysterema, a type of the left hand, and follow after the one which, added to ninety-nine, they say was transferred to his own right hand.

Chapter XLVIII.—Their Cosmogony Framed According to These Mystic Doctrines of Letters.

And by the Mother, they allege, were created first the four elements, which, they say, are fire, water, earth, air; and these have been projected as an image of the tetrad above; and reckoning the energies of these—for instance, as hot, cold, moist, dry—they assert that they accurately portray the Ogdoad. And next they compute ten powers thus. (There are, they say,) seven orbicular bodies, which they likewise call heavens. There is next a circle containing these within its compass, and this also they name an eighth heaven: and in addition to these, they affirm the existence of both a sun and moon. And these being ten in number, they say, are images of the invisible decade that (emanated) from Logos and Zoe. (They affirm,) however, that the dodecade is indicated by what is termed the zodiacal circle. For these twelve zodiacal signs, they say, most evidently shadowed forth the daughter of Anthropos and Ecclesia, namely the Dodecade. And since, he says, the upper heaven has been united from an opposite direction to the revolutionary motion, which is most rapid, of the entire (of the signs); and since (this heaven) within its cavity retards, and by its slowness counterpoises, the velocity of those (signs), so that in thirty years it accomplishes its circuit from sign to sign,—they therefore assert that this (heaven) is an image of Horos, who encircles the mother of these, who has thirty names. And, again, (they affirm) that the moon, which traverses the heaven in thirty days, by reason of (these) days portrays the number of the Æons. And (they say) that the sun, performing its circuit, and terminating its exact return to its first position in its orbit in twelve months, manifests the dodecade. And also (they say) that the days themselves, involving the measure of twelve hours, constitute a type of the empty dodecade; and that the circumference of the actual zodiacal circle consists of three hundred and sixty degrees, and that each zodiacal sign possesses thirty divisions. In this way, therefore, even by means of the circle, they maintain that the image is preserved of the connection of the twelve with the thirty. But, moreover, alleging that the earth was divided into twelve regions, and that according to each particular region it receives one power by the latter's being sent down from the heavens, and that it produces children corresponding in likeness unto the power which transmitted (the likeness) by emanation; (for this reason) they assert that earth is a type of the Dodecade above.

Chapter XLIX.—The Work of the Demiurge Perishable.

And in addition to these (points, they lay down) that the Demiurge of the supernal Ogdoad, desirous of imitating the indefinite, and everlasting, and illimitable (one), and (the one) not subject to the condition of time; and (the Demiurge) not being able to represent the stability and eternity of this (Ogdoad), on account of his being the fruit of the Hysterema, to this end appointed times, and seasons, and numbers, measuring many years in reference to the eternity of this (Ogdoad), thinking by the multitude of times to imitate its indefiniteness. And here they say, when Truth eluded his pursuit, that Falsehood followed close upon him; and that on account of this, when the times were fulfilled, his work underwent dissolution.

Chapter L.—Marcus and Colarbasus Refuted by Irenaeus.

These assertions, then, those who are of the school of Valentinus advance concerning both the creation and the universe, in each case propagating opinions still more empty. And they suppose this to constitute productiveness (in their system), if any one in like manner, making some greater discovery, will appear to work wonders. And finding, (as they insinuate,) each of the particulars of Scripture to accord with the aforesaid numbers, they (attempt to) criminate Moses and the prophets, alleging that these speak allegorically of the measures of the Æons. And inasmuch as these statements are trifling and unstable, it does not appear to me expedient to bring them before (the reader. This, however, is the less requisite,) as now the blessed presbyter Irenaeus has powerfully and elaborately refuted the opinions of these (heretics). And to him we are indebted for a knowledge of their inventions, (and have thereby succeeded in) proving that these heretics, appropriating these opinions from the Pythagorean philosophy, and from over-spun theories of the astrologers, cast an imputation upon Christ, as though He had delivered these (doctrines). But since I suppose that the worthless opinions of these men have been sufficiently explained, and that it has been clearly proved whose disciples are Marcus and Colarbasus, who were successors of the school of Valentinus, let us see what statement likewise Basilides advances.

## Book VII.

Contents.

The following are the contents of the seventh book of the Refutation of all Heresies:— What the opinion of Basilides is, and that, being struck with the doctrines of Aristotle, he out of these framed his heresy.

And what are the statements of Saturnilus, who flourished much about the time of Basilides.

And how Menander advanced the assertion that the world was made by angels.

What is the folly of Marcion, and that his tenet is not new, nor (taken) out of the Holy Scriptures, but that he obtains it from Empedocles.

How Carpocrates acts sillily, in himself also alleging that existing things were made by angels.

That Cerinthus, in no wise indebted to the Scriptures, formed his opinion (not out of them), but from the tenets of the Egyptians.

What are the opinions propounded by the Ebionæans, and that they in preference adhere to Jewish customs.

How Theodotus has been a victim of error, deriving contributions to his system partly from the Ebionæans, (partly from Cerinthus.)

And what were the opinions of Cerdon, who both enunciated the doctrines of Empedocles, and who wickedly induced Marcion to step forward.

And how Lucian, when he had become a disciple of Marcion, having divested himself of all shame, blasphemed God from time to time.

## The Refutation of All Heresies

And Apelles also, having become a disciple of this (heretic), was not in the habit of advancing the same opinions with his preceptor; but being actuated (in the formation of his system) from the tenets of natural philosophers, assumed the substance of the universe as the fundamental principle of things.

Chapter I.—Heresy Compared to (1) the Stormy Ocean, (2) the Rocks of the Sirens; Moral from Ulysses and the Sirens.

The pupils of these men, when they perceive the doctrines of the heretics to be like unto the ocean when tossed into waves by violence of the winds, ought to sail past in quest of the tranquil haven. For a sea of this description is both infested with wild beasts and difficult of navigation, like, as we may say, the Sicilian (Sea), in which the legend reports were Cyclops, and Charybdis, and Scylla, and the rock of the Sirens. Now, the poets of the Greeks allege that Ulysses sailed through (this channel), adroitly using (to his own purpose) the terribleness of these strange monsters. For the savage cruelty (in the aspect) of these towards those who were sailing through was remarkable. The Sirens, however, singing sweetly and harmoniously, beguiled the voyagers, luring, by reason of their melodious voice, those who heard it, to steer their vessels towards (the promontory). The (poets) report that Ulysses, on ascertaining this, smeared with wax the ears of his companions, and, lashing himself to the mast, sailed, free of danger, past the Sirens, hearing their chant distinctly. And my advice to my readers is to adopt a similar expedient, viz., either on account of their infirmity to smear their ears with wax, and sail (straight on) through the tenets of the heretics, not even listening to (doctrines) that are easily capable of enticing them into pleasure, like the luscious lay of the Sirens, or, by binding one's self to the Cross of Christ, (and) hearkening with fidelity (to His words), not to be distracted, inasmuch as he has reposed his trust in Him to whom ere this he has been firmly knit, and (I admonish that man) to continue steadfastly (in this faith).

Chapter II.—The System of Basilides Derived from Aristotle.

Since, therefore, in the six books preceding this, we have explained previous (heretical opinions), it now seems proper not to be silent respecting the (doctrines) of Basilides, which are the tenets of Aristotle the Stagyrite, not (those) of Christ. But even though on a former occasion the opinions propounded by Aristotle have been elucidated, we shall not even now scruple to set them down beforehand in a sort of synopsis, for the purpose of enabling my readers, by means of a nearer comparison of the two systems, to perceive with facility that the doctrines advanced by Basilides are (in reality) the clever quibbles of Aristotle.

Chapter III.—Sketch of Aristotle's Philosophy.

Aristotle, then, makes a threefold division of substance. For one portion of it is a certain genus, and another a certain species, as that (philosopher) expresses it, and a third a certain individual. What is individual, however, (is so) not through any minuteness of body, but because by nature it cannot admit of any division whatsoever. The genus, on the other hand, is a sort of aggregate, made up of many and different germs. And from this genus, just as (from) a certain heap, all the species of existent things derive their distinctions. And the genus constitutes a competent cause for (the production of) all generated entities. In order, however, that the foregoing statement may be clear, I shall prove (my position) through an example. And by means of this it will be possible for us to retrace our steps over the entire speculation of the Peripatetic (sage).

Chapter IV.—Aristotle's General Idea.

We affirm the existence of animal absolutely, not some animal. And this animal is neither ox, nor horse, nor man, nor god; nor is it significant of any of these at all, but is animal absolutely. From this animal the species of all particular animals derive their subsistence. And this animality, itself the summum genus, constitutes (the originating principle) for all animals produced in those (particular) species, and (yet is) not (itself any one) of the things generated. For man is an animal deriving the principle (of existence) from that animality, and horse is an animal deriving the principle of existence from that animality. The horse, and ox, and dog, and each of the rest of the animals, derive the principle (of existence) from the absolute animal, while animality itself is not any of these.

Chapter V.—Nonentity as a Cause.

If, however, this animality is not any of these (species), the subsistence, according to Aristotle, of the things that are generated, derived its reality from non-existent entities. For animality, from whence these singly have been derived, is not any one (of them); and though it is not any one of them, it has yet become someone originating principle of existing things. But who it is that has established this substance as an originating cause of what is subsequently produced, we shall declare when we arrive at the proper place for entertaining a discussion of this sort.

Chapter VI.—Substance, According to Aristotle; The Predicates.

Since, however, as I have stated, substance is threefold, viz., genus, species, (and) individual; and (since) we have set down animality as being the genus, and man the species, as being already distinct from the majority of animals, but notwithstanding still to be identified (with animals of his own kind), inasmuch as not being yet molded into a species of realized substance,—(therefore it is, that) when I impart form under a name to a man derived from the genus, I style him Socrates or Diogenes, or some one of the many denominations (in use). And since (in this way, I repeat,) I comprehend under a name the man who constitutes a species that is generated from the genus, I denominate a substance of this description in☐dividual. For genus has been divided into species, and species into individual. But (as regards) the individual, since it has been comprehended under a name, it is not possible that, according to its own nature, it could be divided into anything else, as we have divided each of the forementioned (genus and species).

Aristotle primarily, and especially, and preeminently entitles this—substance, inasmuch as it cannot either be predicated of any Subject, or exist in a Subject. He, however, predicates of the Subject, just as with the genus, what I said constituted animality, (and which is) predicated by means of a common name of all particular animals, such as ox, horse, and the rest that are placed under (this genus). For it is true to say that man is an animal, and horse an animal, and that ox is an animal, and each of the rest. Now the meaning of the expression "predicated of a Subject" is this, that inasmuch as it is one, it can be predicated in like manner of many (particulars), even though these happen to be diversified in species. For neither does horse nor ox differ from man so far forth as he is an animal, for the definition of animal is said to suit all animals alike. For what is an animal? If we define it, a general definition will comprehend all animals. For animal is an animated Substance, endued with Sensation. Such are ox, man, horse, and each of the rest (of the animal kingdom). But the meaning of the expression "in a Subject" is this, that what is inherent in anything, not as a part, it is impossible should exist separately from that in which it is. But this constitutes each of the accidents (resident) in Substance, and is what is termed Quality. Now, according to this, we say that certain persons are of such a quality; for instance, white, grey, black, just, unjust, temperate, and other (characteristics) similar to these. But it is impossible for any one of these to subsist itself by itself; but it must inhere in something else. If, however, neither animal which I predicate of all individual animals, nor accidents which are discoverable in all things of which they are nonessential qualities, can subsist themselves by themselves, and (yet if) individuals are formed out of these, (it follows, therefore, that) the triply divided Substance, which is not made up out of other things, consists of nonentities. If, then, what is primarily, and pre-eminently, and particularly denominated Substance consists of these, it derives existence from nonentities, according to Aristotle.

Chapter VII.—Aristotle's Cosmogony; His "Psychology;" His "Entelecheia;" His Theology; His Ethics; Basilides Follows Aristotle.

But concerning Substance, the statements now made will suffice. But not only is Substance denominated genus, species, (and) individual, but also matter, and form, and privation. There is, however, (as regards the substance,) in these no difference, even though the division be allowed to stand. Now, inasmuch as Substance is of this description, the arrangement of the world has taken place according to some such plan as the following. The world is divided, according to Aristotle, into very numerous and diversified parts. Now the portion of the world which extends from the earth to the moon is devoid of foresight, guideless, and is under the sway808 of that nature alone which belongs to itself. But another (part of the world which lies) beyond the moon, and extends to the surface of heaven, is arranged in the midst of all order and foresight and governance. Now, the (celestial) superficies constitutes a certain fifth substance and is remote from all those natural elements out of which the cosmical system derives consistence. And this is a certain fifth Substance, according to Aristotle,—as it were, a certain super-mundane essence. And (this essence) has become (a logical necessity) in his system, in order to accord with the (Peripatetic) division of the world. And (the topic of this fifth nature) constitutes a distinct investigation in philosophy. For there is extant a certain disquisition, styled A Lecture on Physical (Phenomena), in which he has elaborately treated concerning the operations which are conducted by nature and not providence, (in the quarter of space extending) from the earth as far as the moon. And there is also extant by him a certain other peculiar treatise on the principles of things (in the region) beyond the moon, and it bears the following inscription: Metaphysics. And another peculiar dissertation has been (written) by him, entitled Concerning a Fifth Substance, and in this work Aristotle unfolds his theological opinions.

There exists some such division of the universe as we have now attempted to delineate in outline, and (corresponding with it is the division) of the Aristotelian philosophy. His work, however, (styled) Concerning the Soul, is obscure. For in the entire three books (where he treats of this subject) it is not possible to say clearly what is Aristotle's opinion concerning the soul. For, as regards the definition which he furnishes of soul, it is easy (enough) to declare this; but what it is that is signified by the definition is difficult to discover. For soul, he says, is an entelecheia of a natural organic body; (but to explain) what this is at all, would require a very great number of arguments and a lengthened investigation. As regards, however, the Deity, the Originator of all those glorious objects in creation, (the nature of) this (First Cause)—even to one conducting his speculations by a more prolonged inquiry than that concerning (the soul)—is more difficult to know than the soul itself. The definition, however, which Aristotle furnishes of the Deity is, I admit, not difficult to ascertain, but it is impossible to comprehend the meaning of it. For, he says, (the Deity) is a "conception of conception;" but this is altogether a non-existent (entity). The world, however, is incorruptible (and) eternal, according to Aristotle. For it has in itself nothing faulty, inasmuch as it is directed by Providence and Nature. And Aristotle has laid down doctrines not only concerning Nature and a cosmical system, and Providence, and God, but he has written (more than this); for there is extant by him likewise a certain treatise on ethical subjects, and these he inscribes Books of Ethics. But throughout these he aims at rendering the habits of his hearers excellent from being worthless. When, therefore, Basilides has been discovered, not in spirit alone, but also in the actual expressions and names, transferring the tenets of Aristotle into our evangelical and saving doctrine, what remains, but that, by restoring what he has appropriated from others, we should prove to the disciples of this (heretic) that Christ will in no wise profit them, inasmuch as they are heathenish?

Chapter VIII.—Basilides and Isidorus Allege Apostolic Sanction for Their Systems; They Really Follow Aristotle.

Basilides, therefore, and Isidorus, the true son and disciple of Basilides, say that Matthias communicated to them secret discourses, which, I being specially instructed, he heard from the Savior. Let us, then, see how clearly Basilides, simultaneously with Isidorus, and the entire band of these (heretics), not only absolutely belies Matthias, but even the Savior Himself. (Time) was, says (Basilides), when there was nothing. Not even, however, did that nothing constitute anything of existent things; but, to express myself undisguisedly and candidly, and without any quibbling, it is altogether nothing. But when, he says, I employ the expression "was," I do not say that it was; but (I speak in this way) in order to signify the meaning of what I wish to elucidate. I affirm then, he says, that it was "altogether nothing." For, he says, that is not absolutely ineffable which is named (so),—although undoubtedly we call this ineffable,—but that which is "non-ineffable." For that which is "non-ineffable" is not denominated ineffable, but is, he says, above every name that is named. For, he says, by no means for the world are these names sufficient, but so manifold are its divisions that there is a deficiency (of names). And I do not take it upon myself to discover, he says, proper denominations for all things. Undoubtedly, however, one ought mentally, not by means of names, to conceive, after an ineffable manner, the peculiarities (of things) denominated. For an equivocal terminology, (when employed by teachers,) has created for their pupils confusion and a source of error concerning objects. (The Basilidians), in the first instance, laying hold on this borrowed and furtively derived tenet from the Peripatetic (sage), play upon the folly of those who herd together with them. For Aristotle, born many generations before Basilides, first lays down a system in The Categories concerning homonymous words. And these heretics bring this (system) to light as if it were peculiarly their own, and as if it were some novel (doctrine), and some secret disclosure from the discourses of Matthias.

Chapter IX.—Basilides Adopts the Aristotelian Doctrine of "Nonentity."

Since, therefore, "nothing" existed,—(I mean) not matter, nor substance, nor what is insubstantial, nor is absolute, nor composite, (nor conceivable, nor inconceivable, (nor what is sensible,) nor devoid of senses, nor man, nor angel, nor a god, nor, in short, any of those objects that have names, or are apprehended by sense, or that are cognized by intellect, but (are) thus (cognized), even with greater minuteness, still, when all things are absolutely removed,—(since, I say, "nothing" existed,) God, "non-existent,"—whom Aristotle styles "conception of conception," but these (Basilidians) "non-existent,"—inconceivably, insensibly, indeterminately, involuntarily, impassively, (and) unactuated by desire, willed to create a world. Now I employ, he says, the expression "willed" for the purpose of signifying (that he did so) involuntarily, and inconceivably, and insensibly. And by the expression "world" I do not mean that which was subsequently formed according to breadth and division, and which stood apart; nay, (far from this,) for (I mean) the germ of a world. The germ, however, of the world had all things in itself. Just as the grain of mustard comprises all things simultaneously, holding them (collected) together within the very smallest (compass), viz., roots, stem, branches, leaves, and innumerable gains which are produced from the plant, (as) seeds again of other plants, and frequently of others (still), that are produced (from them). In this way, "non-existent" God made the world out of nonentities, casting and depositing someone Seed that contained in itself a conglomeration of the germs of the world. But in order that I may render clearer what it is those (heretics) affirm, (I shall mention the following illustration of theirs.) As an egg of some variegated and particolored bird,—for instance the peacock, or some other (bird) still more manifold and particolored,—being one in reality, contains in itself numerous forms of manifold, and particolored, and much compounded substances; so, he says, the nonexistent seed of the world, which has been deposited by the non-existent God, constitutes at the same time the germ of a multitude of forms and a multitude of substances.

Chapter X.—Origin of the World; Basilides' Account of the "Sonship."

All things, therefore whatsoever it is possible to declare, and whatever, being not as yet discovered, one must omit, were likely to receive adaptation to the world which was about to be generated from the Seed. And this (Seed), at the requisite seasons, increases in bulk in a peculiar manner, according to accession, as through the instrumentality of a Deity so great, and of this description. (But this Deity) the creature can neither express nor grasp by perception. (Now, all these things) were inherent, treasured in the Seed, as we afterwards observe in a new-born child the growth of teeth, and paternal substance, and intellect, and everything which, though previously having no existence, accrues unto a man, growing little by little, from a youthful period of life. But since it would be absurd to say that any projection of a non-existent God became anything non-existent (for Basilides altogether shuns and dreads the Substances of things generated in the way of projection for, (he asks,) of what sort of projection is there a necessity, or of what sort of matter must we assume the previous existence, in order that God should construct a world, as the spider his web; or (as) a mortal man, for the purpose of working it, takes a (piece of) brass or of wood, or some other of the parts of matter?),—(projection, I say, being out of the question,) certainly, says (Basilides), God spoke the word, and it was carried into effect. And this, as these men assert, is that which has been stated by Moses: "Let there be light, and there was light." Whence he says, came the light? From nothing. For it has not been written, he says, whence, but this only, (that it came) from the voice of him who speaks the word. And he who speaks the word, he says, was non-existent; nor was that existent which was being produced. The seed of the cosmical system was generated, he says, from nonentities; (and I mean by the seed,) the word which was spoken, "Let there be light." And this, he says, is that which has been stated in the Gospels: "He was the true light, which lighted every man that cometh into the world." He derives his originating principles from that Seed and obtains from the same source his illuminating power. This is that seed which has in itself the entire conglomeration of germs. And Aristotle affirms this to be genius, and it is distributed by him into infinite species; just as from animal, which is non-existent, we sever ox, horse, (and) man. When, therefore, the cosmical Seed becomes the basis (for a subsequent development), those (heretics) assert, (to quote Basilides' own words:) "Whatsoever I affirm," he says, "to have been made after these, ask no question as to whence. For (the Seed) had all seeds treasured and reposing in itself, just as non-existent entities, and which were designed to be produced by a non-existent Deity."

Let us see, therefore, what they say is first, or what second, or what third, (in the development of) what is generated from the cosmical Seed. There existed, he says, in the Seed itself, a Sonship, threefold, in every respect of the same Substance with the non-existent God, (and) begotten from nonentities. Of this Sonship (thus) involving a threefold division, one part was refined, (another gross,) and another requiring purification. The refined portion, therefore, in the first place, simultaneously with the earliest deposition of the Seed by the non-existent one, immediately burst forth and went upwards and hurried above from below, employing a sort of velocity described in poetry,—

"…As wing or thought,"—

and attained, he says, unto him that is nonexistent. For every nature desires that (nonexistent one), on account of a superabundance of beauty and bloom. Each (nature desires this), however, after a different mode. The more gross portion, however, (of the Sonship) continuing still in the Seed, (and) being a certain imitative (principle), was not able to hurry upwards. For (this portion) was much more deficient in the refinement that the Sonship possessed, which through itself hurried upwards, (and so the more gross portion) was left behind. Therefore the more gross Sonship equipped itself with some such wing as Plato, the Preceptor of Aristotle, fastens on the soul in (his) Phædrus. And Basilides styles such, not a wing, but Holy Spirit; and Sonship invested in this (Spirit) confers benefits, and receives them in turn. He confers benefits, because, as a wing of a bird, when removed from the bird, would not of itself soar high up and aloft; nor, again, would a bird, when disengaged from its pinion, at any time soar high up and aloft; (so, in like manner,) the Sonship involved some such relation in reference to the Holy Spirit, and the Spirit in reference to the Sonship. For the Sonship, carried upwards by the Spirit as by a wing, bears aloft (in turn) its pinion, that is, the Spirit. And it approaches the refined Sonship, and the non-existent God, even Him who fabricated the world out of nonentities. He was not, (however,) able to have this (spirit) with (the Sonship) itself; for it was not of the same substance (with God), nor has it (any) nature (in common) with the Sonship. But as pure and dry air is contrary to (their) nature, and destructive to fishes; so, in contrariety to the nature of the Holy Spirit, was that place simultaneously of non-existent Deity and Sonship,—(a place) more ineffable than ineffable (entities), and higher up than all names.

Sonship, therefore, left this (spirit) near that Blessed Place, which cannot be conceived or represented by any expression. (He left the spirit) not altogether deserted or separated from the Sonship; nay, (far from it,) for it is just as when a most fragrant ointment is put into a vessel, that, even though (the vessel) be emptied (of it) with ever so much care, nevertheless some odor of the ointment still remains, and is left behind, even after (the ointment) is separated from the vessel; and the vessel retains an odor of ointment, though (it contain) not the ointment (itself). So the Holy Spirit has continued without any share in the Sonship, and separated (from it), and has in itself, similarly with ointment, its own power, a savor of Sonship. And this is what has been declared: "As the ointment upon the head which descended to the beard of Aaron." This is the savor from the Holy Spirit borne down from above, as far as formlessness, and the interval (of space) in the vicinity of our world. And from this the Son began to ascend, sustained as it were, says (Basilides), upon eagles' wings, and upon the back. For, he says, all (entities) hasten upwards from below, from things inferior to those that are superior. For not one of those things that are among things superior, is so silly as to descend beneath. The third Sonship, however, that which requires purification, has continued, he says, in the vast conglomeration of all germs conferring benefits and receiving them. But in what manner it is that (the third Sonship) receives benefits and confers them, we shall afterwards declare when we come to the proper place for discussing this question.

Chapter XI.—The "Great Archon" Of Basilides.

When, therefore, a first and second ascension of the Sonship took place, and the Holy Spirit itself also remained after the mode mentioned, the firmament was placed between the super-mundane (spaces) and the world. For existing things were distributed by Basilides into two continuous and primary divisions, and are, according to him, denominated partly in a certain (respect) world, and partly in a certain (respect) super-mundane (spaces). But the spirit, a line of demarcation between the world and super-mundane (spaces), is that which is both holy, and has abiding in itself the savor of Sonship. While, therefore, the firmament which is above the heaven is coming into existence, there burst forth, and was begotten from the cosmical Seed, and the conglomeration of all germs, the Great Archon (and) Head of the world, (who constitutes) a certain (species of) beauty, and magnitude, and indissoluble power. For, says he, he is more ineffable than ineffable entities, and more potent than potent ones, and more wise than wise ones, and superior to all the beautiful ones whatever you could mention. This (Archon), when begotten, raised Himself up and soared aloft, and was carried up entire as far as the firmament. And there He paused, supposing the firmament to be the termination of His ascension and elevation, and considering that there existed nothing at all beyond these. And than all the subjacent (entities) whatsoever there were among them which remained mundane, He became more wise, more powerful, more comely, more lustrous, (in fact,) pre-eminent for beauty above any entities you could mention with the exception of the Sonship alone, which is still left in the (conglomeration of) all germs. For he was not aware that there is (a Sonship) wiser and more powerful, and better than Himself. Therefore imagining Himself to be Lord, and Governor, and a wise Master Builder, He turns Himself to (the work of) the creation of every object in the cosmical system. And first, he deemed it proper not to be alone, but made unto Himself, and generated from adjacent (entities), a Son far superior to Himself, and wiser. For all these things had the non-existent Deity previously determined upon, when He cast down the (conglomeration of) all germs. Beholding, therefore, the Son, He was seized with astonishment, and loved (Him), and was struck with amazement. For some beauty of this description appeared to the Great Archon to belong to the Son, and the Archon caused Him to sit on his right (hand). This is, according to these (heretics), what is denominated the Ogdoad, where the Great Archon has his throne. The entire celestial creation, then, that is, the Æther, He

Himself, the Great Wise Demiurge formed. The Son, however, begotten of this (Archon), operates in Him, and offered Him suggestions, being endued with far greater wisdom than the Demiurge Himself.

### Chapter XII.—Basilides Adopts the "Entelecheia" Of Aristotle.

This, then, constitutes the entelecheia of the natural organic body, according to Aristotle, (viz.,) a soul operating in the body, without which the body is able to accomplish nothing; (I mean nothing) that is greater, and more illustrious, and more powerful, and more wise than the body. The account, therefore, which Aristotle has previously rendered concerning the soul and the body, Basilides elucidates as applied to the Great Archon and his Son. For the Archon has generated, according to Basilides, a son; and the soul as an operation and completion, Aristotle asserts to be an entelecheia of a natural organic body. As, therefore, the entelecheia controls the body, so the Son, according to Basilides, controls the God that is more ineffable than ineffable (entities). All things, therefore, have been provided for, and managed by the majesty of the Great Archon; (I mean) whatever objects exist in the ethereal region of space as far as the moon, for from that quarter onwards air is separated from æther. When all objects in the ethereal regions, then, were arranged, again from (the conglomeration of) all germs another Archon ascended, greater, of course, than all subjacent (entities), with the exception, however, of the Sonship that had been left behind, but far inferior to the First Archon. And this (second Archon) is called by them Rhetus. And this

Topos is styled Hebdomad, and this (Archon) is the manager and fabricator of all subjacent (entities). And He has likewise made unto Himself out (of the conglomeration of) all germs, a son who is more prudent and wise than Himself, similarly to what has been stated to have taken place in the case of the First Archon. That which exists in this quarter (of the universe) constitutes, he says, the actual conglomeration and collection of all seeds; and the things which are generated are produced according to nature, as has been declared already by Him who calculates on things future, when they ought (to be), and what sort they ought (to be), and how they ought (to be). And of these no one is Chief, or Guardian, or Creator. For (a) sufficient (cause of existence) for them is that calculation which the Non-Existent One formed when He exercised the function of creation.

Chapter XIII.—Further Explanation of the "Sonship."

When, therefore, according to these (heretics), the entire world and super-mundane entities were finished, and (when) nothing exists laboring under deficiency, there still remains in the (conglomeration of) all germs the third Sonship, which had been left behind in the Seed to confer benefits and receive them. And it must needs be that the Sonship which had been left behind ought likewise to be revealed and reinstated above. And His place should be above the Conterminous Spirit, near the refined and imitative Sonship and the Non-Existent One. But this would be in accordance with what has been written, he says: "And the creation itself groaned together, and travailed in pain together, waiting for the manifestation of the sons of God." Now, we who are spiritual are sons, he says, who have been left here to arrange, and mold, and rectify, and complete the souls which, according to nature, are so constituted as to continue in this quarter of the universe. "Sin, then, reigned from Adam unto Moses," as it has been written. For the Great Archon exercised dominion and possesses an empire with limits extending as far as the firmament. And He imagines Himself alone to be God, and that there exists nothing above Him, for (the reason that) all things have been guarded by unrevealed Siope. This, he says, is the mystery which has not been made known to former generations; but in those days the Great Archon, the Ogdoad, was King and Lord, as it seemed, of the universe. But (in reality) the Hebdomad was king and lord of this quarter of the universe, and the Ogdoad is Arrhetus, whereas the Hebdomad is Rhetus. This, he says, is the Archon of the Hebdomad, who has spoken to Moses, and says: "I am the God of Abraham, and Isaac, and Jacob, and I have not manifested unto them the name of God" (for so they wish that it had been written)—that is, the God, Arrhetus, Archon of the Ogdoad. All the prophets, therefore, who were before the Savior uttered their predictions, he says, from this source (of inspiration). Since, therefore, it was requisite, he says, that we should be revealed as the children of God, in expectation of whose manifestation, he says, the creation habitually groans and travails in pain, the Gospel came into the world, and passed through every Principality, and Power, and Dominion, and every Name that is named. And (the Gospel) came in reality, though nothing descended from above; nor did the blessed Sonship retire from that Inconceivable, and Blessed, (and) Non-Existent

God. Nay, (far from it;) for as Indian naphtha, when lighted merely from a considerably long distance, nevertheless attracts fire (towards it), so from below, from the formlessness of the conglomeration (of all germs), the powers pass upwards as far as the Sonship. For, according to the illustration of the Indian naphtha, the Son of the Great Archon of the Ogdoad, as if he were some (sort of) naphtha, apprehends and seizes conceptions from the Blessed Sonship, whose place of habitation is situated after that of the Conterminous (Spirit). For the power of the Sonship which is in the midst of the Holy Spirit, (that is,) in, the midst of the (Conterminous) Spirit, shares the flowing and rushing thoughts of the Sonship with the Son of the Great Archon.

Chapter XIV.—Whence Came the Gospel; The Number of Heavens According to Basilides; Explanation of Christ's Miraculous Conception.

The Gospel then came, says (Basilides), first from the Sonship through the Son, that was seated beside the Archon, to the Archon, and the Archon learned that He was not God of the universe, but was begotten. But (ascertaining that) He has above Himself the deposited treasure of that Ineffable and Unnameable (and) Non-existent One, and of the Sonship, He was both converted and filled with terror, when He was brought to understand in what ignorance He was (involved). This, he says, is what has been declared: "The fear of the Lord is the beginning of wisdom." For, being orally instructed by Christ, who was seated near, he began to acquire wisdom, (inasmuch as he thereby) learns who is the Non-Existent One, what the Sonship (is), what the Holy Spirit (is), what the apparatus of the universe (is), and what is likely to be the consummation of things. This is the wisdom spoken in a mystery, concerning which, says (Basilides), Scripture uses the following expressions: "Not in words taught of human wisdom, but in (those) taught of the Spirit." The Archon, then, being orally instructed, and taught, and being (thereby) filled with fear, proceeded to make confession concerning the sin which He had committed in magnifying Himself. This, he says, is what is declared: "I have recognized my sin, and I know my transgression, (and) about this I shall confess forever." When, then, the Great Archon had been orally instructed, and every creature of the Ogdoad had been orally instructed and taught, and (after) the mystery became known to the celestial (powers), it was also necessary that afterwards the Gospel should come to the Hebdomad, in order likewise that the Archon of the Hebdomad might be similarly instructed and indoctrinated into the Gospel. The Son of the Great Archon (therefore) kindled in the Son of the Archon of the Hebdomad the light which Himself possessed and had kindled from above from the Sonship. And the Son of the Archon of the Hebdomad had radiance imparted to Him, and He proclaimed the Gospel to the Archon of the Hebdomad. And in like manner, according to the previous account, He Himself was both terrified and induced to make confession. When, therefore, all (beings) in the Hebdomad had been likewise enlightened, and had the Gospel announced to them (for in these regions of the universe there exist, according to these heretics, creatures infinite (in number), viz., Principalities and Powers and Rulers, in regard of which there is extant among the (Basilidians) a very prolix and verbose treatise, where they allege that there are three hundred and sixty-five heavens, and that the great Archon of these is Abrasax, from the fact that his name comprises the computed number 365, so that, of course, the calculation of the title includes all (existing) things, and that for these reasons the year consists of so many days);—but when, he says, these (two events, viz., the illumination of the Hebdomad and the manifestation of the Gospel) had thus taken place, it was necessary, likewise, that afterwards the Formlessness existent in our quarter of creation should have radiance imparted to it, and that the mystery should be revealed to the Sonship, which had been left behind in Formlessness, just like an abortion.

Now this (mystery) was not made known to previous generations, as he says, it has been written, "By revelation was made known unto me the mystery;" and, "I have heard inexpressible words which it is not possible for man to declare." The light, (therefore,) which came down from the Ogdoad above to the Son of the Hebdomad, descended from the Hebdomad upon Jesus the son of Mary, and he had radiance imparted to him by being illuminated with the light that shone upon him. This, he says, is that which has been declared: "The Holy Spirit will come upon thee," (meaning) that which proceeded from the Sonship through the conterminous spirit upon the Ogdoad and Hebdomad, as far as Mary; "and the power of the Highest will overshadow thee," (meaning) the power of the anointing, (which streamed) from the (celestial) height above (through) the Demiurge, as far as the creation, which is (as far as) the Son. And as far as that (Son) he says the world consisted thus. And as far as this, the entire Sonship, which is left behind for benefiting the souls in Formlessness, and for being the recipient in turn of benefits,—(this Sonship, I say,) when it is transformed, followed Jesus, and hastened upwards, and came forth purified. And it becomes most refined, so that it could, as the first (Sonship), hasten upwards through its own instrumentality. For it possesses all the power that, according to nature, is firmly connected with the light which from above shone down (upon earth).

Chapter XV.—God's Dealings with the Creature; Basilides' Notion of (1) the Inner Man, (2) the Gospel; His Interpretation of the Life and Sufferings of Our Lord.

When, therefore, he says, the entire Sonship shall have come, and shall be above the conterminous spirit, then the creature will become the object of mercy. For (the creature) groans until now, and is tormented, and waits for the manifestation of the sons of God, in order that all who are men of the Sonship may ascend from thence. When this takes place, God, he says, will bring upon the whole world enormous ignorance, that all things may continue according to nature, and that nothing may inordinately desire anything of the things that are contrary to nature. But (far from it); for all the souls of this quarter of creation, as many as possess the nature of remaining immortal in this (region) only, continue (in it), aware of nothing superior or better (than their present state). And there will not prevail any rumor or knowledge in regions below, concerning beings whose dwelling is placed above, lest subjacent souls should be wrung with torture from longing after impossibilities. (It would be) just as if a fish were to crave to feed on the mountains along with sheep. (For) a wish of this description would, he says, be their destruction. All things, therefore, that abide in (this) quarter are incorruptible, but corruptible if they are disposed to wander and cross over from the things that are according to nature. In this way the Archon of the Hebdomad will know nothing of superjacent entities. For enormous ignorance will lay hold on this one likewise, in order that sorrow, and grief, and groaning may depart from him; for he will not desire aught of impossible things, nor will he be visited with anguish. In like manner, however, the same ignorance will lay hold also on the Great Archon of the Ogdoad, and similarly on all the creatures that are subject unto him, in order that in no respect anything may desire aught of those things that are contrary to nature and may not (thus) be overwhelmed with sorrow. And so there will be the restitution of all things which, in conformity with nature, have from the beginning a foundation in the seed of the universe, but will be restored at (their own) proper periods. And that each thing, says (Basilides), has its own particular times, the Savior is a sufficient (witness) when He observes, "Mine hour is not yet come." And the Magi (afford similar testimony) when they gaze wistfully upon the (Savior's) star. For (Jesus) Himself was, he says, mentally preconceived at the time of the generation of the stars, and of the complete return to their starting point of the seasons in the vast conglomeration (of all germs). This is, according to these (Basilidians), he who has been conceived as the inner spiritual man in what is natural (now this is the Sonship which left there the soul, not (that it might be) mortal, but that it might abide here according to nature, just as the first Sonship left above in its proper locality the Holy Spirit, (that is, the spirit) which is conterminous),—(this, I say, is he who has been conceived as the inner spiritual man, and) has then been arrayed in his own peculiar soul.

In order, however, that we may not omit any of the doctrines of this (Basilides), I shall likewise explain whatever statements they put forward respecting a gospel. For gospel with them, as has been elucidated, is of supermundane entities the knowledge which the Great Archon did not understand. As, then, it was manifested unto him that there are likewise the Holy Spirit—that is, the conterminous (spirit)—and the Sonship, and the Non-Existent God, the cause of all these, he rejoiced at the communications made to him, and was filled with exultation. According to them, this constitutes the gospel. Jesus, however, was born, according to these (heretics), as we have already declared. And when the generation which has been previously explained took place, all the events in our Lord's life occurred, according to them, in the same manner as they have been described in the Gospels. And these things happened, he says, in order that Jesus might become the first fruits of a distinction of the different orders (of created objects) that had been confused together. For when the world had been divided into an Ogdoad, which is the head of the entire world,—now the great Archon is head of the entire world,—and into a Hebdomad,—which is the head of the Hebdomad, the Demiurge of subjacent entities,—and into this order of creatures (that prevails) amongst us, where exists Formlessness, it was requisite that the various orders of created objects that had been confounded together should be distinguished by a separating process performed by Jesus. (Now this separation) that which was his corporeal part suffered, and this was (the part) of Formlessness and reverted into Formlessness. And that was resuscitated which was his psychical part, and this was (part) of the Hebdomad, and reverted into the Hebdomad. And he revived that (element in his nature) which was the peculiar property of the elevated region where dwells the Great Archon, and (that element) remained beside the Great Archon. And he carried upwards as far as (that which is) above that which was (the peculiar property) of the conterminous spirit, and he remained in the conterminous spirit. And through him there was purified the third Sonship, which had been left for conferring benefits, and receiving them. And (through Jesus) it ascended towards the blessed Sonship and passed through all these. For the entire purpose of these was the blending together of, as it were, the conglomeration of all germs, and the distinction of the various orders of created objects, and the restoration into their proper component parts of things that had been blended together. Jesus, therefore, became the first fruits of the distinction of the various orders of created objects, and his Passion took place for not any other reason than the distinction which was thereby brought about in the various orders of created objects that had been confounded together. For in this manner (Basilides) says that the entire Son☐ship, which had been left in Formlessness for the purpose of conferring benefits and receiving them, was divided into its component elements, according to the manner in which also the distinction of natures had taken place in Jesus. These, then, are the legends which likewise Basilides details after his sojourn in Egypt; and being instructed by the (sages of this country) in so great a system of wisdom, (the heretic) produced fruits of this description.

## Chapter XVI.—The System of Saturnilus.

But one Saturnilus, who flourished about the same period with Basilides, but spent his time in Antioch, (a city) of Syria, propounded opinions akin to whatever (tenets) Menander (advanced). He asserts that there is one Father, unknown to all—He who had made angels, archangels, principalities, (and) powers; and that by certain angels, seven (in number), the world was made, and all things that are in it. And (Saturnilus affirms) that man was a work of angels. There had appeared above from (the Being of) absolute sway, a brilliant image; and when (the angels) were not able to detain this, on account of its immediately, he says, returning with rapidity upwards, they exhorted one another, saying, "Let us make man in our likeness and image." And when the figure was formed, and was not, he says, able, owing to the impotence of the angels, to lift up itself, but continued writhing as a worm, the Power above, compassionating him on account of his having been born in its own image, sent forth a scintillation of life, which raised man up, and caused him to have vitality. (Saturnilus) asserts that this scintillation of life rapidly returns after death to those things that are of the same order of existence; and that the rest, from which they have been generated, are resolved into those. And the Savior he supposed to be unbegotten and incorporeal, and devoid of figure. (Saturnilus,) however, (maintained that Jesus) was manifested as man in appearance only. And he says that the God of the Jews is one of the angels, and, on account of the Father's wishing to deprive of sovereignty all the Archons, that Christ came for the overthrow of the God of the Jews, and for the salvation of those that believe upon Him; and that these have in them the scintillation of life. For he asserted that two kinds of men had been formed by the angels,—one wicked, but the other good. And, since demons from time to time assisted wicked (men, Saturnilus affirms) that the Savior came for the overthrow of worthless men and demons, but for the salvation of good men. And he affirms that marriage and procreation are from Satan. The majority, however, of those who belong to this (heretic's school) abstain from animal food likewise, (and) by this affectation of asceticism (make many their dupes). And (they maintain) that the prophecies have been uttered, partly by the world-making angels, and partly by Satan, who is also the very angel whom they supposed to act in antagonism to the cosmical (angels), and especially to the God of the Jews. These, then, are in truth the tenets of Saturnilus.

Chapter XVII.—Marcion; His Dualism; Derives His System from Empedocles; Sketch of the Doctrine of Empedocles.

But Marcion, a native of Pontus, far more frantic than these (heretics), omitting the majority of the tenets of the greater number (of speculators), (and) advancing into a doctrine still more unabashed, supposed (the existence of) two originating causes of the universe, alleging one of them to be a certain good (principle), but the other an evil one. And himself imagining that he was introducing some novel (opinion), founded a school full of folly, and attended by men of a sensual mode of life, inasmuch as he himself was one of lustful propensities. This (heretic) having thought that the multitude would forget that he did not happen to be a disciple of Christ, but of Empedocles, who was far anterior to himself, framed and formed the same opinions,—namely, that there are two causes of the universe, discord and friendship. For what does Empedocles say respecting the plan of the world? Even though we have previously spoken (on this subject), yet even now also, for the purpose, at all events, of comparing the heresy of this plagiarist (with its source), we shall not be silent.

This (philosopher) affirms that all the elements out of which the world consists and derives its being, are six: two of them material, (viz.,) earth and water; and two of them instruments by which material objects are arranged and altered, (viz.,) fire and air; and two of them, by means of the instruments, operating upon matter and fashioning it, viz., discord and friendship. (Empedocles) expresses himself somehow thus:—

> "The four roots of all things hear thou first:
> Brilliant Jove, and life-giving Juno and Aidoneus,
> And Nestis, who with tears bedews the mortal font."

Jupiter is fire, and life-giving Juno earth, which produces fruits for the support of existence; and Aidoneus air, because although through him we behold all things, yet himself alone we do not see. But Nestis is water, for this is a sole vehicle of (food), and thus becomes a cause of sustenance to all those that are being nourished; (but) this of itself is not able to afford nutriment to those that are being nourished. For if it did possess the power of affording nutriment, animal life, he says, could never be destroyed by famine, inasmuch as water is always superabundant in the world. For this reason, he denominates Nestis water, because, (though indirectly) being a cause of nutriment, it is not (of itself) competent to afford nutriment to those things that are being nourished. These, therefore—to delineate them as by way of outline—are the principles that comprise (Empedocles') entire theory of the world: (viz.,) water and earth, out of which (proceed) generated entities; fire and spirit, (which are) instruments and efficient (causes), but discord and friendship, which are (principles) artistically fabricating (the universe). And friendship is a certain peace, and unanimity, and love, whose entire effort is, that there should be one finished and complete world. Discord, however, invariably separates that one (world), and subdivides it, or makes many things out of one. Therefore, discord is of the entire creation a cause which he styles "oulomenon," that is, destructive. For it is the concern of this (discord), that throughout every age the creation itself should continue to preserve its existing condition. And ruinous discord has been (thus) a fabricator and an efficient cause of the production of all generated entities; whereas friendship (is the cause) of the eduction, and alteration, and restoration of existing things into one system. And in regard of these (causes), Empedocles asserts that they are two immortal and unbegotten principles, and such as have not as yet received an originating cause of existence. (Empedocles) somewhere or other (expresses himself) in the following manner:—

> "For if both once it was, and will be; never, I think,
> Will be the age eternal void of both of these."

(But) what are these (two)? Discord and Friendship; for they did not begin to come into being, but pre-existed and always will exist, because, from the fact of their being unbegotten, they are not able to undergo corruption. But fire, (and water,) and earth, and air, are (entities) that perish and revive. For when these generated (bodies), by reason of Discord, cease to exist, Friendship, laying hold on them, brings them forward, and attaches and associates them herself with the universe. (And this takes place) in order that the Universe may continue one, being always ordered by Friendship in a manner one and the same, and with (uninterrupted) uniformity.

When, however, Friendship makes unity out of plurality, and associates with unity separated entities, Discord, again, forcibly severs them from unity, and makes them many, that is, fire, water, earth, air, (as well as) the animals and plants produced from these, and whatever portions of the world we observe. And in regard of the form of the world, what sort it is, (as) arranged by Friendship, (Empedocles) expresses himself in the following terms:—

> "For not from back two arms arise,
> Not feet, not nimble knees, not genital groin,
> But a globe it was, and equal to itself it is."

An operation of this description Friendship maintains, and makes (one) most beautiful form of the world out of plurality. Discord, however, the cause of the arrangement of each of the parts (of the universe), forcibly severs and makes many things out of that one (form). And this is what Empedocles affirms respecting his own generation:—

"Of these I also am from God a wandering exile."

That is, (Empedocles) denominates as God the unity and unification of that (one form) in which (the world) existed antecedent to the separation and production (introduced) by Discord among the majority of those things (that subsisted) in accordance with the disposition (effected) by Discord. For Empedocles affirms Discord to be a furious, and perturbed, and unstable Demiurge, (thus) denominating Discord the creator of the world. For this constitutes the condemnation and necessity of souls which Discord forcibly severs from unity, and (which it) fashions and operates upon, (according to Empedocles,) who expresses himself after some such mode as, the following:—

"Who perjury piles on sin,
While demons gain a life prolonged;"

meaning by demons long-lived souls, because they are immortal, and live for lengthened ages:—

"For thrice ten thousand years banished from bliss;"

denominating as blissful, those that have been collected by Friendship from the majority of entities into the process of unification (arising out) of the intelligible world. He asserts that those are exiles, and that

"In lapse of time all sorts of mortal men are born,
Changing the irksome ways of life."

He asserts the irksome ways to be the alterations and transfigurations of souls into (successive) bodies. This is what he says:— "Changing the irksome ways of life."

For souls "change," body after body being altered, and punished by Discord, and not permitted to continue in the one (frame), but that the souls are involved in all descriptions of punishment by Discord being changed from body to body. He says:—

"Ethereal force to ocean drives the souls,
And ocean spurts them forth on earth's expanse,
And earth on beams of blazing sun, who flings
(The souls) on æther's depths, and each from each
(A spirit) takes, and all with hatred burn."

This is the punishment which the Demiurge inflicts, just as some brazier molding (a piece of) iron, and dipping it successively from fire into water. For fire is the æther whence the Demiurge transfers the souls into the sea; and land is the earth: whence he uses the words, from water into earth, and from earth into air. This is what (Empedocles) says:—

"And earth on beams
Of blazing sun, who flings (the souls)
On æther's depths, and each from each
A (spirit) takes, and all with hatred burn."

The souls, then, thus detested, and tormented, and punished in this world, are, according to Empedocles, collected by Friendship as being a certain good (power), and (one) that pities the groaning of these, and the disorderly and wicked device of furious Discord. And (likewise Friendship is) eager, and toils to lead forth little by little the souls from the world, and to domesticate them with unity, in order that all things, being conducted by herself, may attain unto unification. Therefore on account of such an arrangement on the part of destructive Discord of this divided world, Empedocles admonishes his disciples to abstain from all sorts of animal food. For he asserts that the bodies of animals are such as feed on the habitations of punished souls. And he teaches those who are hearers of such doctrines (as his), to refrain from intercourse with women. (And he issues this precept) in order that (his disciples) may not co-operate with and assist those works which Discord fabricates, always dissolving and forcibly severing the work of Friendship. Empedocles asserts that this is the greatest law of the management of the universe, expressing himself somehow thus:—

"There's something swayed by Fate, the ancient, Endless law of gods, and sealed by potent oaths."

He thus calls Fate the alteration from unity into plurality, according to Discord, and from plurality into unity, according to Friendship. And, as I stated, (Empedocles asserts) that there are four perishable gods, (viz.,) fire, water, earth, (and) air. (He maintains,) however, that there are two (gods) which are immortal, unbegotten, (and) continually hostile one to the other, (namely) Discord and Friendship. And (he asserts) that Discord always is guilty of injustice and covetousness, and forcible abduction of the things of Friendship, and of appropriation of them to itself. (He alleges,) however, that Friendship, inasmuch as it is always and invariably a certain good (power), and intent on union, recalls and brings towards (itself), and reduces to unity, the parts of the universe that have been forcibly severed, and tormented, and punished in the creation by the Demiurge. Some such system of philosophy as the foregoing is advanced for us by Empedocles concerning the generation of the world, and its destruction, and its constitution, as one consisting of what is good and bad. And he says that there is likewise a certain third power which is cognized by intellect, and that this can be understood from these, (viz., Discord and Friendship,) expressing himself somehow thus:—

> "For if, 'neath hearts of oak, these truths you fix,
> And view them kindly in meditations pure,
> Each one of these, in lapse of time, will haunt you,
> And many others, sprung of these, descend.
> For into every habit these will grow, as Nature prompts;
> But if for other things you sigh, which, countless, linger
> Undisguised 'mid men, and blunt the edge of care,
> As years roll on they'll leave you fleetly,
> Since they yearn to reach their own beloved race;
> For know that all possess perception and a share of mind."

Chapter XVIII.—Source of Marcionism; Empedocles Reasserted as the Suggester of the Heresy.

When, therefore, Marcion or some one of his hounds barks against the Demiurge, and adduces reasons from a comparison of what is good and bad, we ought to say to them, that neither Paul the apostle nor Mark, he of the maimed finger, announced such (tenets). For none of these (doctrines) has been written in the Gospel according to Mark. But (the real author of the system) is Empedocles, son of Meto, a native of Agrigentum. And (Marcion) despoiled this (philosopher) and imagined that up to the present would pass undetected his transference, under the same expressions, of the arrangement of his entire heresy from Sicily into the evangelical narratives. For bear with me, O Marcion: as you have instituted a comparison of what is good and evil, I also to-day will institute a comparison following up your own tenets, as you suppose them to be. You affirm that the Demiurge of the world is evil—why not hide your countenance in shame, (as thus) teaching to the Church the doctrines of Empedocles? You say that there is a good Deity who destroys the works of the Demiurge: then do not you plainly preach to your pupils, as the good Deity, the Friendship of Empedocles. You forbid marriage, the procreation of children, (and) the abstaining from meats which God has created for participation by the faithful, and those that know the truth. (Thinks thou, then,) that thou canst escape detection, (while thus) enjoining the purificatory rites of Empedocles? For in point of fact you follow in every respect this (philosopher of paganism), while you instruct your own disciples to refuse meats, in order not to eat any body (that might be) a remnant of a soul which has been punished by the Demiurge. You dissolve marriages that have been cemented by the Deity. And here again you conform to the tenets of Empedocles, in order that for you the work of Friendship may be perpetuated as one (and) indivisible. For, according to Empedocles, matrimony separates unity, and makes (out of it) plurality, as we have proved.

Chapter XIX.—The Heresy of Prepon; Follows Empedocles; Marcion Rejects the Generation of the Savior.

The principal heresy of Marcion, and (the one of his) which is most free from admixture (with other heresies), is that which has its system formed out of the theory concerning the good and bad (God). Now this, it has been manifested by us, belongs to Empedocles. But since at present, in our times, a certain follower of Marcion, (namely) Prepon, an Assyrian, has endeavored to introduce something more novel, and has given an account of his heresy in a work inscribed to Bardesanes, an Armenian, neither of this will I be silent. In alleging that what is just constitutes a third principle, and that it is placed intermediate between what is good and bad, Prepon of course is not able to avoid (the imputation of inculcating) the opinion of Empedocles. For Empedocles asserts that the world is managed by wicked Discord, and that the other (world) which (is managed) by Friendship, is cognizable by intellect. And (he asserts) that these are the two different principles of good and evil, and that intermediate between these diverse principles is impartial reason, in accordance with which are united the things that have been separated by Discord, (and which,) in accordance with the influence of Friendship, are accommodated to unity. The impartial reason itself, that which is an auxiliary to Friendship, Empedocles denominates "Musa." And he himself likewise entreats her to assist him, and expresses himself somehow thus:—

"For if on fleeting mortals, deathless Muse,
Thy care it be that thoughts our mind engross,
Calliope, again befriend my present prayer,
As I disclose a pure account of happy gods."

Marcion, adopting these sentiments, rejected altogether the generation of our Savior. He considered it to be absurd that under the (category of a) creature fashioned by destructive Discord should have been the Logos that was an auxiliary to Friendship—that is, the Good Deity. (His doctrine,) however, was that, independent of birth, (the Logos) Himself descended from above in the fifteenth year of the reign of Tiberius Caesar, and that, as being intermediate between the good and bad Deity, He proceeded to give instruction in the synagogues. For if He is a Mediator, He has been, he says, liberated from the entire nature of the Evil Deity. Now, as he affirms, the Demiurge is evil, and his works. For this reason, he affirms, Jesus came down unbegotten, in order that He might be liberated from all (admixture of) evil. And He has, he says, been liberated from the nature of the Good One likewise, in order that He may be a Mediator, as Paul states, and as Himself acknowledges: "Why call ye me good? there is one good." These, then, are the opinions of Marcion, by means of which he made many his dupes, employing the conclusions of Empedocles. And he transferred the philosophy invented by that (ancient speculator) into his own system of thought, and (out of Empedocles) constructed his (own) impious heresy. But I consider that this has been sufficiently refuted by us, and that I have not omitted any opinion of those who purloin their opinions from the Greeks, and act despitefully towards the disciples of Christ, as if they had become teachers to them of these (tenets). But since it seems that we have sufficiently explained the doctrines of this (heretic), let us see what Carpocrates says.

Chapter XX.—The Heresy of Carpocrates; Wicked Doctrines Concerning Jesus Christ; Practice Magical Arts; Adopt a Metempsychosis.

Carpocrates affirms that the world and the things in it were made by angels, far inferior to the unbegotten Father; and that Jesus was generated of Joseph, and that, having been born similar to (other) men, He was more just than the rest (of the human race). And (Carpocrates asserts) that the soul (of Jesus), inasmuch as it was made vigorous and undefiled, remembered the things seen by it in its converse with the unbegotten God. And (Carpocrates maintains) that on this account there was sent down upon (Jesus) by that (God) a power, in order that through it He might be enabled to escape the world-making (angels). And (he says) that this power, having passed through all, and having obtained liberty in all, again ascended881 to God (Himself). And (he alleges) that in the same condition with (the soul of Jesus are all the souls) that embrace similar objects of desire with the (power just alluded to). And they assert that the soul of Jesus, (though,) according to law, it was disciplined in

Jewish customs, (in reality) despised them. And (he says) that on this account (Jesus) received powers whereby He rendered null and void the passions incidental to men for their punishment. And (he argues), therefore, that the (soul), which, similarly with that soul of Christ, is able to despise the world-making Archons, receives in like manner power for the performance of similar acts. Wherefore, also, (according to Carpocrates, there are persons who) have attained unto such a degree of pride as to affirm some of themselves to be equal to Jesus Himself, whereas others among them to be even still more powerful. But (they also contend) that some enjoy an excellence above the disciples of that (Redeemer), for instance Peter and Paul, and the rest of the Apostles, and that these are in no respect inferior to Jesus. And (Carpocrates asserts) that the souls of these have originated from that supernal power, and that consequently they, as equally despising the world-making (angels), have been deemed worthy of the same power, and (of the privilege) to ascend to the same (place). If, however, any one would despise earthly concerns more than did that (Savior, Carpocrates says) that such a one would be able to become superior to (Jesus. The followers of this heretic) practice their magical arts and incantations, and spells and voluptuous feasts. And (they are in the habit of invoking the aid of) subordinate demons and dream-senders, and (of resorting to) the rest of the tricks (of sorcery), alleging that they possess power for now acquiring sway over the Archons and makers of this world, nay, even over all the works that are in it.

(Now these heretics) have themselves been sent forth by Satan, for the purpose of slandering before the Gentiles the divine name of the Church. (And the devil's object is,) that men hearing, now after one fashion and now after another, the doctrines of those (heretics), and thinking that all of us are people of the same stamp, may turn away their ears from the preaching of the truth, or that they also, looking, (without abjuring,) upon all the tenets of those (heretics), may speak hurtfully of us. (The followers of Carpocrates) allege that the souls are transferred from body to body, so far as that they may fill up (the measure of) all their sins. When, however, not one (of these sins) is left, (the Carpocratians affirm that the soul) is then emancipated, and departs unto that God above of the world-making angels, and that in this way all souls will be saved. If, however, some (souls), during the presence of the soul in the body for one life, may by anticipation become involved in the full measure of transgressions, they, (according to these heretics,) no longer undergo metempsychosis. (Souls of this sort,) however, on paying off at once all trespasses, will, (the Carpocratians say,) be emancipated from dwelling any more in a body. Certain, likewise, of these (heretics) brand882 their own disciples in the back parts of the lobe of the right ear. And they make counterfeit images of Christ, alleging that these were in existence at the time (during which our Lord was on earth, and that they were fashioned) by Pilate.

Chapter XXI.—The System of Cerinthus Concerning Christ.

But a certain Cerinthus, himself being disciplined in the teaching of the Egyptians, asserted that the world was not made by the primal Deity, but by some virtue which was an offshoot from that Power which is above all things, and which (yet) is ignorant of the God that is above all. And he supposed that Jesus was not generated from a virgin, but that he was born son of Joseph and Mary, just in a manner similar with the rest of men, and that (Jesus) was more just and more wise (than all the human race). And (Cerinthus alleges) that, after the baptism (of our Lord), Christ in form of a dove came down upon him, from that absolute sovereignty which is above all things. And then, (according to this heretic,) Jesus proceeded to preach the unknown Father, and in attestation (of his mission) to work miracles. It was, however, (the opinion of Cerinthus,) that ultimately Christ departed from Jesus, and that Jesus suffered and rose again; whereas that Christ, being spiritual, remained beyond the possibility of suffering.

Chapter XXII.—Doctrine of the Ebionæans.

The Ebionæans, however, acknowledge that the world was made by Him Who is in reality God, but they propound legends concerning the Christ similarly with Cerinthus and Carpocrates. They live conformably to the customs of the Jews, alleging that they are justified according to the law, and saying that Jesus was justified by fulfilling the law. And therefore it was, (according to the Ebionæans,) that (the Savior) was named (the) Christ of God and Jesus, since not one of the rest (of mankind) had observed completely the law. For if even any other had fulfilled the commandments (contained) in the law, he would have been that Christ. And the (Ebionæans allege) that they themselves also, when in like manner they fulfil (the law), are able to become Christs; for they assert that our Lord Himself was a man in a like sense with all (the rest of the human family).

### Chapter XXIII.—The Heresy of Theodotus.

But there was a certain Theodotus, a native of Byzantium, who introduced a novel heresy. He announces tenets concerning the originating cause of the universe, which are partly in keeping with the doctrines of the true Church, in so far as he acknowledges that all things were created by God. Forcibly appropriating, however, (his notions of) Christ from the school of the Gnostics, and of Cerinthus and Ebion, he alleges that (our Lord) appeared in some such manner as I shall now describe. (According to this, Theodotus maintains) that Jesus was a (mere) man, born of a virgin, according to the counsel of the Father, and that after he had lived promiscuously with all men, and had become pre-eminently religious, he subsequently at his baptism in Jordan received Christ, who came from above and descended (upon him) in form of a dove. And this was the reason, (according to Theodotus,) why (miraculous) powers did not operate within him prior to the manifestation in him of that Spirit which descended, (and) which proclaims him to be the Christ. But (among the followers of Theodotus) some are disposed (to think) that never was this man made God, (even) at the descent of the Spirit; whereas others (maintain that he was made God) after the resurrection from the dead.

Chapter XXIV.—The Melchisedecians; The Nicolaitans.

While, however, different questions have arisen among them, a certain (heretic), who himself also was styled Theodotus, and who was by trade a banker, attempted to establish (the doctrine), that a certain Melchisedec constitutes the greatest power, and that this one is greater than Christ. And they allege that Christ happens to be according to the likeness (of this Melchisedec). And they themselves, similarly with those who have been previously spoken of as adherents of Theodotus, assert that Jesus is a (mere) man, and that, in conformity with the same account (already given), Christ descended upon him.

There are, however, among the Gnostics diversities of opinion; but we have decided that it would not be worthwhile to enumerate the silly doctrines of these (heretics), inasmuch as they are (too) numerous and devoid of reason, and full of blasphemy. Now, even those (of the heretics) who are of a more serious turn in regard of the Divinity, and have derived their systems of speculation from the Greeks, must stand convicted (of these charges). But Nicolaus has been a cause of the wide-spread combination of these wicked men. He, as one of the seven (that were chosen) for the diaconate, was appointed by the Apostles. (But Nicolaus) departed from correct doctrine, and was in the habit of inculcating indifferency of both life and food. And when the disciples (of Nicolaus) continued to offer insult to the Holy Spirit, John reproved them in the Apocalypse as fornicators and eaters of things offered unto idols.

## Chapter XXV.—The Heresy of Cerdon.

But one Cerdon himself also, taking occasion in like manner from these (heretics) and Simon, affirms that the God preached by Moses and the prophets was not Father of Jesus Christ. For (he contends) that this (Father) had been known, whereas that the Father of Christ was unknown, and that the former was just, but the latter good. And Marcion corroborated the tenet of this (heretic) in the work which he attempted to write, and which he styled Antitheses. And he was in the habit, (in this book,) of uttering whatever slanders suggested themselves to his mind against the Creator of the universe. In a similar manner likewise (acted) Lucian, the disciple of this (heretic).

## Chapter XXVI.—The Doctrines of Apelles; Philumene, His Prophetess.

But Apelles, sprung from these, thus expresses himself, (saying) that there is a certain good Deity, as also Marcion supposed, and that he who created all things is just. Now he, (according to Apelles,) was the Demiurge of generated entities. And (this heretic also maintains) that there is a third (Deity), the one who was in the habit of speaking to Moses, and that this (god) was of a fiery nature, and that there was another fourth god, a cause of evils. But these he denominates angels. He utters, however, slanders against law and prophets, by alleging that the things that have been written are (of) human (origin), and are false. And (Apelles) selects from the Gospels or (from the writings of) the Apostle (Paul) whatever pleases himself. But he devotes himself to the discourses of a certain Philumene as to the revelations902 of a prophetess. He affirms, however, that Christ descended from the power above; that is, from the good (Deity), and that he is the son of that good (Deity). And (he asserts that Jesus) was not born of a virgin, and that when he did appear he was not devoid of flesh. (He maintains,) however, that (Christ) formed his body by taking portions of it from the substance of the universe: that is, hot and cold, and moist and dry. And (he says that Christ), on receiving in this body cosmical powers, lived for the time he did in (this) world. But (he held that Jesus) was subsequently crucified by the Jews, and expired, and that, being raised up after three days, he appeared to his disciples. And (the Savior) showed them, (so Apelles taught,) the prints of the nails and (the wound) in his side, desirous of persuading them that he was in truth no phantom, but was present in the flesh. After, says (Apelles), he had shown them his flesh, (the Savior) restored it to earth, from which substance it was (derived. And this he did because) he coveted nothing that belonged to another. (Though indeed Jesus) might use for the time being (what belonged to another), he yet in due course rendered to each (of the elements) what peculiarly belonged to them. And so it was, that after he had once more loosed the chains of his body, he gave back heat to what is hot, cold to what is cold, moisture to what is moist, (and) dryness to what is dry. And in this condition (our Lord) departed to the good Father, leaving the seed of life in the world for those who through his disciples should believe in him.

It appears to us that these (tenets) have been sufficiently explained. Since, however, we have determined to leave unrefuted not one of those opinions that have been advanced by any (of the heretics), let us see what (system) also has been invented by the Docetæ.

## Book VIII.

### Contents.

The following are the contents of the eighth book of the Refutation of all Heresies:—

What are the opinions of the Docetæ, and that they have formed the doctrines which they assert from natural philosophy.

How Monoïmus trifles, devoting his attention to poets, and geometricians, and arithmeticians.

How (the system of) Tatian has arisen from the opinions of Valentinus and Marcion, and how this heretic (from this source) has formed his own doctrines. Hermogenes, however, availed himself of the tenets of Socrates, not those of Christ.

How those err who contend for keeping Easter on the fourteenth day.

What the error is of the Phrygians, who suppose that Montanus, and Priscilla, and Maximilla, are prophets.

What the conceit is of the Encratites, and that their opinions have been formed not from the Holy Scriptures, but from themselves, and the Gymnosophists among the Indians.

### Chapter I.—Heresies Hitherto Refuted; Opinions of the Docetæ.

Since the great body of (the heretics) do not employ the counsel of the Lord, by having the beam in the eye, and announce that they see when in reality laboring under blindness, it seems to us expedient in no wise to be silent concerning the tenets of these. Our object is, that by the refutation accomplished by us, the (heretics), being of themselves ashamed, may be brought to know how the Savior has advised (men) first to take away the beam, then to behold clearly the mote that is in thy brother's eye. Having therefore adequately and sufficiently explained the doctrines of the majority (of the heretics) in the seven books before this, we shall not now be silent as regards the (heterodox) opinions that follow (from these). We shall by this means exhibit the abundance of the grace of the Holy Spirit; and we shall refute those (who suppose) that they have acquired steadfastness of doctrine, when it is only in appearance. Now these have styled themselves Docetæ, and propound the following opinions:—

(The Docetæ maintain) that God is the primal (Being), as it were a seed of a fig-tree, which is altogether very diminutive in size, but infinite in power. (This seed constitutes, according to the Docetæ,) a lowly magnitude, incalculable in multitude, (and) laboring under no deficiency as regards generation. (This seed is) a refuge for the terror-stricken, a shelter of the naked, a veil for modesty, (and) the sought-for produce, to which He came in search (for fruit), he says, three times, and did not discover (any). Wherefore, he says, He cursed the fig-tree, because He did not find upon it that sweet fruit—the sought-for produce. And inasmuch as the Deity is, according to them—to express myself briefly—of this description and so great, that is, small and minute, the world, as it seems to them, was made in some such manner as the following: When the branches of the fig-tree became tender, leaves budded (first), as one may (generally) see, and next in succession the fruit. Now, in this (fruit) is preserved treasured the infinite and incalculable seed of the fig-tree. We think, therefore, (say the Docetæ,) that there are three (parts) which are primarily produced by the seed of the fig-tree, (viz.,) stem, which constitutes the fig-tree, leaves, and fruit—the fig itself, as we have previously declared. In this manner, the (Docetic) affirms, have been produced three Æons, which are principles from the primal originating cause of the universe. And Moses has not been silent on this point, when he says, that there are three words of God, "darkness, gloom, tempest, and added no more." For the (Docetic) says, God has made no addition to the three Æons; but these, in every respect, have been sufficient for (the exigencies of) those who have been begotten and are sufficient. God Himself, however, remains with Himself, far separated from the three Æons. When each of these Æons had obtained an originating cause of generation, he grew, as has been declared, by little and little, and (by degrees) was magnified, and (ultimately) became perfect. But they think that that is perfect which is reckoned at ten. When, therefore, the Æons had become equal in number and in perfection, they were, as (the Docetæ) are of opinion, constituted thirty Æons in all, while each of them attains full perfection in a decade. And the three are mutually distinct and hold one (degree of) honor relatively to one another, differing in position merely, because one of them is first, and the other second, and the other of these third. Position, however, afforded them diversity of power. For he who has obtained a position nearest to the primal Deity—who is, as it were, a seed—possessed a more productive power than the rest, inasmuch as he himself who is the immeasurable one, measured himself tenfold in bulk. He, however, who in position is second to the primal Deity, has, inasmuch as he is the incomprehensible one, comprehended himself sixfold. But he who is now third in position is conveyed to an infinite distance, in consequence of the dilatation of his brethren. (And when this third Æon) had thrice realized himself in thought, he encircled himself with, as it were, some eternal chain of union.

Chapter II.—Docetic Notion of the Incarnation; Their Doctrines of Æons; Their Account of Creation; Their Notion of a Fiery God.

And these (heretics) suppose that this is what is spoken by the Savior: "A Sower went forth to sow; and that which fell on the fair and good ground produced, some a hundredfold, and some sixty-fold, and some thirty-fold." And for this reason, the (Docetic) says, (that the Savior) has spoken the words, "He that hath ears to hear, let him hear," because these (truths) are not altogether rumors. All these Æons, both the three and all those infinite (Æons which proceed) from these indefinitely, are hermaphrodite Æons. All these, then, after they had been increased and magnified, and had sprung from that one primary seed, (were actuated by a spirit) of concord and union, and they all coalesced into one Æon. And in this manner, they begot of a single virgin, Mary, a joint offspring, who is a Mediator, (that is,) the Savior of all who are in the (covenant of) mediation. (And this Savior is,) in every respect, coequal in power with the seed of the fig-tree, with the exception that he was generated. Whereas that primary seed, from whence the fig-tree sprung, is unbegotten. When, therefore, those three Æons were adorned with all virtue and with all sanctity, so these teachers suppose, as well as that only begotten child—for he alone was begotten by those infinite Æons from three immediately concerned in his birth, for three immeasurable Æons being unanimous procreated him;—(after, I say, the Æons and only Son were thus adorned,) the entire nature, which is cognized by intellect, was fashioned free from deficiency. Now, all those intelligible and eternal (entities) constituted light. Light, however, was not devoid of form, nor inoperative, nor in want, as it were, of the assistance of any (other power). But (light) proportionately with the multitude of those infinite (Æons) indefinitely (generated) in conformity with the exemplar of the fig-tree, possesses in itself infinite species of various animals indigenous to that quarter of creation, and it shone down upon the underlying chaos. And when this (chaos) was simultaneously illuminated, and had form imparted to it by those diversified species from above, it derived (thereby) solidity, and acquired all those supernal species from the third Æon, who had made himself threefold.

This third Æon, however, beholding all his own distinctive attributes laid hold on collectively by the underlying darkness (which was) beneath, and not being ignorant of the power of darkness, and at the same time of the security and profusion of light, did not allow his brilliant attributes (which he derived) from above for any length of time to be snatched away by the darkness beneath. But (he acted in quite a contrary manner), for he subjected (darkness) to the Æons. After, then, he had formed the firmament over the nether world, "he both divided the darkness from the light, and called the light which was above the firmament day, and the darkness he called night." When all the infinite species, then, as I have said, of the third Æon were intercepted in this the lowest darkness, the figure also of the Æon himself, such as he has been described, was impressed (upon them) along with the rest (of his attributes). (Now this figure is) a life-giving fire, which is generated from light, from whence the Great Archon originated. And respecting this (Archon) Moses observes: "In the beginning God created the heavens and the earth." Moses mentions this fiery God as having spoken from the bush, (batos,) that is, from the darkish air. For the whole of the atmosphere that underlies the darkness is (batos, i.e.,) a medium for the transmission of light. Now Moses has employed, says (the Docetic), the expression batos, because all the species of light pass down from above by means of their having the atmosphere as a medium (batos) of transmission. And in no less degree is capable of being recognized the Word of Jehovah addressed to us from the bush (batos, i.e., an atmospheric medium); for voice, as significant (in language) of a meaning, is a reverberation of air, and without this (atmosphere) human speech is incapable of being recognized. And not only the Word (of Jehovah addressed) to us from the bush (batos), that is, the air, legislates and is a fellow-citizen with (us); but (it does more than this), for both odors and colors manifest to us, through the medium of air, their own (peculiar) qualities.

Chapter III.—Christ Undoes the Work of the Demiurge; Docetic Account of the Baptism and Death of Jesus; Why He Lived for Thirty Years on Earth.

This fiery deity, then, after he became fire from light, proceeded to create the world in the manner which Moses describes. He himself, however, as devoid of subsistence, employs the darkness as (his) substance, and perpetually insults those eternal attributes of light which, (being) from above, had been laid hold on by (the darkness) beneath. Up to the time, therefore, of the appearance of the Savior, there prevailed, by reason of the Deity of fiery light, (that is,) the Demiurge, a certain extensive delusion of souls. For the species are styled souls, because they are refrigerations from the (Æons) above, and continue in darkness. But when (the souls) are altered from bodies to bodies, they remain under the guardianship of the Demiurge. And that these things are so, says (the Docetic), it is possible also to perceive from Job, when he uses the following words: "And I am a wanderer, changing both place after place, and house after house." And (we may learn, according to the Docetæ, the same) from the expressions of the Savior, "And if ye will receive it, this is Elias that was for to come. He that hath ears to hear, let him hear." But by the instrumentality of the Savior this transference of souls from body to body was made to cease, and faith is preached for remission of sins. After some such manner, that only begotten Son, when He gazes upon the forms of the supernal Æons, which were transferred from above into darkish bodies, coming down, wished to descend and deliver them. When (the Son), however, became aware that the Æons, those (that subsist) collectively, are unable to behold the Pleroma of all the Æons, but that in a state of consternation they fear lest they may undergo corruption as being themselves perishable, and that they are overwhelmed by the magnitude and splendor of power;—(when the Son, I say, perceived this,) He contracted Himself—as it were a very great flash in a very small body, nay, rather as a ray of vision condensed beneath the eyelids, and (in this condition) He advances forth as far as heaven and the effulgent stars. And in this quarter of creation, He again collects himself beneath the lids of vision according as He wishes it. Now the light of vision accomplishes the same effect; for though it is everywhere, and (renders visible) all things, it is yet imperceptible to us. We, however, merely see lids of vision, while corners (of the eye), a tissue which is broad, tortuous, (and) exceedingly fibrous, a membrane of the cornea; and underneath this, the pupil, which is shaped as a berry, is net-like and round. (And we observe) whatever other membranes there are that belong to the light of the eye, and enveloped in which it lies concealed.

Thus, says (the Docetic), the only-begotten (and) eternal Child from above arrayed Himself in a form to correspond with each individual Æon of the three Æons; and while he was within the triacontad of Æons, He entered into this world924 just as we have described Him, unnoticed, unknown, obscure, and disbelieved. In order, therefore, say the Docetæ, that He may be clad in the darkness that is prevalent in more distant quarters of creation—(now by darkness he means) flesh—an angel journeyed with Him from above, and announced the glad tidings to Mary, says (the Docetic), as it has been written. And the (child) from her was born, as it has been written. And He who came from above put on that which was born; and so did He all things, as it has been written (of Him) in the Gospels. He washed in Jordan, and when He was baptized He received a figure and a seal in the water of (another spiritual body beside) the body born of the Virgin. (And the object of this was,) when the Archon condemned his own peculiar figment (of flesh) to death, (that is,) to the cross, that that soul which had been nourished in the body (born of the Virgin) might strip off that body and nail it to the (accursed) tree. (In this way the soul) would triumph by means of this (body) over principalities and powers, and would not be found naked, but would, instead of that flesh, assume the (other) body, which had been represented in the water when he was being baptized. This is, says (the Docetic), what the Savior affirms: "Except a man be born of water and spirit, he will not enter into the kingdom of heaven, because that which is born of the flesh is flesh." From the thirty Æons, therefore, (the Son) assumed thirty forms. And for this reason, that eternal One existed for thirty years on the earth, because each Æon was in a peculiar manner manifested during (his own) year. And the souls are all those forms that have been laid hold on by each of the thirty Æons; and each of these is so constituted as to discern Jesus, who is of a nature (similar to their own). (And it was the nature of this Jesus) which that only-begotten and eternal One assumed from everlasting places. These (places), however, are diverse. Consequently, a proportionate number of heresies, with the utmost emulation, seek Jesus. Now all these heresies have their own peculiar Jesus; but he is seen differently according as the place is different towards which, he says, each soul is borne and hastens. (Now each soul) supposes that (the Jesus seen from its particular place) is alone that (Jesus) who is its own peculiar kinsman and fellow-citizen. And on first beholding (this Jesus, that soul) recognizes Him as its own peculiar brother, but the rest as bastards. Those, then, that derive their nature from the places below, are not able to see the forms of the Savior which are above them. Those, however, he says, who are from above, from the intermediate decade and the most excellent ogdoad—whence, say (the Docetæ), we are—have themselves known not in part, but entirely, Jesus the Savior. And those, who are from above, are alone perfect, but all the rest are only partially so.

Chapter IV.—Docetic Doctrine Derived from the Greek Sophists.

These (statements), therefore, I consider sufficient to properly constituted minds for the purpose of attaining unto a knowledge of the complicated and unstable heresy of the Docetæ. (But) those who have propounded attempted arguments about inaccessible and incomprehensible Matter, have styled themselves Docetæ. Now, we consider that some of these are acting foolishly, we will not say in appearance, but in reality. At all events, we have proved that a beam from such matter is carried in the eye, if by any means they may be enabled to perceive it. If, however, they do not (discern it, our object is) that they should not make others blind. But the fact is, that the sophists of the Greeks in ancient times have previously devised, in many particulars, the doctrines of these (Docetæ), as it is possible for my readers (who take the trouble) to ascertain. These, then, are the opinions propounded by the Docetæ. As to what likewise, however, are the tenets of Monoïmus, we shall not be silent.

## The Refutation of All Heresies

Chapter V.—Monoïmus; Man, the Universe, According to Monoïmus; His System of the Monad.

Monoïmus the Arabian was far removed from the glory of the high-sounding poet. (For Monoïmus) supposes that there is some such man as the poet (calls) Oceanus, expressing himself somehow thus:—

"Oceans, source of gods and source of men."

Changing these (sentiments) into other words, Monoïmus says that man is the universe. Now the universe is the originating cause of all things, unbegotten, incorruptible, (and) eternal. And (he says) that the son of (the) man previously spoken of is begotten, and subject to passion, (and) that he is generated independently of time, (as well as) undesignedly, (and) without being predestinated. For such, he says, is the power of that man. And he being thus constituted in power, (Monoïmus alleges) that the son was born quicker than thought and volition. And this, he says, is what has been spoken in the Scriptures, "He was, and was generated." And the meaning of this is: Man was, and his son was generated; just as one may say, Fire was, and, independently of time, and undesignedly, and without being predestinated, light was generated simultaneously with the existence of the fire. And this man constitutes a single monad, which is uncompounded and indivisible, (and yet at the same time) compounded (and) divisible. (And this monad is) in all respects friendly (and) in all respects peaceful, in all respects quarrelsome (and) in all respects contentious with itself, dissimilar (and) similar. (This monad is likewise,) as it were, a certain musical harmony, which comprises all things in itself, as many as one may express and may omit when not considering; and it manifests all things, and generates all things. This (is) Mother, this (is) Father—two immortal names. As an illustration, however, consider, he says, as a greatest image of the perfect man, the one jot—that one tittle. And this one tittle is an uncompounded, simple, and pure monad, which derives its composition from nothing at all. (And yet this tittle is likewise) compounded, multiform, branching into many sections, and consisting of many parts. That one indivisible tittle is, he says, one tittle of the (letter) iota, with many faces, and innumerable eyes, and countless names, and this (tittle) is an image of that perfect invisible man.

Chapter VI.—Monoïmus' "Iota;" His Notion of the "Son of Man."

The monad, (that is,) the one tittle, is therefore, he says, also a decade. For by the actual power of this one tittle, are produced duad, and triad, and tetrad, and pentad, and hexad, and heptad, and ogdoad, and ennead, up to ten. For these numbers, he says, are capable of many divisions, and they reside in that simple and uncompounded single tittle of the iota. And this is what has been declared: "It pleased (God) that all fulness should dwell in the Son of man bodily." For such compositions of numbers out of the simple and uncompounded one tittle of the iota become, he says, corporeal realities. The Son of man, therefore, he says, has been generated from the perfect man, whom no one knew; every creature who is ignorant of the Son, however, forms an idea of Him as the offspring of a woman. And certain very obscure rays of this Son which approach this world, check and control alteration (and) generation. And the beauty of that Son of man is up to the present incomprehensible to all men, as many as are deceived in reference to the offspring of the woman. Therefore nothing, he says, of the things that are in our quarter of creation has been produced by that man, nor will aught (of these) ever be (generated from him). All things, however, have been produced, not from the entirety, but from some part of that Son of man. For he says the Son of man is a jot in one tittle, which proceeds from above, is full, and completely replenishes all (rays flowing down from above). And it comprises in itself whatever things the man also possesses (who is) the Father of the Son of man.

Chapter VII.—Monoïmus on the Sabbath; Allegorizes the Rod of Moses; Notion Concerning the Decalogue.

The world, then, as Moses says, was made in six days, that is, by six powers, which (are inherent) in the one tittle of the iota. (But) the seventh (day, which is) a rest and Sabbath, has been produced from the Hebdomad, which is over earth, and water, and fire, and air. And from these (elements) the world has been formed by the one tittle. For cubes, and octahedrons, and pyramids, and all figures similar to these, out of which consist fire, air, water, (and) earth, have arisen from numbers which are comprehended in that simple tittle of the iota. And this (tittle) constitutes a perfect son of a perfect man. When, therefore, he says, Moses mentions that the rod was changeably brandished for the (introduction of the) plagues throughout Egypt—now these plagues, he says, are allegorically expressed symbols of the creation—he did not (as a symbol) for more plagues than ten shape the rod. Now this (rod) constitutes one tittle of the iota, and is (both) twofold (and) various. This succession of ten plagues is, he says, the mundane creation. For all things, by being stricken, bring forth and bear fruit, just like vines. Man, he says, bursts forth, and is forcibly separated from man by being severed by a certain stroke. (And this takes place) in order that (man) may be generated, and may declare the law which Moses ordained, who received (it) from God. Conformably with that one tittle, the law constitutes the series of the ten commandments which expresses allegorically the divine mysteries of (those) precepts. For, he says, all knowledge of the universe is contained in what relates to the succession of the ten plagues and the series of the ten commandments. And no one is acquainted with this (knowledge) who is (of the number) of those that are deceived concerning the offspring of the woman. If, however, you say that the Pentateuch constitutes the entire law, it is from the Pentad which is comprehended in the one tittle. But the entire is for those who have not been altogether perfected in understanding a mystery, a new and not antiquated feast, legal, (and) everlasting, a Passover of the Lord God kept unto our generations, by those who are able to discern (this mystery), at the commencement of the fourteenth day, which is the beginning of a decade from which, he says, they reckon. For the monad, as far as fourteen, is the summary of that one (tittle) of the perfect number. For one, two, three, four, become ten; and this is the one tittle. But from fourteen until one-and-twenty, he asserts that there is an Hebdomad which inheres in the one tittle of the world, and constitutes an unleavened creature in all these. For in what respect, he says, would the one tittle require any substance such as leaven (derived) from without for the Lord's Passover, the eternal feast, which is given for generation upon generation? For the entire world and all causes of creation constitute a Passover, (i.e.,) a feast of the Lord. For God rejoices in the conversion of the creation, and this is accomplished by ten strokes of the one tittle. And this (tittle) is Moses' rod, which was given by God into the hand of Moses. And with this (rod Moses) smites the Egyptians, for the purpose of altering bodies,—as, for instance, water into blood; and the rest of (material) things similarly with these,—(as, for example,) the locusts, which is a symbol of grass. And by this he means the alteration of the elements into flesh; "for all flesh," he says, "is grass."938 These men, nevertheless receive even the entire law after some such manner; adopting very probably, as I think, the opinions of those of the Greeks who affirm that there are Substance, and Quality, and Quantity, and Relation, and Place, and Time, and Position, and Action, and Possession, and Passion.

Chapter VIII.—Monoïmus Explains His Opinions in a Letter to Theophrastus; Where to Find God; His System Derived from Pythagoras.

Monoïmus himself, accordingly, in his letter to Theophrastus, expressly makes the following statement: "Omitting to seek after God, and creation, and things similar to these, seek for Him from (out of) thyself, and learn who it is that absolutely appropriates (unto Himself) all things in thee, and says, 'My God (is) my mind, my understanding, my soul, my body.' And learn from whence are sorrow, and joy, and love, and hatred, and involuntary wakefulness, and involuntary drowsiness, and involuntary anger, and involuntary affection; and if," he says, "you accurately investigate these (points), you will discover (God) Himself, unity and plurality, in thyself, according to that tittle, and that He finds the outlet (for Deity) to be from thyself." Those (heretics), then, (have made) these (statements). But we are under no necessity of comparing such (doctrines) with what have previously been subjects of meditation on the part of the Greeks, inasmuch as the assertions advanced by these (heretics) evidently derive their origin from geometrical and arithmetical art. The disciples, however, of Pythagoras, expounded this (art) after a more excellent method, as our readers may ascertain by consulting those passages (of our work) in which we have previously furnished expositions of the entire wisdom of the Greeks. But since the heresy of Monoïmus has been sufficiently refuted, let us see what are the fictitious doctrines which the rest also (of these heretics) devise, in their desire to set up for themselves an empty name.

Chapter IX.—Tatian.

Tatian, however, although being himself a disciple of Justinus the Martyr, did not entertain similar opinions with his master. But he attempted (to establish) certain novel (tenets) and affirmed that there existed certain invisible Æons. And he framed a legendary account (of them), similarly to those (spoken of) by Valentinus. And similarly with Marcion, he asserts that marriage is destruction. But he alleges that Adam is not saved on account of his having been the author of disobedience. And so far for the doctrines of Tatian.

Chapter X.—Hermogenes; Adopts the Socratic Philosophy; His Notion Concerning the Birth and Body of Our Lord.

But a certain Hermogenes, himself also imagining that he propounded some novel opinion, said that God made all things out of coeval and ungenerated matter. For that it was impossible that God could make generated things out of things that are not. And that God is always Lord, and always Creator, and matter always a subservient (substance), and that which is assuming phases of being—not, however, the whole of it. For when it was being continually moved in a rude and disorderly manner, He reduced (matter) into order by the following expedient. As He gazed (upon matter) in a seething condition, like (the contents of) a pot when a fire is burning underneath, He effected a partial separation. And taking one portion from the whole, He subdued it, but another He allowed to be whirled in a dis☐orderly manner. And he asserts that what was (thus) subdued is the world, but that another portion remains wild, and is denominated chaotic matter. He asserts that this constitutes the substance of all things, as if introducing a novel tenet for his disciples. He does not, however, reflect that this happens to be the Socratic discourse, which (indeed) is worked out more elaborately by Plato than by Hermogenes. He acknowledges, however, that Christ is the Son of the God who created all things; and along with (this admission), he confesses that he was born of a virgin and of (the) Spirit, according to the voice of the Gospels.

And (Hermogenes maintains that Christ), after His passion, was raised up in a body, and that He appeared to His disciples, and that as He went up into heaven He left His body in the sun, but that He Himself proceeded on to the Father. Now (Hermogenes) resorts to testimony, thinking to support himself by what is spoken, (viz.) what the Psalmist David says: "In the sun he hath placed his tabernacle, and himself (is) as a bridegroom coming forth from his nuptial chamber, (and) he will rejoice as a giant to run his course." These, then, are the opinions which also Hermogenes attempted to establish.

Chapter XI.—The Quartodecimans.

And certain other (heretics), contentious by nature, (and) wholly uninformed as regards knowledge, as well as in their manner more (than usually) quarrelsome, combine (in maintaining) that Easter should be kept on the fourteenth day of the first month, according to the commandment of the law, on whatever day (of the week) it should occur. (But in this) they only regard what has been written in the law, that he will be accursed who does not so keep (the commandment) as it is enjoined. They do not, however, attend to this (fact), that the legal enactment was made for Jews, who in times to come should kill the real Passover. And this (paschal sacrifice, in its efficacy,) has spread unto the Gentiles, and is discerned by faith, and not now observed in letter (merely). They attend to this one commandment, and do not look unto what has been spoken by the apostle: "For I testify to every man that is circumcised, that he is a debtor to keep the whole law." In other respects, however, these consent to all the traditions delivered to the Church by the Apostles.

Chapter XII.—The Montanists; Priscilla and Maximilla Their Prophetesses; Some of Them Noetians.

But there are others who themselves are even more heretical in nature (than the foregoing), and are Phrygians by birth. These have been rendered victims of error from being previously captivated by (two) wretched women, called a certain Priscilla and Maximilla, whom they supposed (to be) prophetesses. And they assert that into these the Paraclete Spirit had departed; and antecedently to them, they in like manner consider Montanus as a prophet. And being in possession of an infinite number of their books, (the Phrygians) are overrun with delusion; and they do not judge whatever statements are made by them, according to (the criterion of) reason; nor do they give heed unto those who are competent to decide; but they are heedlessly swept onwards, by the reliance which they place on these (impostors). And they allege that they have learned something more through these, than from law, and prophets, and the Gospels. But they magnify these wretched women above the Apostles and every gift of Grace, so that some of them presume to assert that there is in them a something superior to Christ. These acknowledge God to be the Father of the universe, and Creator of all things, similarly with the Church, and (receive) as many things as the Gospel testifies concerning Christ. They introduce, however, the novelties of fasts, and feasts, and meals of parched food, and repasts of radishes, alleging that they have been instructed by women. And some of these assent to the heresy of the Noetians, and affirm that the Father himself is the Son, and that this (one) came under generation, and suffering, and death. Concerning these I shall again offer an explanation, after a more minute manner; for the heresy of these has been an occasion of evils to many. We therefore are of opinion, that the statements made concerning these (heretics) are sufficient, when we shall have briefly proved to all that the majority of their books are silly, and their attempts (at reasoning) weak, and worthy of no consideration. But it is not necessary for those who possess a sound mind to pay attention (either to their volumes or their arguments).

Chapter XIII.—The Doctrines of the Encratites.

Others, however, styling themselves Encratites, acknowledge some things concerning God and Christ in like manner with the Church. In respect, however, of their mode of life, they pass their days inflated with pride. They suppose that by meats they magnify themselves, while abstaining from animal food, (and) being water-drinkers, and forbidding to marry, and devoting themselves during the remainder of life to habits of asceticism. But persons of this description are estimated Cynics rather than Christians, inasmuch as they do not attend unto the words spoken against them through the Apostle Paul. Now he, predicting the novelties that were to be hereafter introduced ineffectually by certain (heretics), made a statement thus: "The Spirit speaks expressly, In the latter times certain will depart from sound doctrine, giving heed to seducing spirits and doctrines of devils, uttering falsehoods in hypocrisy, having their own conscience seared with a hot iron, forbidding to marry, to abstain from meats, which God has created to be partaken of with thanksgiving by the faithful, and those who know the truth; because every creature of God is good, and nothing to be rejected which is received with thanksgiving; for it is sanctified by the word of God and prayer." This voice, then, of the blessed Paul, is sufficient for the refutation of those who live in this manner, and plume themselves on being just; (and) for the purpose of proving that also, this (tenet of the Encratites) constitutes a heresy. But even though there have been denominated certain other heresies—I mean those of the Cainites, Ophites, or Noachites, and of others of this description—I have not deemed it requisite to explain the things said or done by these, lest on this account they may consider themselves somebody, or deserving of consideration. Since, however, the statements concerning these appear to be sufficient, let us pass on to the cause of evils to all, (viz.,) the heresy of the Noetians. Now, after we have laid bare the root of this (heresy), and stigmatized openly the venom, as it were, lurking within it, let us seek to deter from an error of this description those who have been impelled into it by a violent spirit, as it were by a swollen torrent.

Book IX.

Contents.

The following are the contents of the ninth book of the Refutation of all Heresies:—

What the blasphemous folly is of Noetus, and that he devoted himself to the tenets of Heraclitus the Obscure, not to those of Christ.

And how Callistus, intermingling the heresy of Cleomenes, the disciple of Noetus, with that of Theodotus, constructed another more novel heresy, and what sort the life of this (heretic) was.

What was the recent arrival (at Rome) of the strange spirit Elchasai, and that there served as a concealment of his peculiar errors his apparent adhesion to the law, when in point of fact he devotes himself to the tenets of the Gnostics, or even of the astrologists, and to the arts of sorcery.

What the customs of the Jews are, and how many diversities of opinion there are (amongst them).

Chapter I.—An Account of Contemporaneous Heresy.

A lengthened conflict, then, having been maintained concerning all heresies by us who, at all events, have not left any unrefuted, the greatest struggle now remains behind, viz., to furnish an account and refutation of those heresies that have sprung up in our own day, by which certain ignorant and presumptuous men have attempted to scatter abroad the Church, and have introduced the greatest confusion among all the faithful throughout the entire world. For it seems expedient that we, making an onslaught upon the opinion which constitutes the prime source of (contemporaneous) evils, should prove what are the originating principles of this (opinion), in order that its offshoots, becoming a matter of general notoriety, may be made the object of universal scorn.

# The Refutation of All Heresies

Chapter II.—Source of the Heresy of Noetus; Cleomenes His Disciple; Its Appearance at Rome During the Episcopates of Zephyrinus and Callistus; Noetianism Opposed at Rome by Hippolytus.

There has appeared one, Noetus by name, and by birth a native of Smyrna. This person introduced a heresy from the tenets of Heraclitus. Now a certain man called Epigonus becomes his minister and pupil, and this person during his sojourn at Rome disseminated his godless opinion. But Cleomenes, who had become his disciple, an alien both in way of life and habits from the Church, was wont to corroborate the (Noetian) doctrine. At that time, Zephyrinus imagines that he administers the affairs of the Church—an uninformed and shamefully corrupt man. And he, being persuaded by proffered gain, was accustomed to conniving at those who were present for the purpose of becoming disciples of Cleomenes. But (Zephyrinus) himself, being in process of time enticed away, hurried headlong into the same opinions; and he had Callistus as his adviser, and a fellow-champion of these wicked tenets. But the life of this (Callistus), and the heresy invented by him, I shall after a little explain. The school of these heretics during the succession of such bishops, continued to acquire strength and augmentation, from the fact that Zephyrinus and Callistus helped them to prevail. Never at any time, however, have we been guilty of collusion with them; but we have frequently offered them opposition, and have refuted them, and have forced them reluctantly to acknowledge the truth. And they, abashed and constrained by the truth, have confessed their errors for a short period, but after a little, wallow once again in the same mire.

Chapter III.—Noetianism an Offshoot from the Heraclitic Philosophy.

But since we have exhibited the succession of their genealogy, it seems expedient next that we should also explain the depraved teaching involved in their doctrines. For this purpose we shall first adduce the opinions advanced by Heraclitus "the Obscure," and we shall next make manifest what are the portions of these opinions that are of Heraclitean origin. Such parts of their system its present champions are not aware belong to the "Obscure" philosopher, but they imagine them to belong to Christ. But if they might happen to fall in with the following observations, perhaps they thus might be put out of countenance, and induced to desist from this godless blasphemy of theirs. Now, even though the opinion of Heraclitus has been expounded by us previously in the Philosophumena, it nevertheless seems expedient now also to set down side by side in contrast the two systems, in order that by this closer refutation they may be evidently instructed. I mean the followers of this (heretic), who imagine themselves to be disciples of Christ, when in reality they are not so, but of "the Obscure."

Chapter IV.—An Account of the System of Heraclitus.

Heraclitus then says that the universe is one, divisible and indivisible; generated and ungenerated; mortal and immortal; reason, eternity; Father, Son, and justice, God. "For those who hearken not to me, but the doctrine, it is wise that they acknowledge all things to be one," says Heraclitus; and because all do not know or confess this, he utters a reproof somewhat in the following terms: "People do not understand how what is diverse (nevertheless) coincides with itself, just like the inverse harmony of a bow and lyre." But that Reason always exists, inasmuch as it constitutes the universe, and as it pervades all things, he affirms in this manner. "But in regard of this Reason, which always exists, men are continually devoid of understanding, both before they have heard of it and in first hearing of it. For though all things take place according to this Reason, they seem like persons devoid of any experience regarding it. Still they attempt both words and works of such a description as I am giving an account of, by making a division according to nature, and declaring how things are." And that a Son is the universe and throughout endless ages an eternal king of all things, he thus asserts: "A sporting child, playing at his dice, is eternity; the kingdom is that of a child." And that the Father of all things that have been generated is an unbegotten creature who is creator, let us hear Heraclitus affirming in these words: "Contrariety is a progenitor of all things, and king of all; and it exhibited some as gods, but others as men, and made some slaves, whereas others free." And (he likewise affirms) that there is "a harmony, as in a bow and lyre." That obscure harmony (is better), though unknown and invisible to men, he asserts in these words: "An obscure harmony is preferable to an obvious one." He commends and admires before what is known, that which is unknown and invisible in regard of its power. And that harmony visible to men, and not incapable of being dis covered, is better, he asserts in these words: "Whatever things are objects of vision, hearing, and intelligence, these I pre-eminently honor," he says; that is, he prefers things visible to those that are invisible. From such expressions of his it is easy to understand the spirit of his philosophy. "Men," he says, "are deceived in reference to the knowledge of manifest things similarly with Homer, who was wiser than all the Greeks. For even children killing vermin deceived him, when they said, 'What we have seen and seized, these we leave behind; whereas what we neither have seen nor seized, these we carry away.'"

Chapter V.—Heraclitus' Estimate of Hesiod; Paradoxes of Heraclitus; His Eschatology; The Heresy of Noetus of Heraclitean Origin; Noetus' View of the Birth and Passion of Our Lord.

In this manner Heraclitus assigns to the visible an equality of position and honor with the invisible, as if what was visible and what was invisible were confessedly some one thing. For he says, "An obscure harmony is preferable to an obvious one;" and, "Whatsoever things are objects of vision, hearing, and intelligence," that is, of the (corporeal) organs,—"these," he says, "I pre-eminently honor," not (on this occasion, though previously), having preeminently honored invisible things. Therefore neither darkness, nor light, nor evil, nor good, Heraclitus affirms, is different, but one and the same thing. At all events, he censures Hesiod because he knew not day and night. For day, he says, and night are one, expressing himself somehow thus: "The teacher, however, of a vast amount of information is Hesiod, and people suppose this poet to be possessed of an exceedingly large store of knowledge, and yet he did not know (the nature of) day and night, for they are one." As regards both what is good and what is bad, (they are, according to Heraclitus, likewise) one. "Physicians, undoubtedly," says Heraclitus, "when they make incisions and cauterize, though in every respect they wickedly torture the sick, complain that they do not receive fitting remuneration from their patients, notwithstanding that they perform these salutary operations upon diseases." And both straight and twisted are, he says, the same. "The way is straight and curved of the carders of wool;" and the circular movement of an instrument in the fuller's shop called "a screw" is straight and curved, for it revolves up and circularly at the same time. "One and the same," he says, "are, therefore, straight and curved." And upward and downward, he says, are one and the same. "The way up and the way down are the same." And he says that what is filthy and what is pure are one and the same, and what is drinkable and unfit for drink are one and the same. "Sea," he says, "is water very pure and very foul, drinkable to fishes no doubt, and salutary for them, but not fit to be used as drink by men, and (for them) pernicious." And, confessedly, he asserts that what is immortal is mortal, and that what is mortal is immortal, in the following expressions: "Immortals are mortal, and mortals are immortal, that is, when the one derive life from death, and the other death from life." And he affirms also that there is a resurrection of this palpable flesh in which we have been born; and he knows God to be the cause of this resurrection, expressing himself in this manner: "Those that are here will God enable to arise and become guardians of quick and dead." And he likewise affirms that a judgment of the world and all things in it takes place by fire, expressing himself thus: "Now, thunder pilots all things," that is, directs them, meaning by the thunder everlasting fire. But he also asserts that this fire is endued with intelligence, and a cause of the management of the Universe, and he denominates it craving and satiety. Now craving is, according to him, the arrangement of the world, whereas satiety its destruction. "For," says he, "the fire, coming upon the earth, will judge and seize all things."

But in this chapter Heraclitus simultaneously explains the entire peculiarity of his mode of thinking, but at the same time the (characteristic quality) of the heresy of Noetus. And I have briefly demonstrated Noetus to be not a disciple of Christ, but of Heraclitus. For this philosopher asserts that the primal world is itself the Demiurge and creator of itself in the following passage: "God is day, night; winter, summer; war, peace; surfeit, famine." All things are contraries—this appears his meaning—"but an alteration takes place, just as if incense were mixed with other sorts of incense, but denominated according to the pleasurable sensation produced by each sort. Now it is evident to all that the silly successors of Noetus, and the champions of his heresy, even though they have not been hearers of the discourses of Heraclitus, nevertheless, at any rate when they adopt the opinions of Noetus, undisguisedly acknowledge these (Heraclitean) tenets. For they advance statements after this manner—that one and the same God is the Creator and Father of all things; and that when it pleased Him, He nevertheless appeared, (though invisible,) to just men of old. For when He is not seen He is invisible; and He is incomprehensible when He does not wish to be comprehended, but comprehensible when he is comprehended. Wherefore it is that, according to the same account, He is invincible and vincible, unbegotten and begotten, immortal and mortal. How shall not persons holding this description of opinions be proved to be disciples of Heraclitus? Did not (Heraclitus) the Obscure anticipate Noetus in framing a system of philosophy, according to identical modes of expression?

Now, that Noetus affirms that the Son and Father are the same, no one is ignorant. But he makes his statement thus: "When indeed, then, the Father had not been born, He yet was justly styled Father; and when it pleased Him to undergo generation, having been begotten, He Himself became His own Son, not another's." For in this manner he thinks to establish the sovereignty of God, alleging that Father and Son, so called, are one and the same (substance), not one individual produced from a different one, but Himself from Himself; and that He is styled by name Father and Son, according to vicissitude of times. But that He is one who has appeared (amongst us), both having submitted to generation from a virgin, and as a man having held converse among men. And, on account of the birth that had taken place, He confessed Himself to those beholding Him a Son, no doubt; yet He made no secret to those who could comprehend Him of His being a Father. That this person suffered by being fastened to the tree, and that He commended His spirit unto Himself, having died to appearance, and not being (in reality) dead. And He raised Himself up the third day, after having been interred in a sepulcher, and wounded with a spear, and perforated with nails. Cleomenes asserts, in common with his band of followers, that this person is God and Father of the universe, and thus introduces among many an obscurity (of thought) such as we find in the philosophy of Heraclitus.

Chapter VI.—Conduct of Callistus and Zephyrinus in the Matter of Noetianism; Avowed Opinion of Zephyrinus Concerning Jesus Christ; Disapproval of Hippolytus; As a Contemporaneous Event, Hippolytus Competent to Explain It.

Callistus attempted to confirm this heresy,—a man cunning in wickedness, and subtle where deceit was concerned, (and) who was impelled by restless ambition to mount the episcopal throne. Now this man molded to his purpose Zephyrinus, an ignorant and illiterate individual, and one unskilled in ecclesiastical definitions. And inasmuch as Zephyrinus was accessible to bribes, and covetous, Callistus, by luring him through presents, and by illicit demands, was enabled to seduce him into whatever course of action he pleased. And so it was that Callistus succeeded in inducing Zephyrinus to create continually disturbances among the brethren, while he himself took care subsequently, by knavish words, to attach both factions in good-will to himself. And, at one time, to those who entertained true opinions, he would in private allege that they held similar doctrines (with himself), and thus make them his dupes; while at another time he would act similarly towards those (who embraced) the tenets of Sabellius. But Callistus perverted Sabellius himself, and this, too, though he had the ability of rectifying this heretic's error. For (at any time) during our admonition Sabellius did not evince obduracy; but as long as he continued alone with Callistus, he was wrought upon to relapse into the system of Cleomenes by this very Callistus, who alleges that he entertains similar opinions to Cleomenes. Sabellius, however, did not then perceive the knavery of Callistus; but he afterwards came to be aware of it, as I shall narrate presently.

Now Callistus brought forward Zephyrinus himself, and induced him publicly to avow the following sentiments: "I know that there is one God, Jesus Christ; nor except Him do I know any other that is begotten and amenable to suffering." And on another occasion, when he would make the following statement: "The Father did not die, but the Son." Zephyrinus would in this way continue to keep up ceaseless disturbance among the people. And we, becoming aware of his sentiments, did not give place to him, but reproved and withstood him for the truth's sake. And he hurried headlong into folly, from the fact that all consented to his hypocrisy—we, however, did not do so—and called us worshippers of two gods, disgorging, independent of compulsion, the venom lurking within him. It would seem to us desirable to explain the life of this heretic, inasmuch as he was born about the same time with ourselves, in order that, by the exposure of the habits of a person of this description, the heresy attempted to be established by him may be easily known, and may perchance be regarded as silly, by those endued with intelligence. This Callistus became a "martyr" at the period when Fuscianus was prefect of Rome, and the mode of his "martyrdom" was as follows.

Chapter VII.—The Personal History of Callistus; His Occupation as a Banker; Fraud on Carpophorus; Callistus Absconds; Attempted Suicide; Condemned to the Treadmill; ReCondemnation by Order of the Prefect Fuscianus; Banished to Sardinia; Release of Callistus by the Interference Of Marcion; Callistus Arrives at Rome; Pope Victor Removes Callistus to Antium; Return of

## St. Hippolytus

Callistus on Victor's Death; Zephyrinus Friendly to Him; Callistus Accused by Sabellius; Hippolytus' Account of the Opinions of Callistus; The Callistian School at Rome, and Its Practices; This Sect in Existence in Hippolytus' Time.

Callistus happened to be a domestic of one Carpophorus, a man of the faith belonging to the household of Caesar. To this Callistus, as being of the faith, Carpophorus committed no inconsiderable amount of money, and directed him to bring in profitable returns from the banking business. And he, receiving the money, tried (the experiment of) a bank in what is called the Piscina Publica. And in process of time were entrusted to him not a few deposits by widows and brethren, under the ostensive cause of lodging their money with Carpophorus. Callistus, however, made away with all (the moneys committed to him), and became involved in pecuniary difficulties. And after having practiced such conduct as this, there was not wanting one to tell Carpophorus, and the latter stated that he would require an account from him. Callistus, perceiving these things, and suspecting danger from his master, escaped away by stealth, directing his flight towards the sea. And finding a vessel in Portus ready for a voyage, he went on board, intending to sail wherever she happened to be bound for. But not even in this way could he avoid detection, for there was not wanting one who conveyed to Carpophorus intelligence of what had taken place. But Carpophorus, in accordance with the information he had received, at once repaired to the harbor (Portus), and made an effort to hurry into the vessel after Callistus. The boat, however, was anchored in the middle of the harbor; and as the ferryman was slow in his movements, Callistus, who was in the ship, had time to descry his master at a distance. And knowing that himself would be inevitably captured, he became reckless of life; and, considering his affairs to be in a desperate condition, he proceeded to cast himself into the sea. But the sailors leaped into boats and drew him out, unwilling to come, while those on shore were raising a loud cry. And thus Callistus was handed over to his master, and brought to Rome, and his master lodged him in the Pistrinum.

But as time wore on, as happens to take place in such cases, brethren repaired to Carpophorus, and entreated him that he would release the fugitive serf from punishment, on the plea of their alleging that Callistus acknowledged himself to have money lying to his credit with certain persons. But Carpophorus, as a devout man, said he was indifferent regarding his own property, but that he felt a concern for the deposits; for many shed tears as they remarked to him, that they had committed what they had entrusted to Callistus, under the ostensive cause of lodging the money with himself. And Carpophorus yielded to their persuasions, and gave directions for the liberation of Callistus. The latter, however, having nothing to pay, and not being able again to abscond, from the fact of his being watched, planned an artifice by which he hoped to meet death. Now, pretending that he was repairing as it were to his creditors, he hurried on their Sabbath-day to the synagogue of the Jews, who were congregated, and took his stand, and created a disturbance among them. They, however, being disturbed by him, offered him insult, and inflicted blows upon him, and dragged him before Fuscianus, who was prefect of the city. And (on being asked the cause of such treatment), they replied in the following terms: "Romans have conceded to us the privilege of publicly reading those laws of ours that have been handed down from our fathers. This person, however, by coming into (our place of worship), prevented (us so doing), by creating a disturbance among us, alleging that he is a Christian." And Fuscianus happens at the time to be on the judgment-seat; and on intimating his indignation against Callistus, on account of the statements made by the Jews, there was not wanting one to go and acquaint Carpophorus concerning these transactions. And he, hastening to the judgment-seat of the prefect, exclaimed, "I implore of you, my lord Fuscianus, believe not thou this fellow; for he is not a Christian, but seeks occasion of death, having made away with a quantity of my money, as I shall prove." The Jews, however, supposing that this was a stratagem, as if Carpophorus were seeking under this pretext to liberate Callistus, with the greater enmity clamored against him in presence of the prefect. Fuscianus, however, was swayed by these Jews, and having scourged Callistus, he gave him to be sent to a mine in Sardinia.

But after a time, there being in that place other martyrs, Marcia, a concubine of Commodus, who was a God-loving female, and desirous of performing some good work, invite into her presence the blessed Victor, who was at that time a bishop of the Church, and inquired of him what martyrs were in Sardinia. And he delivered to her the names of all, but did not give the name of Callistus, knowing the villainous acts he had ventured upon. Marcia, obtaining her request from Commodus, hands the letter of emancipation to Hyacinthus, a certain eunuch, rather advanced in life. And he, on receiving it, sailed away into Sardinia, and having delivered the letter to the person who at that time was governor of the territory, he succeeded in having the martyrs released, with the exception of Callistus. But Callistus himself, dropping on his knees, and weeping, entreated that he likewise might obtain a release. Hyacinthus, therefore, overcome by the captive's importunity, requests the governor to grant a release, alleging that permission had been given to himself from Marcia (to liberate Callistus), and that he would make arrangements that there should be no risk in this to him. Now (the governor) was persuaded, and liberated Callistus also. And when the latter arrived at Rome, Victor was very much grieved at what had taken place; but since he was a compassionate man, he took no action in the matter. Guarding, however, against the reproach (uttered) by many,—for the attempts made by this Callistus were not distant occurrences,—and because Carpophorus also still continued adverse, Victor sends Callistus to take up his abode in Antium, having settled on him a certain monthly allowance for food. And after Victor's death, Zephyrinus, having had Callistus as a fellow-worker in the management of his clergy, paid him respect to his own damage; and transferring this person from Antium, appointed him over the cemetery.

And Callistus, who was in the habit of always associating with Zephyrinus, and, as I have previously stated, of paying him hypocritical service, disclosed, by force of contrast, Zephyrinus to be a personable neither to form a judgment of things said, nor discerning the design of Callistus, who was accustomed to converse with Zephyrinus on topics which yielded satisfaction to the latter. Thus, after the death of Zephyrinus, supposing that he had obtained (the position) after which he so eagerly pursued, he excommunicated Sabellius, as not entertaining orthodox opinions. He acted thus from apprehension of me, and imagining that he could in this manner obliterate the charge against him among the churches, as if he did not entertain strange opinions. He was then an impostor and knave, and in process of time hurried away many with him. And having even venom imbedded in his heart, and forming no correct opinion on any subject, and yet withal being ashamed to speak the truth, this Callistus, not only on account of his publicly saying in the way of reproach to us, "Ye are Ditheists," but also on account of his being frequently accused by Sabellius, as one that had transgressed his first faith, devised some such heresy as the following. Callistus alleges that the Logos Himself is Son, and that Himself is Father; and that though denominated by a different title, yet that in reality He is one indivisible spirit. And he maintains that the Father is not one person and the Son another, but that they are one and the same; and that all things are full of the Divine Spirit, both those above and those below. And he affirms that the Spirit, which became incarnate in the virgin, is not different from the Father, but one and the same. And he adds, that this is what has been declared by the Savior: "Believes thou not that I am in the Father, and the Father in me?" For that which is seen, which is man, he considers to be the Son; whereas the Spirit, which was contained in the Son, to be the Father. "For," says (Callistus), "I will not profess belief in two Gods, Father and Son, but in one. For the Father, who subsisted in the Son Himself, after He had taken unto Himself our flesh, raised it to the nature of Deity, by bringing it into union with Himself, and made it one; so that Father and Son must be styled one God, and that this

Person being one, cannot be two." And in this way Callistus contends that the Father suffered along with the Son; for he does not wish to assert that the Father suffered, and is one Person, being careful to avoid blasphemy against the Father. (How careful he is!) senseless and knavish fellow, who improvises blasphemies in every direction, only that he may not seem to speak in violation of the truth, and is not abashed at being at one time betrayed into the tenet of Sabellius, whereas at another into the doctrine of Theodotus.

The impostor Callistus, having ventured on such opinions, established a school of theology in antagonism to the Church, adopting the foregoing system of instruction. And he first invented the device of conniving with men in regard of their indulgence in sensual pleasures, saying that all had their sins forgiven by himself. For he who is in the habit of attending the congregation of anyone else, and is called a Christian, should he commit any transgression; the sin, they say, is not reckoned unto him, provided only he hurries off and attaches himself to the school of Callistus. And many persons were gratified with his regulation, as being stricken in conscience, and at the same time having been rejected by numerous sects; while also some of them, in accordance with our condemnatory sentence, had been by us forcibly ejected from the Church. Now such disciples as these passed over to these followers of Callistus, and served to crowd his school. This one propounded the opinion, that, if a bishop was guilty of any sin, if even a sin unto death, he ought not to be deposed. About the time of this man, bishops, priests, and deacons, who had been twice married, and thrice married, began to be allowed to retain their place among the clergy. If also, however, any one who is in holy orders should become married, Callistus permitted such a one to continue in holy orders as if he had not sinned. And in justification, he alleges that what has been spoken by the Apostle has been declared in reference to this person: "Who art thou that judges another man's servant?" But he asserted that likewise the parable of the tares is uttered in reference to this one: "Let the tares grow along with the wheat;" or, in other words, let those who in the Church are guilty of sin remain in it. But also he affirmed that the ark of Noe was made for a symbol of the Church, in which were both dogs, and wolves, and ravens, and all things clean and unclean; and so he alleges that the case should stand in like manner with the Church. And as many parts of Scripture bearing on this view of the subject as he could collect, he so interpreted.

    And the hearers of Callistus being delighted with his tenets, continue with him, thus mocking both themselves as well as many others, and crowds of these dupes stream together into his school. Wherefore also his pupils are multiplied, and they plume themselves upon the crowds (attending the school) for the sake of pleasures which Christ did not permit. But in contempt of Him, they place restraint on the commission of no sin, alleging that they pardon those who acquiesce (in Callistus' opinions). For even also he permitted females, if they were unwedded, and burned with passion at an age at all events unbecoming, or if they were not disposed to overturn their own dignity through a legal marriage, that they might have whomsoever they would choose as a bedfellow, whether a slave or free, and that a woman, though not legally married, might consider such a companion as a husband. Whence women, reputed believers, began to resort to drugs for producing sterility, and to gird themselves round, so to expel what was being conceived on account of their not wishing to have a child either by a slave or by any paltry fellow, for the sake of their family and excessive wealth. Behold, into how great impiety that lawless one has proceeded, by inculcating adultery and murder at the same time! And withal, after such audacious acts, they, lost to all shame, attempt to call themselves a Catholic Church! And some, under the supposition that they will attain prosperity, concur with them. During the episcopate of this one, second baptism was for the first time presumptuously attempted by them. These, then, (are the practices and opinions which) that most astonishing Callistus established, whose school continues, preserving its customs and tradition, not discerning with whom they ought to communicate, but indiscriminately offering communion to all. And from him they have derived the denomination of their cognomen; so that, on account of Callistus being a foremost champion of such practices, they should be called Callistians.

Chapter VIII.—Sect of the Elchasaites; Hippolytus' Opposition to It.

The doctrine of this Callistus having been noised abroad throughout the entire world, a cunning man, and full of desperation, one called Alcibiades, dwelling in Apamea, a city of Syria, examined carefully into this business. And considering himself a more formidable character, and more ingenious in such tricks, than Callistus, he repaired to Rome; and he brought some book, alleging that a certain just man, Elchasai, had received this from Seræ, a town of Parthia, and that he gave it to one called Sobiaï. And the contents of this volume, he alleged, had been revealed by an angel whose height was 24 schœnoi, which make 96 miles, and whose breadth is 4 schœnoi, and from shoulder to shoulder 6 schœnoi; and the tracks of his feet extend to the length of three and a half schœnoi, which are equal to fourteen miles, while the breadth is one schœnos and a half, and the height half a schœnos. And he alleges that also there is a female with him, whose measurement, he says, is according to the standards already mentioned. And he asserts that the male (angel) is Son of God, but that the female is called Holy Spirit. By detailing these prodigies he imagines that he confounds fools, while at the same time he utters the following sentence: "that there was preached unto men a new remission of sins in the third year of Trajan's reign." And Elchasai determines the nature of baptism, and even this I shall explain. He alleges, as to those who have been involved in every description of lasciviousness, and filthiness, and in acts of wickedness, if only any of them be a believer, that he determines that such a one, on being converted, and obeying the book, and believing its contents, should by baptism receive remission of sins.

Elchasai, however, ventured to continue these knaveries, taking occasion from the aforesaid tenet of which Callistus stood forward as a champion. For, perceiving that many were delighted at this sort of promise, he considered that he could opportunely make the attempt just alluded to. And notwithstanding we offered resistance to this, and did not permit many for any length of time to become victims of the delusion. For we carried conviction to the people, when we affirmed that this was the operation of a spurious spirit, and the invention of a heart inflated with pride, and that this one like a wolf had risen up against many wandering sheep, which Callistus, by his arts of deception, had scattered abroad. But since we have commenced, we shall not be silent as regards the opinions of this man. And, in the first place, we shall expose his life, and we shall prove that his supposed discipline is a mere pretense. And next, I shall adduce the principal heads of his assertions, in order that the reader, looking fixedly on the treatises of this (Elchasai), may be made aware what and what sort is the heresy which has been audaciously attempted by this man.

Chapter IX.—Elchasai Derived His System from Pythagoras; Practiced Incantations.

This Elchasai puts forward as a decoy a polity (authorized in the) Law, alleging that believers ought to be circumcised and live according to the Law, (while at the same time) he forcibly rends certain fragments from the aforesaid heresies. And he asserts that Christ was born a man in the same way as common to all, and that Christ was not for the first time on earth when born of a virgin, but that both previously and that frequently again He had been born and would be born. Christ would thus appear and exist among us from time to time, undergoing alterations of birth, and having his soul transferred from body to body. Now Elchasai adopted that tenet of Pythagoras to which I have already alluded. But the Elchasaites have reached such an altitude of pride, that even they affirm themselves to be endued with a power of foretelling futurity, using as a starting point, obviously, the measures and numbers of the aforesaid Pythagorean art. These also devote themselves to the tenets of mathematicians, and astrologers, and magicians, as if they were true. And they resort to these, so as to confuse silly people, thus led to suppose that the heretics participate in a doctrine of power. And they teach certain incantations and formularies for those who have been bitten by dogs, and possessed of demons, and seized with other diseases; and we shall not be silent respecting even such practices of these heretics. Having then sufficiently explained their principles, and the causes of their presumptuous attempts, I shall pass on to give an account of their writings, through which my readers will become acquainted with both the trifling and godless efforts of these Elchasaites.

Chapter X.—Elchasai's Mode of Administering Baptism; Formularies.

To those, then, that have been orally instructed by him, he dispenses baptism in this manner, addressing to his dupes some such words as the following: "If, therefore, (my) children, one shall have intercourse with any sort of animal whatsoever, or a male, or a sister, or a daughter, or hath committed adultery, or been guilty of fornication, and is desirous of obtaining remission of sins, from the moment that he hearkens to this book let him be baptized a second time in the name of the Great and Most High God, and in the name of His Son, the Mighty King. And by baptism let him be purified and cleansed and let him adjure for himself those seven witnesses that have been described in this book—the heaven, and the water, and the holy spirits, and the angels of prayer, and the oil, and the salt, and the earth." These constitute the astonishing mysteries of Elchasai, those ineffable and potent secrets which he delivers to deserving disciples. And with these that lawless one is not satisfied, but in the presence of two and three witnesses he puts the seal to his own wicked practices. Again expressing himself thus: "Again I say, O adulterers and adulteresses, and false prophets, if you are desirous of being converted, that your sins may be forgiven you, as soon as ever you hearken unto this book, and be baptized a second time along with your garments, shall peace be yours, and your portion with the just." But since we have stated that these resort to incantations for those bitten by dogs and for other mishaps, we shall explain these. Now Elchasai uses the following formulary: "If a dog rabid and furious, in which inheres a spirit of destruction, bite any man, or woman, or youth, or girl, or may worry or touch them, in the same hour let such a one run with all their wearing apparel, and go down to a river or to a fountain wherever there is a deep spot. Let (him or her) be dipped with all their wearing apparel, and offer supplication to the Great and Most High God in faith of heart, and then let him thus adjure the seven witnesses described in this book: 'Behold, I call to witness the heaven and the water, and the holy spirits, and the angels of prayer, and the oil, and the salt, and the earth. I testify by these seven witnesses that no more shall I sin, nor commit adultery, nor steal, nor be guilty of injustice, nor be covetous, nor be actuated by hatred, nor be scornful, nor shall I take pleasure in any wicked deeds.' Having uttered, therefore, these words, let such a one be baptized with the entire of his wearing apparel in the name of the Mighty and Most High God."

Chapter XI.—Precepts of Elchasai.

But in very many other respects he talks folly, inculcating the use of these sentences also for those afflicted with consumption, and that they should be dipped in cold water forty times during seven days; and he prescribes similar treatment for those possessed of devils. Oh inimitable wisdom and incantations gorged with powers! Who will not be astonished at such and such force of words? But since we have stated that they also bring into requisition astrological deceit, we shall prove this from their own formularies; for Elchasai speaks thus: "There exist wicked stars of impiety. This declaration has been now made by us, O ye pious ones and disciples: beware of the power of the days of the sovereignty of these stars, and engage not in the commencement of any undertaking during the ruling days of these. And baptize not man or woman during the days of the power of these stars, when the moon, (emerging) from among them, courses the sky, and travels along with them. Beware of the very day up to that on which the moon passes out from these stars, and then baptize and enter on every beginning of your works. But, moreover, honor the day of the Sabbath, since that day is one of those during which prevails (the power) of these stars. Take care, however, not to commence your works the third day from a Sabbath, since when three years of the reign of the emperor Trojan are again completed from the time that he subjected the Parthians to his own sway,—when, I say, three years have been completed, war rages between the impious angels of the northern constellations; and on this account all kingdoms of impiety are in a state of confusion."

Chapter XII.—The Heresy of the Elchasaites a Derivative One.

Inasmuch as (Elchasai) considers, then, that it would be an insult to reason that these mighty and ineffable mysteries should be trampled underfoot, or that they should be committed to many, he advises that as valuable pearls they should be preserved, expressing himself thus: "Do not recite this account to all men, and guard carefully these precepts, because all men are not faithful, nor are all women straightforward." Books containing these (tenets), however, neither the wise men of the Egyptians secreted in shrines, nor did Pythagoras, a sage of the Greeks, conceal them there. For if at that time Elchasai had happened to live, what necessity would there be that Pythagoras, or Thales, or Solon, or the wise Plato, or even the rest of the sages of the Greeks, should become disciples of the Egyptian priests, when they could obtain possession of such and such wisdom from Alcibiades, as the most astonishing interpreter of that wretched Elchasai? The statements, therefore, that have been made for the purpose of attaining a knowledge of the madness of these, would seem sufficient for those endued with sound mind. And so it is, that it has not appeared expedient to quote more of their formularies, seeing that these are very numerous and ridiculous. Since, however, we have not omitted those practices that have risen up in our own day, and have not been silent as regards those prevalent before our time, it seems proper, in order that we may pass through all their systems, and leave nothing untold, to state what also are the (customs) of the Jews, and what are the diversities of opinion among them, for I imagine that these as yet remain behind for our consideration. Now, when I have broken silence on these points, I shall pass on to the demonstration of the Doctrine of the Truth, in order that, after the lengthened argumentative struggle against all heresies, we, devoutly pressing forward towards the kingdom's crown, and believing the truth, may not be unsettled.

Chapter XIII.—The Jewish Sects.

Originally there prevailed but one usage among the Jews; for one teacher was given unto them by God, namely Moses, and one law by this same Moses. And there was one desert region and one Mount Sinai, for one God it was who legislated for these Jews. But, again, after they had crossed the river Jordan, and had inherited by lot the conquered country, they in various ways rent in sunder the law of God, each devising a different interpretation of the declarations made by God. And in this way they raised up for themselves teachers, (and) invented doctrines of an heretical nature, and they continued to advance into (sectarian) divisions. Now it is the diversity of these Jews that I at present propose to explain. But though for even a considerable time they have been rent into very numerous sects, yet I intend to elucidate the more principal of them, while those who are of a studious turn will easily become acquainted with the rest. For there is a division amongst them into three sorts; and the adherents of the first are the Pharisees, but of the second the Sadducees, while the rest are Essenes. These practice a more devotional life, being filled with mutual love, and being temperate. And they turn away from every act of inordinate desire, being averse even to hearing of things of the sort. And they renounce matrimony, but they take the boys of others, and thus have an offspring begotten for them. And they lead these adopted children into an observance of their own peculiar customs, and in this way bring them up and impel them to learn the sciences. They do not, however, forbid them to marry, though themselves refraining from matrimony. Women, however, even though they may be disposed to adhere to the same course of life, they do not admit, inasmuch as in no way whatsoever have they confidence in women.

### Chapter XIV.—The Tenets of the Esseni.

And they despise wealth, and do not turn away from sharing their goods with those that are destitute. No one amongst them, however, enjoys a greater amount of riches than another. For a regulation with them is, that an individual coming forward to join the sect must sell his possessions, and present the price of them to the community. And on receiving the money, the head of the order distributes it to all according to their necessities. Thus, there is no one among them in distress. And they do not use oil, regarding it as a defilement to be anointed. And there are appointed overseers, who take care of all things that belong to them in common, and they all appear always in white clothing.

### Chapter XV.—The Tenets of the Esseni Continued.

But there is not one city of them, but many of them settle in every city. And if any of the adherents of the sect may be present from a strange place, they consider that all things are in common for him, and those whom they had not previously known they receive as if they belonged to their own household and kindred. And they traverse their native land, and on each occasion that they go on a journey they carry nothing except arms. And they have also in their cities a president, who expends the moneys collected for this purpose in procuring clothing and food for them. And their robe and its shape are modest. And they do not own two cloaks, or a double set of shoes; and when those that are in present use become antiquated, then they adopt others. And they neither buy nor sell anything at all; but whatever any one has he gives to him that has not, and that which one has not he receives.

Chapter XVI.—The Tenets of the Esseni Continued.

And they continue in an orderly manner, and with perseverance pray from early dawn, and they do not speak a word unless they have praised God in a hymn. And in this way, they each go forth and engage in whatever employment they please; and after having worked up to the fifth hour they leave off. Then again they come together into one place, and encircle themselves with linen girdles, for the purpose of concealing their private parts. And in this manner they perform ablutions in cold water; and after being thus cleansed, they repair together into one apartment,—now no one who entertains a different opinion from themselves assembles in the house,—and they proceed to partake of breakfast. And when they have taken their seats in silence, they set down loaves in order, and next someone sort of food to eat along with the bread, and each receives from these a sufficient portion. No one, however, tastes these before the priest utters a blessing, and prays over the food. And after breakfast, when he has a second time offered up supplication, as at the beginning, so at the conclusion of their meal they praise God in hymns. Next, after they have laid aside as sacred the garments in which they have been clothed while together taking their repast within the house—(now these garments are linen)—and having resumed the clothes which they had left in the vestibule, they hasten to agreeable occupations until evening. And they partake of supper, doing all things in like manner to those already mentioned. And no one will at any time cry aloud, nor will any other tumultuous voice be heard. But they each converse quietly, and with decorum one concedes the conversation to the other, so that the stillness of those within the house appears a sort of mystery to those outside. And they are invariably sober, eating and drinking all things by measure.

Chapter XVII.—The Tenets of the Esseni Continued.

All then pay attention to the president; and whatever injunctions he will issue, they obey as law. For they are anxious that mercy and assistance be extended to those that are burdened with toil. And especially they abstain from wrath and anger, and all such passions, inasmuch as they consider these to be treacherous to man. And no one amongst them is in the habit of swearing; but whatever any one says, this is regarded more binding than an oath. If, however, one will swear, he is condemned as one unworthy of credence. They are likewise solicitous about the readings of the law and prophets; and moreover also, if there is any treatise of the faithful, about that likewise. And they evince the utmost curiosity concerning plants and stones, rather busying themselves as regards the operative powers of these, saying that these things were not created in vain.

## Chapter XVIII.—The Tenets of the Esseni Continued.

But to those who wish to become disciples of the sect, they do not immediately deliver their rules, unless they have previously tried them. Now for the space of a year they set before (the candidates) the same food, while the latter continue to live in a different house outside the Essenes' own place of meeting. And they give (to the probationists) a hatchet and the linen girdle, and a white robe. When, at the expiration of this period, one affords proof of self-control, he approaches nearer to the sect's method of living, and he is washed more purely than before. Not as yet, however, does he partake of food along with the Essenes. For, after having furnished evidence as to whether he is able to acquire self-control,—but for two years the habit of a person of this description is on trial,—and when he has appeared deserving, he is thus reckoned amongst the members of the sect. Previous, however, to his being allowed to partake of a repast along with them, he is bound under fearful oaths. First, that he will worship the Divinity; next, that he will observe just dealings with men, and that he will in no way injure anyone, and that he will not hate a person who injures him, or is hostile to him, but pray for them. He likewise swears that he will always aid the just, and keep faith with all, especially those who are rulers. For, they argue, a position of authority does not happen to anyone without God. And if the Essene himself be a ruler, he swears that he will not conduct himself at any time arrogantly in the exercise of power, nor be prodigal, nor resort to any adornment, or a greater state of magnificence than the usage permits. He likewise swears, however, to be a lover of truth, and to reprove him that is guilty of falsehood, neither to steal, nor pollute his conscience for the sake of iniquitous gain, nor conceal aught from those that are members of his sect, and to divulge nothing to others, though one should be tortured even unto death. And in addition to the foregoing promises, he swears to impart to no one a knowledge of the doctrines in a different manner from that in which he has received them himself.

Chapter XIX.—The Tenets of the Esseni Continued.

With oaths, then, of this description, they bind those who come forward. If, however, anyone may be condemned for any sin, he is expelled from the order; but one that has been thus excommunicated sometimes perishes by an awful death. For, inasmuch as he is bound by the oaths and rites of the sect, he is not able to partake of the food in use among other people. Those that are excommunicated, occasionally, therefore, utterly destroy the body through starvation. And so it is, that when it comes to the last the Essenes sometimes pity many of them who are at the point of dissolution, inasmuch as they deem a punishment even unto death, thus inflicted upon these culprits, a sufficient penalty.

Chapter XX.—The Tenets of the Esseni Concluded.

But as regards judicial decisions, the Essenes are most accurate and impartial. And they deliver their judgments when they have assembled together, numbering at the very least one hundred; and the sentence delivered by them is irreversible. And they honor the legislator next after God; and if anyone is guilty of blasphemy against this framer of laws, he is punished. And they are taught to yield obedience to rulers and elders; and if ten occupy seats in the same room, one of them will not speak unless it will appear expedient to the nine. And they are careful not to spit out into the midst of persons present, and to the right hand. They are more solicitous, however, about abstaining from work on the Sabbath-day than all other Jews. For not only do they prepare their victuals for themselves one day previously, so as not (on the Sabbath) to kindle a fire, but not even would they move a utensil from one place to another (on that day), nor ease nature; nay, some would not even rise from a couch. On other days, however, when they wish to relieve nature, they dig a hole a foot long with the mattock,—for of this description is the hatchet, which the president in the first instance gives those who come forward to gain admission as disciples,—and cover (this cavity) on all sides with their garment, alleging that they do not necessarily insult the sunbeams. They then replace the upturned soil into the pit; and this is their practice, choosing the lonelier spots. But after they have performed this operation, immediately they undergo ablution, as if the excrement pollutes them.

## Chapter XXI.—Different Sects of the Esseni.

The Essenes have, however, in the lapse of time, undergone divisions, and they do not preserve their system of training after a similar manner, inasmuch as they have been split up into four parties. For some of them discipline themselves above the requisite rules of the order, so that even they would not handle a current coin of the country, saying that they ought not either to carry, or behold, or fashion an image: wherefore no one of those goes into a city, lest (by so doing) he should enter through a gate at which statues are erected, regarding it a violation of law to pass beneath images. But the adherents of another party, if they happen to hear any one maintaining a discussion concerning God and His laws—supposing such to be an uncircumcised person, they will closely watch him and when they meet a person of this description in any place alone, they will threaten to slay him if he refuses to undergo the rite of circumcision. Now, if the latter does not wish to comply with this request, an Essene spares not, but even slaughters. And it is from this occurrence that they have received their appellation, being denominated (by some) Zelotæ, but by others Sicarii. And the adherents of another party call no one Lord except the Deity, even though one should put them to the torture, or even kill them. But there are others of a later period, who have to such an extent declined from the discipline (of the order), that, as far as those are concerned who continue in the primitive customs, they would not even touch these. And if they happen to come in contact with them, they immediately resort to ablution, as if they had touched one belonging to an alien tribe.

But here also there are very many of them of so great longevity, as even to live longer than a hundred years. They assert, therefore, that a cause of this arises from their extreme devotion to religion, and their condemnation of all excess in regard of what is served up (as food), and from their being temperate and incapable of anger. And so it is that they despise death, rejoicing when they can finish their course with a good conscience. If, however, any one would even put to the torture persons of this description, in order to induce any amongst them either to speak evil of the law, or eat what is offered in sacrifice to an idol, he will not affect his purpose; for one of this party submits to death and endures torment rather than violate his conscience.

Chapter XXII.—Belief of the Esseni in the Resurrection; Their System a Suggestive One.

Now the doctrine of the resurrection has also derived support among these; for they acknowledge both that the flesh will rise again, and that it will be immortal, in the same manner as the soul is already imperishable. And they maintain that the soul, when separated in the present life, (departs) into one place, which is well ventilated and lightsome, where, they say, it rests until judgment. And this locality the Greeks were acquainted with by hearsay and called it "Isles of the Blessed." And there are other tenets of these which many of the Greeks have appropriated, and thus have from time to time formed their own opinions. For the disciplinary system in regard of the Divinity, according to these (Jewish sects), is of greater antiquity than that of all nations. And so it is that the proof is at hand, that all those (Greeks) who ventured to make assertions concerning God, or concerning the creation of existing things, derived their principles from no other source than from Jewish legislation. And among these may be particularized Pythagoras especially, and the Stoics, who derived (their systems) while resident among the Egyptians, by having become disciples of these Jews. Now they affirm that there will be both a judgment and a conflagration of the universe, and that the wicked will be eternally punished. And among them is cultivated the practice of prophecy, and the prediction of future events.

Chapter XXIII.—Another Sect of the Esseni: the Pharisees.

There is then another order of the Essenes who use the same customs and prescribed method of living with the foregoing sects, but make an alteration from these in one respect, viz., marriage. Now they maintain that those who have abrogated matrimony commit some terrible offence, which is for the destruction of life, and that they ought not to cut off the succession of children; for, that if all entertained this opinion, the entire race of men would easily be exterminated. However, they make a trial of their betrothed women for a period of three years; and when they have been three times purified, with a view of proving their ability of bringing forth children, so then they wed. They do not, however, cohabit with pregnant women, evincing that they marry not from sensual motives, but from the advantage of children. And the women likewise undergo ablution in a similar manner (with their husbands), and are themselves also arrayed in a linen garment, after the mode in which the men are with their girdles. These things, then, are the statements which I have to make respecting the Esseni.

But there are also others who themselves practice the Jewish customs; and these, both in respect of caste and in respect of the laws, are called Pharisees. Now the greatest part of these is to be found in every locality, inasmuch as, though all are styled Jews, yet, on account of the peculiarity of the opinions advanced by them, they have been denominated by titles proper to each. These, then, firmly hold the ancient tradition, and continue to pursue in a disputative spirit a close investigation into the things regarded according to the Law as clean and not clean. And they interpret the regulations of the Law, and put forward teachers, whom they qualify for giving instruction in such things. These Pharisees affirm the existence of fate, and that some things are in our power, whereas others are under the control of destiny. In this way they maintain that some actions depend upon ourselves, whereas others upon fate. But (they assert) that God is a cause of all things, and that nothing is managed or happens without His will. These likewise acknowledge that there is a resurrection of flesh, and that soul is immortal, and that there will be a judgment and conflagration, and that the righteous will be imperishable, but that the wicked will endure everlasting punishment in unquenchable fire.

## Chapter XXIV.—The Sadducees.

These, then, are the opinions even of the Pharisees. The Sadducees, however, are for abolishing fate, and they acknowledge that God does nothing that is wicked, nor exercises providence over (earthly concerns);

but they contend that the choice between good and evil lies within the power of men. And they deny that there is a resurrection not only of flesh, but also they suppose that the soul does not continue after death. The soul they consider nothing but mere vitality, and that it is on account of this that man has been created. However, (they maintain) that the notion of the resurrection has been fully realized by the single circumstance, that we close our days after having left children upon earth. But (they still insist) that after death one expects to suffer nothing, either bad or good; for that there will be a dissolution both of soul and body, and that man passes into non-existence, similarly also with the material of the animal creation. But as regards whatever wickedness a man may have committed in life, provided he may have been reconciled to the injured party, he has been a gainer (by transgression), inasmuch as he has escaped the punishment (that otherwise would have been inflicted) by men. And whatever acquisitions a man may have made, and (in whatever respect), by becoming wealthy, he may have acquired distinction, he has so far been a gainer. But (they abide by their assertion), that God has no solicitude about the concerns of an individual here. And while the Pharisees are full of mutual affection, the Sadducees, on the other hand, are actuated by self-love. This sect had its stronghold especially in the region around Samaria. And these also adhere to the customs of the law, saying that one ought so to live, that he may conduct himself virtuously, and leave children behind him on earth. They do not, however, devote attention to prophets, but neither do they to any other sages, except to the law of Moses only, in regard of which, however, they frame no interpretations. These, then, are the opinions which also the Sadducees choose to teach.

Chapter XXV.—The Jewish Religion.

Since, therefore, we have explained even the diversities among the Jews, it seems expedient likewise not to pass over in silence the system of their religion. The doctrine, therefore, among all Jews on the subject of religion is fourfold-theological, natural, moral, and ceremonial. And they affirm that there is one God, and that He is Creator and Lord of the universe: that He has formed all these glorious works which had no previous existence; and this, too, not out of any coeval substance that lay ready at hand, but His Will—the efficient cause—was to create, and He did create. And (they maintain) that there are angels, and that these have been brought into being for ministering unto the creation; but also that there is a sovereign Spirit that always continues beside God, for glory and praise. And that all things in the creation are endued with sensation, and that there is nothing inanimate. And they earnestly aim at serious habits and a temperate life, as one may ascertain from their laws. Now these matters have long ago been strictly defined by those who in ancient times have received the divinely-appointed law; so that the reader will find himself astonished at the amount of temperance, and of diligence, lavished on customs legally enacted in reference to man. The ceremonial service, however, which has been adapted to divine worship in a manner befitting the dignity of religion, has been practiced amongst them with the highest degree of elaboration. The superiority of their ritualism it is easy for those who wish it to ascertain, provided they read the book which furnishes information on these points. They will thus perceive how that with solemnity and sanctity the Jewish priests offer unto God the first-fruits of the gifts bestowed by Him for the use and enjoyment of men; how they fulfil their ministrations with regularity and steadfastness, in obedience to His commandments. There are, however, some (liturgical usages adopted) by these, which the Sadducees refuse to recognize, for they are not disposed to acquiesce in the existence of angels or spirits.

Still all parties alike expect Messiah, inasmuch as the Law certainly, and the prophets, preached beforehand that He was about to be present on earth. Inasmuch, however, as the Jews were not cognizant of the period of His advent, there remains the supposition that the declarations (of Scripture) concerning His coming have not been fulfilled. And so it is, that up to this day they continue in anticipation of the future coming of the Christ,—from the fact of their not discerning Him when He was present in the world. And (yet there can be little doubt but) that, on beholding the signs of the times of His having been already amongst us, the Jews are troubled; and that they are ashamed to confess that He has come, since they have with their own hands put Him to death, because they were stung with indignation in being convicted by Himself of not having obeyed the laws. And they affirm that He who was thus sent forth by God is not this Christ (whom they are looking for); but they confess that another Messiah will come, who as yet has no existence; and that he will usher in some of the signs which the law and the prophets have shown beforehand, whereas, regarding the rest (of these indications), they suppose that they have fallen into error. For they say that his generation will be from the stock of David, but not from a virgin and the Holy Spirit, but from a woman and a man, according as it is a rule for all to be procreated from seed. And they allege that this Messiah will be King over them,—a warlike and powerful individual, who, after having gathered together the entire people of the Jews, and having done battle with all the nations, will restore for them Jerusalem the royal city. And into this city He will collect together the entire Hebrew race, and bring it back once more into the ancient customs, that it may fulfil the regal and sacerdotal functions, and dwell in confidence for periods of time of sufficient duration. After this repose, it is their opinion that war would next be waged against them after being thus congregated; that in this conflict Christ would fall by the edge of the sword; and that, after no long time, would next succeed the termination and conflagration of the universe; and that in this way their opinions concerning the resurrection would receive completion, and a recompense be rendered to each man according to his works.

Chapter XXVI.—Conclusion to the Work Explained.

It now seems to us that the tenets of both all the Greeks and barbarians have been sufficiently explained by us, and that nothing has remained unrefuted either of the points about which philosophy has been busied, or of the allegations advanced by the heretics. And from these very explanations the condemnation of the heretics is obvious, for having either purloined their doctrines, or derived contributions to them from some of those tenets elaborately worked out by the Greeks, and for having advanced (these opinions) as if they originated from God. Since, therefore, we have hurriedly passed through all the systems of these, and with much labor have, in the nine books, proclaimed all their opinions, and have left behind us for all men a small viaticum in life, and to those who are our contemporaries have afforded a desire of learning (with) great joy and delight, we have considered it reasonable, as a crowning stroke to the entire work, to introduce the discourse (already mentioned) concerning the truth, and to furnish our delineation of this in one book, namely the tenth. Our object is, that the reader, not only when made acquainted with the overthrow of those who have presumed to establish heresies, may regard with scorn their idle fancies, but also, when brought to know the power of the truth, may be placed in the way of salvation, by reposing that faith in God which He so worthily deserves.

Book X.

Contents.

The following are the contents of the tenth book of the Refutation of all Heresies:— An Epitome of all Philosophers. An Epitome of all Heresies. And, in conclusion to all, what the Doctrine of the Truth is.

Chapter I.—Recapitulation.

After we have, not with violence, burst through the labyrinth of heresies, but have unraveled (their intricacies) through a refutation merely, or, in other words, by the force of truth, we approach the demonstration of the truth itself. For then the artificial sophisms of error will be exposed in all their inconsistency, when we shall succeed in establishing whence it is that the definition of the truth has been derived. The truth has not taken its principles from the wisdom of the Greeks, nor borrowed its doctrines, as secret mysteries, from the tenets of the Egyptians, which, albeit silly, are regarded amongst them with religious veneration as worthy of reliance. Nor has it been formed out of the fallacies which enunciate the incoherent (conclusions arrived at through the) curiosity of the Chaldeans. Nor does the truth owe its existence to astonishment, through the operations of demons, for the irrational frenzy of the Babylonians. But its definition is constituted after the manner in which every true definition is, viz., as simple and unadorned. A definition such as this, provided it is made manifest, will of itself refute error. And although we have very frequently pro☐pounded demonstrations, and with sufficient fulness elucidated for those willing (to learn) the rule of the truth; yet even now, after having discussed all the opinions put forward by the Greeks and heretics, we have decided it not to be, at all events, unreasonable to introduce, as a sort of finishing stroke to the (nine) books preceding, this demonstration throughout the tenth book.

Chapter II.—Summary of the Opinions of Philosophers.

Having, therefore, embraced (a consideration of) the tenets of all the wise men among the Greeks in four books, and the doctrines propounded by the heresiarchs in five, we shall now exhibit the doctrine concerning the truth in one, having first presented in a summary the suppositions entertained severally by all. For the dogmatists of the Greeks, dividing philosophy into three parts, in this manner devised from time to time their speculative systems; some denominating their system Natural, and others Moral, but others Dialectical Philosophy. And the ancient thinkers who called their science Natural Philosophy, were those mentioned in book i. And the account which they furnished was after this mode: Some of them derived all things from one, whereas others from more things than one. And of those who derived all things from one, some derived them from what was devoid of quality, whereas others from what was endued with quality. And among those who derived all things from quality, some derived them from fire, and some from air, and some from water, and some from earth. And among those who derived the universe from more things than one, some derived it from numerable, but others from infinite quantities. And among those who derived all things from numerable quantities, some derived them from two, and others from four, and others from five, and others from six. And among those who derived the universe from infinite quantities, some derived entities from things similar to those generated, whereas others from things dissimilar. And among these some derived entities from things incapable of, whereas others from things capable of, passion. From a body devoid of quality and endued with unity, the Stoics, then, accounted for the generation of the universe. For, according to them, matter devoid of quality, and in all its parts susceptible of change, constitutes an originating principle of the universe. For, when an alteration of this ensues, there is generated fire, air, water, earth. The followers, however, of Hippasus, and Anaximander, and Thales the Milesian, are disposed to think that all things have been generated from one (an entity), endued with quality. Hippasus of Metapontum and Heraclitus the Ephesian declared the origin of things to be from fire, whereas Anaximander from air, but Thales from water, and Xenophanes from earth. "For from earth," says he, "are all things, and all things terminate in the earth."

Chapter III.—Summary of the Opinions of Philosophers Continued.

But among those who derive all entities from more things than one, and from numerable quantities, the poet Homer asserts that the universe consists of two substances, namely earth and water; at one time expressing himself thus:—

"The source of gods was Sea and Mother Earth."
And on another occasion thus:—
"But indeed ye all might become water and earth."
And Xenophanes of Colophon seems to coincide with him, for he says:—
"We all are sprung from water and from earth."
Euripides, however, (derives the universe) from earth and air, as one may ascertain from the following assertion of his:—
"Mother of all, air and earth, I sing."
But Empedocles derives the universe from four principles, expressing himself thus:—
"Four roots of all things hear thou first:
Brilliant Jove, and life-giving Juno and Aidoneus,

And Nestis, that with tears bedews the Mortal Font."

Ocellus, however, the Lucanian, and Aristotle, derive the universe from five principles; for, along with the four elements, they have assumed the existence of a fifth, and (that this is) a body with a circular motion; and they say that from this, things celestial have their being. But the disciples of Empedocles supposed the generation of the universe to have proceeded from six principles. For in the passage where he says, "Four roots of all things hear thou first," he produces generation out of four principles. When, however, he subjoins,—

"Ruinous Strife apart from these, equal in every point,

And with them Friendship equal in length and breadth,"—

he also delivers six principles of the universe, four of them material—earth, water, fire, and air; but two of them formative—Friendship and Discord. The followers, however, of Anaxagoras of Clazomenæ, and of Democritus, and of Epicurus, and multitudes of others, have given it as their opinion that the generation of the universe proceeds from infinite numbers of atoms; and we have previously made partial mention of these philosophers. But Anaxagoras derives the universe from things similar to those that are being produced; whereas the followers of Democritus and Epicurus derived the universe from things both dissimilar (to the entities produced), and devoid of passion, that is, from atoms. But the followers of Heraclides of Pontus, and of Asclepiades, derived the universe from things dissimilar (to the entities produced), and capable of passion, as if from incongruous corpuscles. But the disciples of Plato affirm that these entities are from three principles—God, and Matter, and Exemplar. He divides matter, however, into four principles—fire, water, earth, and air. And (he says) that God is the Creator of this (matter), and that Mind is its exemplar.

Chapter IV.—Summary of the Opinions of Philosophers Continued.

Persuaded, then, that the principle of physiology is confessedly discovered to be encumbered with difficulties for all these philosophers, we ourselves also shall fearlessly declare concerning the examples of the truth, as to how they are, and as we have felt confident that they are. But we shall previously furnish an explanation, in the way of epitome, of the tenets of the heresiarchs, in order that, by our having set before our readers the tenets of all made well known by this (plan of treatment), we may exhibit the truth in a plain and familiar (form).

Chapter V.—The Naasseni.

But since it so appears expedient, let us begin first from the public worshippers of the serpent. The Naasseni call the first principle of the universe a Man, and that the same also is a Son of Man; and they divide this man into three portions. For they say one part of him is rational, and another psychical, but a third earthly. And they style him Adamas, and suppose that the knowledge appertaining to him is the originating cause of the capacity of knowing God. And the Naassene asserts that all these rational, and psychical, and earthly qualities have retired into Jesus, and that through Him these three substances simultaneously have spoken unto the three genera of the universe. These allege that there are three kinds of existence—angelic, psychical, and earthly; and that there are three churches—angelic, psychical, and earthly; and that the names for these are—chosen, called, and captive. These are the heads of doctrine advanced by them, as far as one may briefly comprehend them. They affirm that James, the brother of the Lord, delivered these tenets to Mariamne, by such a statement belying both.

Chapter VI.—The Peratæ.

The Peratæ, however, viz., Ademes the Carystian, and Euphrates the Peratic, say that there is someone world,—this is the denomination they use,—and affirming that it is divided into three parts. But of the threefold division, according to them, there is one principle, just like an immense fountain, capable of being by reason divided into infinite segments. And the first segment, and the one of more proximity, according to them, is the triad, and is called a perfect good, and a paternal magnitude. But the second portion of the triad is a certain multitude of, as it were, infinite powers. The third part, however, is formal. And the first is unbegotten; whence they expressly affirm that there are three Gods, three Logoi, three minds, (and) three men. For when the division has been accomplished, to each part of the world they assign both Gods, and Logoi, and men, and the rest. But from above, from uncreatedness and the first segment of the world, when afterwards the world had attained to its consummation, the Peratic affirms that there came down, in the times of Herod, a certain man with a threefold nature, and a threefold body, and a threefold power, named Christ, and that He possesses from the three parts of the world in Himself all the concretions and capacities of the world. And they are disposed to think that this is what has been declared, "in whom dwelleth all the fulness of the Godhead bodily." And they assert that from the two worlds situated above—namely, both the unbegotten one and self-begotten one—there were borne down into this world in which we are, germs of all sorts of powers. And (they say) that Christ came down from above from uncreatedness, in order that, by His descent, all things that have been divided into three parts may be saved. For, says the Peratic, the things that have been borne down from above will ascend through Him; and the things that have plotted against those that have been borne down are heedlessly rejected, and sent away to be punished. And the Peratic states that there are two parts which are saved—that is, those that are situated above—by having been separated from corruption, and that the third is destroyed, which he calls a formal world. These also are the tenets of the Peratæ.

Chapter VII.—The Sethians.

But to the Sethians it seems that there exist three principles, which have been precisely defined. And each of the principles is fitted by nature for being able to be generated, as in a human soul every art whatsoever is developed which is capable of being learned. The result is the same as when a child, by being long conversant with a musical instrument, becomes a musician; or with geometry a geometrician, or with any other art, with a similar result. And the essences of the principles, the Sethians say, are light and darkness. And in the midst of these is pure spirit; and the spirit, they say, is that which is placed intermediate between darkness, which is below, and light, which is above. It is not spirit, as a current of wind or a certain gentle breeze which may be felt, but just as if some fragrance of ointment or incense made out of a refined mixture,—a power diffusing itself by some impulse of fragrance which is inconceivable and superior to what one can express. Since, therefore, the light is above and the darkness below, and the spirit is intermediate between these, the light, also, as a ray of sun, shines from above on the underlying darkness. And the fragrance of the spirit is wafted onwards, occupying an intermediate position, and proceeds forth, just as is diffused the odor of incense-offerings (laid) upon the fire. Now the power of the things divided threefold being of this description, the power simultaneously of the spirit and of the light is below, in the darkness that is situated beneath. The darkness, however, they say, is a horrible water, into which the light along with the spirit is absorbed, and thus translated into a nature of this description. The darkness being then endued with intelligence, and knowing that when the light has been removed from it the darkness continues desolate, devoid of radiance and splendor, power and efficiency, as well as impotent, (therefore,) by every effort of reflection and of reason, this makes an exertion to comprise in itself brilliancy, and a scintillation of light, along with the fragrance of the spirit. And of this they introduce the following image, expressing themselves thus: Just as the pupil of the eye appears dark beneath the underlying humors, but is illuminated by the spirit, so the darkness earnestly strives after the spirit, and has with itself all the powers which wish to retire and return. Now these are indefinitely infinite, from which, when commingled, all things are figured and generated like seals. For just as a seal, when brought into contact with wax, produces a figure, (and yet the seal) itself remains of itself what it was, so also the powers, by coming into communion (one with the other), form all the infinite kinds of animals. The Sethians assert that, therefore, from the primary concourse of the three principles was generated an image of the great seal, namely heaven and earth, having a form like a womb, possessing a navel in the midst. And so that the rest of the figures of all things were, like heaven and earth, fashioned similar to a womb.

And the Sethians say that from the water was produced a first-begotten principle, namely a vehement and boisterous wind, and that it is a cause of all generation, which creates a sort of heat and motion in the world from the motion of the waters. And they maintain that this wind is fashioned like the hissing of a serpent into a perfect image. And on this the world gazes and hurries into generation, being inflamed as a womb; and from thence they are disposed to think that the generation of the universe has arisen. And they say that this wind constitutes a spirit, and that a perfect God has arisen from the fragrance of the waters, and that of the spirit, and from the brilliant light. And they affirm that mind exists after the mode of generation from a female—(meaning by mind) the supernal spark—and that, having been mingled beneath with the compounds of body, it earnestly desires to flee away, that escaping it may depart and not find dissolution on account of the deficiency in the waters. Wherefore it is in the habit of crying aloud from the mixture of the waters, according to the Psalmist, as they say, "For the entire anxiety of the light above is, that it may deliver the spark which is below from the Father beneath," that is, from wind. And the Father creates heat and disturbance, and produces for Himself a Son, namely mind, which, as they allege, is not the peculiar offspring of Himself. And these heretics affirm that the Son, on beholding the perfect Logos of the supernal light, underwent a transformation, and in the shape of a serpent entered into a womb, in order that he might be able to recover that Mind which is the scintillation from the light. And that this is what has been declared, "Who, being in the form of God, thought it not robbery to be equal with God; but made Himself of no reputation, and took upon Him the form of a servant." And the wretched and baneful Sethians are disposed to think that this constitutes the servile form alluded to by the Apostle. These, then, are the assertions which likewise these Sethians advance.

Chapter VIII.—Simon Magus.

But that very sapient fellow Simon makes his statement thus, that there is an indefinite power, and that this is the root of the universe. And this indefinite power, he says, which is fire, is in itself not anything which is simple, as the gross bulk of speculators maintain, when they assert that there are four incomposite elements, and have supposed fire, as one of these, to be uncompounded. Simon, on the other hand, alleges that the nature of fire is twofold; and one portion of this twofold (nature) he calls a something secret, and another (a something) manifest. And he asserts that the secret is concealed in the manifest parts of the fire, and that the manifest parts of the fire have been produced from the secret. And he says that all the parts of the fire, visible and invisible, have been supposed to be in possession of a capacity of perception. The world, therefore, he says, that is begotten, has been produced from the unbegotten fire. And it commenced, he says, to exist thus: The Unbegotten One took six primal roots of the principle of generation from the principle of that fire. For he maintains that these roots have been generated in pairs from the fire; and these he denominates Mind and Intelligence, Voice and Name, Ratiocination and Reflection. And he asserts that in the six roots, at the same time, resides the indefinite power, which he affirms to be Him that stood, stands, and will stand. And when this one has been formed into a figure, He will, according to this heretic, exist in the six powers substantially and potentially. And He will be in magnitude and perfection one and the same with that unbegotten and indefinite power, possessing no attribute in any respect more deficient than that unbegotten, and unalterable, and indefinite power. If, however, He who stood, stands, and will stand, continues to exist only potentially in the six powers, and has not assumed any definite figure, He becomes, says Simon, utterly evanescent, and perishes. And this takes place in the same manner as the grammatical or geometrical capacity, which, though it has been implanted in man's soul, suffers extinction when it does not obtain (the assistance of) a master of either of these arts, who would indoctrinate that soul into its principles. Now Simon affirms that he himself is He who stood, stands, and will stand, and that He is a power that is above all things. So far, then, for the opinions of Simon likewise.

Chapter IX.—Valentinus.

Valentinus, however, and the adherents of this school, though they agree in asserting that the originating principle of the universe is the Father, still they are impelled into the adoption of a contrary opinion respecting Him. For some of them maintain that (the Father) is solitary and generative; whereas others hold the impossibility, (in His as in other cases,) of procreation without a female. They therefore add Sige as the spouse of this Father, and style the Father Himself Bythus. From this Father and His spouse some allege that there have been six projections,—viz., Nous and Aletheia, Logos and Zoe, Anthropos and Ecclesia,—and that this constitutes the procreative Ogdoad. And the Valentinians maintain that those are the first projections which have taken place within the limit, and have been again denominated "those within the Pleroma;" and the second are "those without the Pleroma;" and the third, "those without the Limit." Now the generation of these constitutes the Hysterema Acamoth. And he asserts that what has been generated from an Æon, that exists in the Hysterema and has been projected (beyond the Limit), is the Creator. But Valentinus is not disposed to affirm what is thus generated to be primal Deity, but speaks in detractive terms both of Him and the things made by Him. And (he asserts) that Christ came down from within the Pleroma for the salvation of the spirit who had erred. This spirit, (according to the Valentinians,) resides in our inner man; and they say that this inner man obtains salvation on account of this indwelling spirit. Valentinus, however, (to uphold the doctrine,) determines that the flesh is not saved, and styles it "a leathern tunic," and the perishable portion of man. I have (already) declared these tenets in the way of an epitome, inasmuch as in their systems there exists enlarged matter for discussion, and a variety of opinions. In this manner, then, it seems proper also to the school of Valentinus to propound their opinions.

## Chapter X.—Basilides.

But Basilides also himself affirms that there is a non-existent God, who, being non-existent, has made the non-existent world, that has been formed out of things that are not, by casting down a certain seed, as it were a grain of mustard-seed, having in itself stem, leaves, branches, and fruit. Or this seed is as a peacock's egg, comprising in itself the varied multitude of colors. And this, say the Basilidians, constitutes the seed of the world, from which all things have been produced. For they maintain that it comprises in itself all things, as it were those that as yet are non-existent, and which it has been predetermined to be brought into existence by the non-existent Deity. There was, then, he says, in the seed itself a threefold Sonship, in all respects of the same substance with the nonexistent God, which has been begotten from things that are not. And of this Sonship, divided into three parts, one portion of it was refined, and another gross, and another requiring purification. The refined portion, when first the earliest putting down of the seed was accomplished by the non-existent God, immediately burst forth, and ascended upwards, and proceeded towards the non-existent Deity. For every nature yearns after that God on account of the excess of His beauty, but different (creatures desire Him) from different causes. The more gross portion, however, still continues in the seed; and inasmuch as it is a certain imitative nature, it was not able to soar upwards, for it was more gross than the subtle part. The more gross portion, however, equipped itself with the Holy Spirit, as it were with wings; for the Sonship, thus arrayed, shows kindness to this Spirit, and in turn receives kindness. The third Sonship, however, requires purification, and therefore this continued in the conglomeration of all germs, and this displays and receives kindness. And (Basilides asserts) that there is something which is called "world," and something else (which is called) supra-mundane; for entities are distributed by him into two primary divisions. And what is intermediate between these he calls "Conterminous Holy Spirit," and (this Spirit) has in itself the fragrance of the Sonship.

From the conglomeration of all germs of the cosmical seed burst forth and was begotten the Great Archon, the head of the world, an Æon of inexpressible beauty and size. This (Archon) having raised Himself as far as the firmament, supposed that there was not another above Himself. And accordingly He became more brilliant and powerful than all the underlying Æons, with the exception of the Sonship that had been left beneath, but which He was not aware was more wise than Himself. This one having His attention turned to the creation of the world, first begat a son unto Himself, superior to Himself; and this son He caused to sit on His own right hand, and this these Basilidians allege is the Ogdoad. The Great Archon Himself, then, produces the entire celestial creation. And other Archon ascended from (the conglomeration of) all the germs, who was greater than all the underlying Æon, except the Sonship that had been left behind, yet far inferior to the former one. And they style this second Archon a Hebdomad. He is Maker, and Creator, and Controller of all things that are beneath Him, and this Archon produced for Himself a Son more prudent and wiser than Himself. Now they assert that all these things exist according to the predetermination of that nonexistent God, and that there exist also worlds and intervals that are infinite. And the Basilidians affirm that upon Jesus, who was born of Mary, came the power of the Gospel, which descended and illuminated the Son both of the Ogdoad and of the Hebdomad. And this took place for the purpose of enlightening and distinguishing from the different orders of beings, and purifying the Sonship that had been left behind for conferring benefits on souls, and the receiving benefits in turn. And they say that themselves are sons, who are in the world for this cause, that by teaching they may purify souls, and along with the Sonship may ascend to the Father above, from whom proceeded the first Sonship. And they allege that the world endures until the period when all souls may have repaired thither along with the Sonship. These, however, are the opinions which Basilides, who detailed them as prodigies, is not ashamed to advance.

Chapter XI.—Justinus.

But Justinus also himself attempted to establish similar opinions with these and expresses himself thus: That there are three unbegotten principles of the universe, two males and one female. And of the males one principle is denominated "Good." Now this alone is called after this mode, and is endued with a foreknowledge of the universe. And the other is Father of all generated entities, and is devoid of foreknowledge, and unknown, and invisible, and is called Elohim. The female principle is devoid of foreknowledge, passionate, with two minds, and with two bodies, as we have minutely detailed in the previous discourses concerning this heretic's system. This female principle, in her upper parts, as far as the groin, is, the Justinians say, a virgin, whereas from the groin downwards a snake. And such is denominated Edem and Israel. This heretic alleges that these are the principles of the universe, from which all things have been produced. And he asserts that Elohim, without foreknowledge, passed into inordinate desire for the half virgin, and that having had intercourse with her, he begot twelve angels; and the names of these he states to be those already given. And of these the paternal ones are connected with the father, and the maternal with the mother. And Justinus maintains that these are (the trees of Paradise), concerning which Moses has spoken in an allegorical sense the things written in the law. And Justinus affirms that all things were made by Elohim and Edem. And (he says) that animals, with the rest of the creatures of this kind, are from the a part resembling a beast, whereas man from the parts above the groin. And Edem (is supposed by Justinus) to have deposited in man himself the soul, which was her own power, (but Elohim the spirit.) And Justinus alleges that this Elohim, after having learned his origin, ascended to the Good Being, and deserted Edem. And this heretic asserts that Edem, enraged on account of such (treatment), concocted all this plot against the spirit of Elohim which he deposited in man. And (Justinus informs us) that for this reason the Father sent Baruch, and issued directions to the prophets, in order that the spirit of Elohim might be delivered, and that all might be seduced away from Edem. But (this heretic) alleges that even Hercules was a prophet, and that he was worsted by Omphale, that is, by Babel; and the Justinians call the latter Venus. And (they say) that afterwards, in the days of Herod, Jesus was born son of Mary and Joseph, to whom he alleges Baruch had spoken. And (Justinus asserts) that Edem plotted against this (Jesus), but could not deceive him; and for this reason, that she caused him to be crucified. And the spirit of Jesus, (says Justinus,) ascended to the Good Being. And (the Justinians maintain) that the spirits of all who thus obey those silly and futile discourses will be saved, and that the body and soul of Edem have been left behind. But the foolish Justinus calls this (Edem) Earth.

Chapter XII.—The Docetæ.

Now the Docetæ advance assertions of this description: that the primal Deity is as a seed of the fig-tree; and that from this proceeded three Æons as the stem, and the leaves and the fruit; and that these projected thirty Æons, each (of them) ten; and that they were all united in decades, but differed only in positions, as some were before others. And (the Docetæ assert) that infinite Æons were indefinitely projected, and that all these were hermaphrodites. And (they say) that these Æons formed a design of simultaneously going together into one Æon, and that from this the intermediate Æon and from the Virgin Mary they begot a Savior of all. And this Redeemer was like in every respect to the first seed of the fig-tree, but inferior in this respect, from the fact of His having been begotten; for the seed whence the fig-tree springs is unbegotten. This, then, was the great light of the Æons—it was entirely radiance—which receives no adornment, and comprises in itself the forms of all animals. And the Docetæ maintain that this light, on proceeding into the underlying chaos, afforded a cause (of existence) to the things that were produced, and those actually existing, and that on coming down from above it impressed on chaos beneath the forms of everlasting species. For the third Æon, which had tripled itself, when he perceives that all his characteristic attributes were forcibly drawn off into the nether darkness, and not being ignorant both of the terror of darkness and the simplicity of light, proceeded to create heaven; and after having rendered firm what intervened, He separated the darkness from the light. As all the species of the third Æon were, he says, overcome by the darkness, the figure even of this Æon became a living fire, having been generated by light. And from this (source), they allege, was generated the Great Archon, regarding whom Moses converses, saying that He is a fiery Deity and Demiurge, who also continually alters the forms of all (Æons) into bodies. And the (Docetæ) allege that these are the souls for whose sake the Savior was begotten, and that He points out the way through which the souls will escape that are (now) overpowered (by darkness). And (the Docetæ maintain) that Jesus arrayed Himself in that only-begotten power, and that for this reason He could not be seen by any, on account of the excessive magnitude of His glory. And they say that all the occurrences took place with Him as it has been written in the Gospels.

Chapter XIII.—Monoïmus.

But the followers of Monoïmus the Arabian assert that the originating principle of the universe is a primal man and son of man; and that, as Moses states, the things that have been produced were produced not by the primal man, but by the Son of that primal man, yet not by the entire Son, but by part of Him. And (Monoïmus asserts) that the Son of man is iota, which stands for ten, the principal number in which is (inherent) the subsistence of all number (in general, and) through which every number (in particular) consists, as well as the generation of the universe, fire, air, water, and earth. But inasmuch as this is one iota and one tittle, and what is perfect (emanates) from what is perfect, or, in other words, a tittle flows down from above, containing all things in itself; (therefore,) whatsoever things also the man possesses, the Father of the Son of man possesses likewise. Moses, therefore, says that the world was made in six days, that is, by six powers, out of which the world was made by the one tittle. For cubes, and octahedrons, and pyramids, and all figures similar to these, having equal superficies, out of which consist fire, air, water, and earth, have been produced from numbers comprehended in that simple tittle of the iota, which is Son of man. When, therefore, says (Monoïmus), Moses mentions the rod's being brandished for the purpose of bringing the plagues upon Egypt, he alludes allegorically to the (alterations of the) world of iota; nor did he frame more than ten plagues. If, however, says he, you wish to become acquainted with the universe, search within yourself who is it that says, "My soul, my flesh, and my mind," and who is it that appropriates each one thing unto himself, as another (would do) for himself. Understand that this is a perfect one arising from (one that is) perfect, and that he considers as his own all so-called nonentities and all entities. These, then, are the opinions of Monoïmus also.

## Chapter XIV.—Tatian.

Tatian, however, similarly with Valentinus and the others, says that there are certain invisible Æons, and that by some one of these the world below has been created, and the things existing in it. And he habituates himself to a very cynical mode of life, and almost in nothing differs from Marcion, as appertaining both to his slanders, and the regulations enacted concerning marriage.

## Chapter XV.—Marcion and Cerdo.

But Marcion, of Pontus, and Cerdon, his preceptor, themselves also lay down that there are three principles of the universe—good, just, and matter. Some disciples, however, of these add a fourth, saying, good, just, evil, and matter. But they all affirm that the good (Being) has made nothing at all, though some denominate the just one likewise evil, whereas others that his only title is that of just. And they allege that (the just Being) made all things out of subjacent matter, for that he made them not well, but irrationally. For it is requisite that the things made should be similar to the maker; wherefore also they thus employ the evangelical parables, saying, "A good tree cannot bring forth evil fruit," and the rest of the passage. Now Marcion alleges that the conceptions badly devised by the (just one) himself constituted the allusion in this passage. And (he says) that Christ is the Son of the good Being, and was sent for the salvation of souls by him whom he styles the inner than. And he asserts that he appeared as a man though not being a man, and as incarnate though not being incarnate. And he maintains that his manifestation was only phantastic, and that he underwent neither generation nor passion except in appearance. And he will not allow that flesh rises again; but in affirming marriage to be destruction, he leads his disciples towards a very cynical life. And by these means he imagines that he annoys the Creator, if he should abstain from the things that are made or appointed by Him.

### Chapter XVI.—Apelles.

But Apelles, a disciple of this heretic, was displeased at the statements advanced by his preceptor, as we have previously declared, and by another theory supposed that there are four gods. And the first of these he alleges to be the "Good Being," whom the prophets did not know, and Christ to be His Son. And the second God, he affirms to be the Creator of the universe, and Him he does not wish to be a God. And the third God, he states to be the fiery one that was manifested; and the fourth to be an evil one. And Apelles calls these angels; and by adding (to their number) Christ likewise, he will assert Him to be a fifth God. But this heretic is in the habit of devoting his attention to a book which he calls "Revelations" of a certain Philumene, whom he considers a prophetess. And he affirms that Christ did not receive his flesh from the Virgin, but from the adjacent substance of the world. In this manner he composed his treatises against the law and the prophets, and attempts to abolish them as if they had spoken falsehoods, and had not known God. And Apelles, similarly with Marcion, affirms that the different sorts of flesh are destroyed.

### Chapter XVII.—Cerinthus.

Cerinthus, however, himself having been trained in Egypt, determined that the world was not made by the first God, but by a certain angelic power. And this power was far separated and distant from that sovereignty which is above the entire circle of existence, and it knows not the God (that is) above all things. And he says that Jesus was not born of a virgin, but that He sprang from Joseph and Mary as their son, similar to the rest of men; and that He excelled in justice, and prudence, and understanding above all the rest of mankind. And Cerinthus maintains that, after Jesus' baptism, Christ came down in the form of a dove upon Him from the sovereignty that is above the whole circle of existence, and that then He proceeded to preach the unknown Father, and to work miracles. And he asserts that, at the conclusion of the passion, Christ flew away from Jesus, but that Jesus suffered, and that Christ remained incapable of suffering, being a spirit of the Lord.

Chapter XVIII.—The Ebionæans.

But the Ebionæans assert that the world is made by the true God, and they speak of Christ in a similar manner with Cerinthus. They live, however, in all respects according to the law of Moses, alleging that they are thus justified.

Chapter XIX.—Theodotus.

But Theodotus of Byzantium introduced a heresy of the following description, alleging that all things were created by the true God; whereas that Christ, he states, in a manner similar to that advocated by the Gnostics already mentioned, made His appearance according to some mode of this description. And Theodotus affirms that Christ is a man of a kindred nature with all men, but that He surpasses them in this respect, that, according to the counsel of God, He had been born of a virgin, and the Holy Ghost had overshadowed His mother. This heretic, however, maintained that Jesus had not assumed flesh in the womb of the Virgin, but that afterwards Christ descended upon Jesus at His baptism in form of a dove. And from this circumstance, the followers of Theodotus affirm that at first miraculous powers did not acquire operating energy in the Savior Himself. Theodotus, however, determines to deny the divinity of Christ. Now, opinions of this description were advanced by Theodotus.

Chapter XX.—Melchisedecians.

And others also make all their assertions similarly with those which have been already specified, introducing one only alteration, viz., in respect of regarding Melchisedec as a certain power. But they allege that Melchisedec himself is superior to all powers; and according to his image, they are desirous of maintaining that Christ likewise is generated.

Chapter XXI.—The Phrygians or Montanists.

The Phrygians, however, derive the principles of their heresy from a certain Montanus, and Priscilla, and Maximilla, and regard these wretched women as prophetesses, and Montanus as a prophet. In respect, however, of what appertains to the origin and creation of the universe, the Phrygians are supposed to express themselves correctly; while in the tenets which they enunciate respecting Christ, they have not irrelevantly formed their opinions. But they are seduced into error in common with the heretics previously alluded to, and devote their attention to the discourses of these above the Gospels, thus laying down regulations concerning novel and strange fasts.

Chapter XXII.—The Phrygians or Montanists Continued.

But others of them, being attached to the heresy of the Noetians, entertain similar opinions to those relating to the silly women of the Phrygians, and to Montanus. As regards, however, the truths appertaining to the Father of the entire of existing things, they are guilty of blasphemy, because they assert that He is Son and Father, visible and invisible, begotten and unbegotten, mortal and immortal. These have taken occasion from a certain Noetus to put forward their heresy.

Chapter XXIII.—Noetus and Callistus.

But in like manner, also, Noetus, being by birth a native of Smyrna, and a fellow addicted to reckless babbling, as well as crafty withal, introduced (among us) this heresy which originated from one Epigonus. It reached Rome, and was adopted by Cleomenes, and so has continued to this day among his successors. Noetus asserts that there is one Father and God of the universe, and that He made all things, and was imperceptible to those that exist when He might so desire. Noetus maintained that the Father then appeared when He wished; and He is invisible when He is not seen, but visible when He is seen. And this heretic also alleges that the Father is unbegotten when He is not generated, but begotten when He is born of a virgin; as also that He is not subject to suffering, and is immortal when He does not suffer or die. When, however, His passion came upon Him, Noetus allows that the Father suffers and dies. And the Noetians suppose that this Father Himself is called Son, (and vice versa,) in reference to the events which at their own proper periods happen to them severally. Callistus corroborated the heresy of these Noetians, but we have already carefully explained the details of his life. And Callistus himself produced likewise a heresy, and derived its starting-points from these Noetians,—namely, so far as he acknowledges that there is one Father and God, viz., the Creator of the universe, and that this (God) is spoken of, and called by the name of Son, yet that in substance He is one Spirit. For Spirit, as the Deity, is, he says, not any being different from the Logos, or the Logos from the Deity; therefore this one person, (according to Callistus,) is divided nominally, but substantially not so. He supposes this one Logos to be God, and affirms that there was in the case of the Word an incarnation. And he is disposed (to maintain), that He who was seen in the flesh and was crucified is Son, but that the Father it is who dwells in Him. Callistus thus at one time branches off into the opinion of Noetus, but at another into that of Theodotus, and holds no sure doctrine. These, then, are the opinions of Callistus.

### Chapter XXIV.—Hermogenes.

But one Hermogenes himself also being desirous of saying something, asserted that God made all things out of matter coeval with Himself, and subject to His design. For Hermogenes held it to be an impossibility that God should make the things that were made, except out of existent things.

### Chapter XXV.—The Elchasaites.

But certain others, introducing as it were some novel tenet, appropriated parts of their system from all heresies, and procured a strange volume, which bore on the title page the name of one Elchasai. These, in like manner, acknowledge that the principles of the universe were originated by the Deity. They do not, however, confess that there is but one Christ, but that there is one that is superior to the rest, and that He is transfused into many bodies frequently, and was now in Jesus. And, in like manner, these heretics maintain that at one time Christ was begotten of God, and at another time became the Spirit, and at another time was born of a virgin, and at another time not so. And they affirm that likewise this Jesus afterwards was continually being transfused into bodies, and was manifested in many (different bodies) at different times. And they resort to incantations and baptisms in their confession of elements. And they occupy themselves with bustling activity in regard of astrological and mathematical science, and of the arts of sorcery. But also they allege themselves to have powers of prescience.

St. Hippolytus

## Chapter XXVI.—Jewish Chronology.

...From Haran, a city of Mesopotamia, (Abraham, by the command) of God, transfers his residence into the country which is now called Palestine and Judea, but then the region of Canaan. Now, concerning this territory, we have in part, but still not negligently, rendered an account in other discourses. From the circumstance, then, (of this migration) is traceable the beginning of an increase (of population) in Judea, which obtained its name from Judah, fourth son of Jacob, whose name was also called Israel, from the fact that a race of kings would be descended from him. Abraham removes from Mesopotamia (when 75 years old, and) when 100 years old he begat Isaac. But Isaac, when 60 years of age, begat Jacob. And Jacob, when 86 years old, begat Levi; and Levi, at 40 years of age, begat Caath; and Caath was four years of age when he went down with Jacob into Egypt. Therefore the entire period during which Abraham sojourned, and the entire family descended from him by Isaac, in the country then called Canaanitis, was 215 years. But the father of this Abraham is Thare, and of this Thare the father is Nachor, and of this Nachor the father is Serag, and of this Serag the father is Reu, and of this Reu the father is Peleg, and of this Peleg the father is Heber. And so it comes to pass that the Jews are denominated by the name of Hebrews. In the time of Phaleg, however, arose the dispersion of nations. Now these nations were 72,1065 corresponding with the number of Abraham's children. And the names of these nations we have likewise set down in other books, not even omitting this point in its own proper place. And the reason of our particularity is our desire to manifest to those who are of a studious disposition the love which we cherish towards the Divinity, and the indubitable knowledge respecting the Truth, which in the course of our labors we have acquired possession of. But of this Heber the father is Salah; and of this Salah the father is Caïnan; and of this Caïnan the father is Arphaxad, whose father is Shem; and of this Shem the father is Noah. And in Noah's time there occurred a flood throughout the entire world, which neither Egyptians, nor Chaldeans, nor Greeks recollect; for the inundations which took place in the age of Ogyges and Deucalion prevailed only in the localities where these dwelt. There are, then, in the case of these (patriarchs— that is, from Noah to Heber inclusive)—5 generations, and 495 years. This Noah, inasmuch as he was a most religious and God-loving man, alone, with wife and children, and the three wives of these, escaped the flood that ensued. And he owed his preservation to an ark; and both the dimensions and relics of this ark are, as we have explained, shown to this day in the mountains called Ararat, which are situated in the direction of the country of the Adiabeni. It is then possible for those who are disposed to investigate the subject industriously, to perceive how clearly has been demonstrated the existence of a nation of worshippers of the true God, more ancient than all the Chaldeans, Egyptians, and Greeks. What necessity, however, is there at present to specify those who, anterior to Noah, were both devout men, and permitted to hold converse with the true God, inasmuch as, so far as the subject taken in hand is concerned, this testimony in regard of the antiquity of the people of God is sufficient?

## Chapter XXVII.—Jewish Chronology Continued.

But since it does not seem irrational to prove that these nations that had their attention engrossed with the speculations of philosophy are of more modern date than those that had habitually worshipped the true God, it is reasonable that we should state both whence the family of these latter originated; and that when they took up their abode in these countries, they did not receive a name from the actual localities, but claimed for themselves names from those who were primarily born, and had inhabited these. Noah had three sons—Shem, Ham, and Japheth. From these the entire family of man was multiplied, and every quarter of the earth owes its inhabitants in the first instance to these. For the word of God to them prevailed, when the Lord said, "Be fruitful, and multiply, and replenish the earth." So great efficacy had that one word that from the three sons of Noah are begotten in the family 72 children,—(viz.,) from Shem, 25; from Japheth, 15; and from Ham, 32. Unto Ham, however, these 32 children are born in accordance with previous declarations. And among Ham's children are: Canaan, from whom came the Canaanites; Mizraim, from whom the Egyptians; Cush, from whom the Ethiopians; and Phut, from whom the Libyans. These, according to the language prevalent among them, are up to the present day styled by the appellation of their ancestors; nay, even in the Greek tongue they are called by the names by which they have been now denominated. But even supposing that neither these localities had been previously inhabited, nor that it could be proved that a race of men from the beginning existed there, nevertheless these sons of Noah, a worshipper of God, are quite sufficient to prove the point at issue. For it is evident that Noah himself must have been a disciple of devout people, for which reason he escaped the tremendous, though transient, threat of water.

How, then, should not the worshippers of the true God be of greater antiquity than all Chaldeans, Egyptians, and Greeks, for we must bear in mind that the father of these Gentiles was born from this Japheth, and received the name Javan, and became the progenitor of Greeks and Ionians? Now, if the nations that devoted themselves to questions concerning philosophy are shown to belong to a period altogether more recent than the race of the worshippers of God as well as the time of the deluge, how would not the nations of the barbarians, and as many tribes as in the world are known and unknown, appear to belong to a more modern epoch than these? Therefore ye Greeks, Egyptians, Chaldeans, and the entire race of men, become adepts in this doctrine, and learn from us, who are the friends of God, what the nature of God is, and what His well-arranged creation. And we have cultivated this system, not expressing ourselves in mere pompous language, but executing our treatises in terms that prove our knowledge of truth and our practice of good sense, our object being the demonstration of His Truth.

Chapter XXVIII.—The Doctrine of the Truth.

The first and only (one God), both Creator and Lord of all, had nothing coeval with Himself; not infinite chaos, nor measureless water, nor solid earth, nor dense air, not warm fire, nor refined spirit, nor the azure canopy of the stupendous firmament. But He was One, alone in Himself. By an exercise of His will He created things that are, which antecedently had no existence, except that He willed to make them. For He is fully acquainted with whatever is about to take place, for foreknowledge also is present to Him. The different principles, however, of what will come into existence, He first fabricated, viz., fire and spirit, water and earth, from which diverse elements He proceeded to form His own creation. And some objects He formed of one essence, but others He compounded from two, and others from three, and others from four. And those formed of one substance were immortal, for in their case dissolution does not follow, for what is one will never be dissolved. Those, on the other hand, which are formed out of two, or three, or four substances, are dissoluble; wherefore also are they named mortal. For this has been denominated death; namely, the dissolution of substances connected. I now therefore think that I have sufficiently answered those endued with a sound mind, who, if they are desirous of additional instruction, and are disposed accurately to investigate the substances of these things, and the causes of the entire creation, will become acquainted with these points should they peruse a work of ours comprised (under the title), Concerning the Substance of the Universe. I consider, however, that at present it is enough to elucidate those causes of which the Greeks, not being aware, glorified, in pompous phraseology, the parts of creation, while they remained ignorant of the Creator. And from these the heresiarchs have taken occasion, and have transformed the statements previously made by those Greeks into similar doctrines, and thus have framed ridiculous heresies.

Chapter XXIX.—The Doctrine of the Truth Continued.

Therefore this solitary and supreme Deity, by an exercise of reflection, brought forth the Logos first; not the word in the sense of being articulated by voice, but as a ratiocination of the universe, conceived and residing in the divine mind. Him alone He produced from existing things; for the Father Himself constituted existence, and the being born from Him was the cause of all things that are produced. The Logos was in the Father Himself, bearing the will of His progenitor, and not being unacquainted with the mind of the Father. For simultaneously with His procession from His Progenitor, inasmuch as He is this Progenitor's first-born, He has, as a voice in Himself, the ideas conceived in the Father. And so it was, that when the Father ordered the world to come into existence, the Logos one by one completed each object of creation, thus pleasing God. And some things which multiply by generation He formed male and female; but whatsoever beings were designed for service and ministration He made either male, or not requiring females, or neither male nor female. For even the primary substances of these, which were formed out of nonentities, viz., fire and spirit, water and earth, are neither male nor female; nor could male or female proceed from any one of these, were it not that God, who is the source of all authority, wished that the Logos might render assistance in accomplishing a production of this kind. I confess that angels are of fire, and I maintain that female spirits are not present with them. And I am of opinion that sun and moon and stars, in like manner, are produced from fire and spirit, and are neither male nor female. And the will of the Creator is, that swimming and winged animals are from water, male and female. For so

God, whose will it was, ordered that there should exist a moist substance, endued with productive power. And in like manner God commanded, that from earth should arise reptiles and beasts, as well males and females of all sorts of animals; for so the nature of the things produced admitted. For as many things as He willed, God made from time to time. These things He created through the Logos, it not being possible for things to be generated otherwise than as they were produced. But when, according as He willed, He also formed (objects), He called them by names, and thus notified His creative effort. And making these, He formed the ruler of all, and fashioned him out of all composite substances. The Creator did not wish to make him a god, and failed in His aim; nor an angel,—be not deceived,—but a man. For if He had willed to make thee a god, He could have done so. Thou hast the example of the Logos. His will, however, was, that you should be a man, and He has made thee a man. But if thou art desirous of also becoming a god, obey Him that has created thee, and resist not now, in order that, being found faithful in that which is small, you may be enabled to have entrusted to you also that which is great.

The Logos alone of this God is from God himself; wherefore also the Logos is God, being the substance of God. Now the world was made from nothing; wherefore it is not God; as also because this world admits of dissolution whenever the Creator so wishes it. But God, who created it, did not, nor does not, make evil. He makes what is glorious and excellent; for He who makes it is good. Now man, that was brought into existence, was a creature endued with a capacity of self-determination, yet not possessing a sovereign intellect, nor holding sway over all things by reflection, and authority, and power, but a slave to his passions, and comprising all sorts of contrarieties in himself. But man, from the fact of his possessing a capacity of self-determination, brings forth what is evil, that is, accidentally; which evil is not consummated except you actually commit some piece of wickedness. For it is in regard of our desiring anything that is wicked, or our meditating upon it, that what is evil is so denominated. Evil had no existence from the beginning, but came into being subsequently. Since man has free will, a law has been defined for his guidance by the Deity, not without answering a good purpose. For if man did not possess the power to will and not to will, why should a law be established? For a law will not be laid down for an animal devoid of reason, but a bridle and a whip; whereas to man has been given a precept and penalty to perform, or for not carrying into execution what has been enjoined. For man thus constituted has a law been enacted by just men in primitive ages. Nearer our own day was there established a law, full of gravity and justice, by Moses, to whom allusion has been already made, a devout man, and one beloved of God. Now the Logos of God controls all these; the first begotten Child of the Father, the voice of the Dawn antecedent to the Morning Star. Afterwards just men were born, friends of God; and these have been styled prophets, on account of their foreshowing future events. And the word of prophecy was committed unto them, not for one age only; but also the utterances of events predicted throughout all generations, were vouchsafed in perfect clearness. And this, too, not at the time merely when seers furnished a reply to those present; but also events that would happen throughout all ages, have been manifested beforehand;

because, in speaking of incidents gone by, the prophets brought them back to the recollection of humanity; whereas, in showing forth present occurrences, they endeavored to persuade men not to be remiss; while, by foretelling future events, they have rendered each one of us terrified on beholding events that had been predicted long before, and on expecting likewise those events predicted as still future. Such is our faith, O all ye men,—ours, I say, who are not persuaded by empty expressions, nor caught away by sudden impulses of the heart, nor beguiled by the plausibility of eloquent discourses, yet who do not refuse to obey words that have been uttered by divine power. And these injunctions has God given to the Word. But the Word, by declaring them, promulgated the divine commandments, thereby turning man from disobedience, not bringing him into servitude by force of necessity, but summoning him to liberty through a choice involving spontaneity.

This Logos the Father in the latter days sent forth, no longer to speak by a prophet, and not wishing that the Word, being obscurely proclaimed, should be made the subject of mere conjecture, but that He should be manifested, so that we could see Him with our own eyes. This Logos, I say, the Father sent forth, in order that the world, on beholding Him, might reverence Him who was delivering precepts not by the person of prophets, nor terrifying the soul by an angel, but who was Himself—He that had spoken—corporally present amongst us. This Logos we know to have received a body from a virgin, and to have remodeled the old man by a new creation. And we believe the Logos to have passed through every period in this life, in order that He Himself might serve as a law for every age, and that, by being present (amongst) us, He might exhibit His own manhood as an aim for all men. And that by Himself in person He might prove that God made nothing evil, and that man possesses the capacity of self-determination, inasmuch as he is able to will and not to will, and is endued with power to do both. This Man we know to have been made out of the compound of our humanity. For if He were not of the same nature with ourselves, in vain does He ordain that we should imitate the Teacher. For if that Man happened to be of a different substance from us, why does He lay injunctions similar to those He has received on myself, who am born weak; and how is this the act of one that is good and just? In order, however, that He might not be supposed to be different from us, He even underwent toil, and was willing to endure hunger, and did not refuse to feel thirst, and sunk into the quietude of slumber. He did not protest against His Passion, but became obedient unto death, and manifested His resurrection. Now in all these acts He offered up, as the first-fruits, His own manhood, in order that thou, when thou art in tribulation, mayest not be disheartened, but, confessing thyself to be a man (of like nature with the Redeemer), mayest dwell in expectation of also receiving what the Father has granted unto this Son.

Chapter XXX.—The Author's Concluding Address.

Such is the true doctrine in regard of the divine nature, O ye men, Greeks and Barbarians, Chaldeans and Assyrians, Egyptians and Libyans, Indians and

Ethiopians, Celts, and ye Latins, who lead armies, and all ye that inhabit Europe, and Asia, and Libya. And to you I am become an adviser, inasmuch as I am a disciple of the benevolent Logos, and hence humane, in order that you may hasten and by us may be taught who the true God is, and what is His well-ordered creation. Do not devote your attention to the fallacies of artificial discourses, nor the vain promises of plagiarizing heretics, but to the venerable simplicity of unassuming truth. And by means of this knowledge you shall escape the approaching threat of the fire of judgment, and the rayless scenery of gloomy Tartarus, where never shines a beam from the irradiating voice of the Word!

You shall escape the boiling flood of hell's eternal lake of fire and the eye ever fixed in menacing glare of fallen angels chained in Tartarus as punishment for their sins; and you shall escape the worm that ceaselessly coils for food around the body whose scum has bred it. Now such (torments) as these shalt thou avoid by being instructed in a knowledge of the true God. And thou shalt possess an immortal body, even one placed beyond the possibility of corruption, just like the soul. And thou shalt receive the kingdom of heaven, thou who, whilst thou didst sojourn in this life, didst know the Celestial King. And thou shalt be a companion of the Deity, and a co-heir with Christ, no longer enslaved by lusts or passions, and never again wasted by disease. For thou hast become God: for whatever sufferings thou didst undergo while being a man, these He gave to thee, because thou was of mortal mold, but whatever it is consistent with God to impart, these God has promised to bestow upon thee, because thou hast been deified, and begotten unto immortality. This constitutes the import of the proverb,

"Know thyself;" i.e., discover God within thyself, for He has formed thee after His own image. For with the knowledge of self is conjoined the being an object of God's knowledge, for thou art called by the Deity Himself. Be not therefore inflamed, O ye men, with enmity one towards another, nor hesitate to retrace with all speed your steps. For Christ is the God above all, and He has arranged to wash away sin from human beings, rendering regenerate the old man. And God called man His likeness from the beginning, and has evinced in a figure His love towards thee. And provided thou obeys His solemn injunctions, and becomes a faithful follower of Him who is good, thou shalt resemble Him, inasmuch as thou shalt have honor conferred upon thee by Him. For the Deity, (by condescension,) does not diminish aught of the divinity of His divine perfection; having made thee even God unto His glory!

Elucidations.

---

I.
(Who first propounded these heresies, p. 11.)

Hippolytus seems to me to have felt the perils to the pure Gospel of many admissions made by Clement and other Alexandrian doctors as to the merits of some of the philosophers of the Gentiles. Very gently, but with prescient genius, he adopts this plan of tracing the origin and all the force of heresies to "philosophy falsely so called." The existence of this "cloud of locusts" is (1) evidence of the antagonism of Satan; (2) of the prophetic spirit of the apostles; (3) of the tremendous ferment produced by the Gospel leaven as soon as it was hid in the "three measures of meal" by "the Elect Lady," the Ecclesia Dei; (4) of the fidelity of the witnesses,—that grand, heroic glory of the Ante-Nicene Fathers,—who never suffered these heresies to be mistaken for the faith, or to corrupt the Scriptures; and (5) finally of the power of the Holy Spirit, who gave them victory over errors, and enabled them to define truth in all the crystalline beauty of that "Mountain of Light," that true Koh-i-noor, the Nicene Symbol. Thus, also, Christ's promises were fulfilled.

II.
(Caulacau, p. 52.)

See Irenaeus, p. 350, vol. i., this series, where I have explained this jargon of heresy. But I think it worthwhile to make use here of two notes on the subject, which I made in 1845, with little foresight of these tasks in 1885. Fleury (tom. ii.) makes this statement: "Les Nicolaites donnaient une infinité de noms barbares aux princes et aux puissances qu'ils mettaient en chaque ciel. Ils en nommaient un caulaucauch, abusant d'un passage d'Isaie, où se lisent ces mots hebreux: cau-la-cau, caula-cau, pour representer l'insolence avec laquelle les impies se moquaient du prophète, en répétant plusieurs fois quelques-unes de ses paroles." Compare Guerricus, thus: "Vox illa tædii et desperationis, quæ apud Isaiam (xxviii. 13) legitur, quia, viz., moram faciente Domino, frequentibus nuntiis ejus increduli et illusores insultare videntur: manda remanda," etc. See the spurious

Bernardina, "de Adventu Dom., serm. i.," S. Bernard., opp. Paris (ed. Mabillon), vol. ii. p. 1799.

III.
(The Phrygians call Papa, p. 54.)

Hippolytus had little idea, when he wrote this, what the word Papa was destined to signify in medieval Rome. The Abba of Holy Writ has its equivalent in many Oriental languages, as well as in the Greek and Latin, through which it has passed into all the dialects of Europe. It was originally given to all presbyters, as implied in their name of elders, and was a title of humility when it became peculiar to the bishops, as (1 Pet. v. 3) non Domini sed patres. St. Paul (1 Cor. iv. 15) shows that "in Christ"—that is, under Him—we may have such "fathers;" and thus, while he indicates the true sense of the precept, he leads us to recognize a prophetic force and admonition in our Savior's words (Matt. xxiii.), "Call no man your father upon the earth." Thus interpreted, these words seem to be a warning against the sense to which this name, Papa, became, long afterwards, restricted, in Western Europe: Notre St. Père, le Pape, as they say in France. This was done by the decree of the ambitious Hildebrand, Gregory VII. (who died a.d. 1085), when, in a synod held at Rome, he defined that "the title Pope should be peculiar to one only in the Christian world." The Easterns, of course, never paid any respect to this novelty and dictation, and to this day their patriarchs are popes; and not only so, for the parish priests of the Greek churches are called by the same name. I was once cordially invited to take a repast "with the pope," on visiting a Greek church on the shores of the Adriatic. It is said, however, that a distinction is made between the words πάπας and παπᾶς; the latter being peculiar to inferiors, according to the refinements of Goar, a Western critic. Valeat quantum. But I must here note, that as "words are things," and as infinite damage has been done to history and to Christian truth by tolerating this empiricism of Rome, I have restored scientific accuracy, in this series, whenever reference is made to the primitive bishops of Rome, who were no more "Popes" than Cincinnatus was an emperor. It is time that theological science should accept, like other sciences, the language of truth and the terminology of demonstrated fact. The early bishops of Rome were geographically important, and were honored as sitting in the only apostolic see of the West; but they were almost inconsiderable in the structural work of the ante-Nicene ages, and have left no appreciable impress on its theology. After the Council of Nice they were recognized as patriarchs, though equals among brethren, and nothing more. The ambition of Boniface III. led him to name himself "universal bishop." This was at first a mere name "of intolerable pride," as his predecessor Gregory had called it, but Nicholas I. (a.d. 858) tried to make it real, and, by means of the false decretals, created himself the first "Pope" in the modern sense, imposing his despotism on the West, and identifying it with the polity of Western churches, which alone submitted to it. Thus, it was never Catholic, and came into existence only by nullifying the Nicene Constitutions, and breaking away from Catholic communion with the parent churches of the East. Compare Casaubon (Exercit., xiv. p. 280, etc.) in his comments on Baronius. I have thus stated with scientific precision what all candid critics and historians, even the

Gallicans included, enable us to prove. Why, then, keep up the language of fiction and imposture, so confusing to young students? I believe the youthful Oxonians whom our modern Tertullian carried with him into the papal schism, could never have been made dupes but for the persistent empiricism of orthodox writers who practically adopt in words what they refute in argument, calling all bishops of Rome "Popes," and even including St. Peter's blessed name in this fallacious designation. In this series I adhere to the logic of facts, calling (1) all the bishops of Rome from Linus to Sylvester simply bishops; and (2) all their successors to Nicholas I. "patriarchs" under the Nicene Constitutions, which they professed to honor, though, after Gregory the Great, they were ever vying with Constantinople to make themselves greater. (3) Nicholas, who trampled on the Nicene Constitutions, and made the false decretals the canon law of the Western churches, was therefore the first "Pope" who answers to the Tridentine definitions. Even these, however, were never able to make dogmatic the claim of "supremacy," which was first done by Pius IX. in our days. A canonical Primacy is one thing: a self-asserted Supremacy is quite another, as the French doctors have abundantly demonstrated.

IV.
(Contemporaneous heresy, p. 125.)

Here begins that "duplicating of our knowledge" of primitive Rome of which Bunsen speaks so justly. A thorough mastery of this book will prepare us to understand the great Cyprian in all his relations with the Roman Province, and not less to comprehend the affairs of Novatian. Bunsen, with all respect, does not comprehend the primitive system, and reads it backward, from the modern system, which travesties antiquity even in its apparent conformities. These conformities are only the borrowing of old names for new contrivances. Thus, he reads the cardinals of the eleventh century into the simple presbytery of comprovincial bishops of the third century, just as he elsewhere lugs in the Ave Maria of modern Italy to expound the Evening Hymn to the Trinity. In a professed Romanist, like De Maistre, this would be resented as jugglery. But let us come to facts. Bunsen's preliminary remarks are excellent. But when he comes to note an "exceptional system" in the Roman "presbytery," he certainly confuses all things. Let us recur to Tertullian. See how much was already established in his day, which the Council of Nicæa recognized a century later as (τὰ ἀρχαῖα ἔθη) old primitive institutions. In all things the Greek churches were the exemplar and the model for other churches to follow. "Throughout the provinces of Greece," he says, "there are held, in definite localities, those councils," etc. "If we also, in our diverse provinces, observe," etc. Now, these councils, or "meetings," in spite of the emperors or the senate who issued mandates against them, as appears from the same passage, were, in the Roman Province, made up of the comprovincial bishops: and their gatherings seem to have been called "the Roman presbytery;" for, as is evident, the bishops and elders were alike called "presbyters," the word being as common to both orders as the word pastors or clergymen in our days. According to the thirty-fourth of the "Canons Apostolical," as Bunsen remarks, "the bishops of the suburban towns, including Portus, also formed at that time an integral part of the Roman presbytery." This word also refers to all the presbyters of the diocese of Rome itself; and I doubt not originally the laity had their place, as they did in Carthage: "the apostles, elders, and brethren" being the formula of Scripture; or, "with the whole Church," which includes them,—omni plebe adstante. Now, all this accounts, as Bunsen justly observes, for the fact that one of the "presbytery" should be thus repeatedly called presbyter and "at the same time have the charge of the church at Portus, for which (office) there was no other title than the old one of bishop; for such was the title of every man who presided over the congregation in any city,—at Ostia, at Tusculum, or in the other suburban cities.

Now let us turn to the thirty-fourth "Apostolical Canon" (so called), and note as follows: "It is necessary that the bishops of every nation should know who is chief among them, and should recognize him as their head by doing nothing of great moment without his consent; and that each of them should do such things only as pertain to his own parish and the districts under him. And neither let him do anything without the consent of all, for thus shall there be unity of heart, and thus shall God be glorified through our Lord Jesus Christ." I do not pause to expound this word parish, for I am elucidating Hippolytus by Bunsen's aid, and do not intend to interpolate my own theory of the primitive episcopate.

Let the "Apostolical Constitutions" go for what they are worth: I refer to them only under lead of Dr. Bunsen. But now turn to the Nicene Council (Canon VI.) as follows: "Let the ancient customs prevail in Egypt,

Libya, and Pentapolis, so that the Bishop of Alexandria have jurisdiction in all these provinces, since the like is customary in Rome also. Likewise in Antioch and the other provinces, let the churches retain their privileges." Here the Province of Rome is recognized as an ancient institution, while its jurisdiction and privileges are equalized with those of other churches. Now, Rufinus, interpreting this canon, says it means, "the ancient custom of Alexandria and Rome shall still be observed; that the one shall have the care or government of the Egyptian, and the other that of the suburbicary churches." Bunsen refers us to Bingham, and from him we learn that the suburbicary region, as known to the Roman magistrates, included only "a hundred miles about Rome." This seems to have been canonically extended even to Sicily on the south, but certainly not to Milan on the north. Suffice it, Hippolytus was one of those suburbicarian bishops who sat in the Provincial Council of Rome; without consent of which the Bishop of Rome could not, canonically, do anything of importance, as the canon above cited ordains. Such are the facts necessary to a comprehension of conflicts excited by "the contemporaneous heresy," here noted.

V.
(Affairs of the Church, p. 125.)

"Zephyrinus imagines that he administers the affairs of the Church—an uninformed and shamefully corrupt man." This word imagines is common with

Hippolytus in like cases, 157 and Dr. Wordsworth gives an ingenious explanation of this usage. But it seems to me to be based upon the relations of Hippolytus as one of the synod or "presbytery," without consent of which the bishop could do nothing important. Zephyrinus, on the contrary, imagined himself competent to decide as to the orthodoxy of a tenet or of a teacher, without his comprovincials. This, too, relieves our author from the charge of egotism when he exults in the defeat of such a bishop. He says, it is true, "Callistus threw off Sabellius through fear of me," and we may readily believe that; but he certainly means to give honor to others in the Province when he says, "We resisted Zephyrinus and Callistus;" "We nearly converted Sabellius;" "All were carried away by the hypocrisy of Callistus, except ourselves." This man cried out to his episcopal brethren, "Ye are Ditheists," apparently in open council. His council prevailed over him by the wise leadership of Hippolytus, however; and he says of the two guilty bishops, "Never, at any time, have we been guilty of collusion with them." They only imagined, therefore, that they were managing the "affairs of the Church." The fidelity of their comprovincials preserved the faith of the Apostles in apostolic Rome.

VI.
(We offered them opposition, p. 125.)

Here we see that Hippolytus had no idea of the sense some put upon the *convenire* of his master Irenaeus. It was not "necessary" for them to conform their doctrines to that of the Bishop of Rome, evidently; nor to "the

Church of Rome" as represented by him. To the church which presided over a province, indeed, recourse was to be had by all belonging to that province; but it is our author's grateful testimony, that to the council of comprovincials, and not to any one bishop therein, Rome owed its own adhesion to orthodoxy at this crisis. All this illustrates the position of Tertullian, who never thinks of ascribing to Rome any other jurisdiction than that belonging to other provinces. As seats of testimony, the apostolic sees, indeed, are all to be honored. "In Greece, go to Corinth; in Asia Minor, to Ephesus; if you are adjacent to Italy, you have Rome; whence also (an apostolic) authority is at hand for us in Africa." Such is his view of "contemporaneous affairs."

VII. (Heraclitus the Obscure, p. 126.)

"Well might he weep," says Tayler Lewis, "as Lucian represents him, over his overflowing universe of perishing phenomena, where nothing stood;...nothing was fixed, but, as in a mixture, all things were confounded." He was "the weeping philosopher." Here let me add Henry Nelson Coleridge's remarks on the Greek seed-plot of those philosophies which were begotten of the Egyptian mysteries, and which our author regards as, in turn, engendering "all heresies," when once their leaders felt, like Simon Magus, a power in the Gospel of which they were jealous, and of which they wished to make use without submitting to its yoke. "Bishop Warburton," says Henry Nelson Coleridge, "discovered, perhaps, more ingenuity than sound judgment in his views of the nature of the Greek mysteries; entertaining a general opinion that their ultimate object was to teach the initiated a pure theism, and to inculcate the certainty and the importance of a future state of rewards and punishments. I am led by the arguments of Villoison and Ste. Croix to doubt the accuracy of this." In short, he supposes a "pure pantheism," or Spinosism, the substance of their teaching.

VIII.
(Imagine themselves to be disciples of Christ, p. 126.)

This and the foregoing chapter offer us a most overwhelming testimony to the independence of councils. In the late "Council of Sacristans" at the Vatican, where truth perished, Pius IX. refused to all the bishops of what he accounted "the Catholic universe" what the seven suburbicarian bishops were able to enforce as a right, in the primitive age, against two successive Bishops of Rome, who were patrons of heresy. These heretical prelates persisted; but the Province remained in communion with the other apostolic provinces, while rejecting all communion with them. All this will help us in studying Cyprian's treatise On Unity, and it justifies his own conduct.

IX.
(The episcopal throne, p. 128.)

The simple primitive cathedra, of which we may learn something from the statue of Hippolytus, was, no doubt, "a throne" in the eyes of an ambitious man. Callistus is here charged, by one who knew him and his history, with obtaining this position by knavish words and practices. The question may well arise, in our Christian love for antiquity, How could such things be, even in the age of martyrdoms? Let us recollect, that under the good Bishop Pius, when his brother wrote the Hermas, the peril of wealth and love of money began to be imminent at Rome. Tertullian testifies to the lax discipline of that see when he was there. Minucius Felix lets us into the impressions made by the Roman Christians upon surrounding heathen: they were a set of conies burrowing in the earth; a "light-shunning people," lurking in the catacombs. And yet, while this fact shows plainly that good men were not ambitious to come forth from these places of exile and suffering, and expose themselves needlessly to death, it leads us to comprehend how ambitious men, *studiosi novarum rerum*, could remain above ground, conforming very little to the discipline of Christ, making friends with the world, and yet using their nominal religion on the principle that "gain is godliness." There were some wealthy Christians; there were others, like Marcia in the palace, sufficiently awakened to perceive their own wickedness, and anxious to do favors to the persecuted flock, by way, perhaps, of compounding for sins not renounced. And when we come to the Epistles of Cyprian, we shall see what opportunities were given to desperate men to make themselves a sort of brokers to the Christian community; for selfish ends helping them in times of peril, and rendering themselves, to the less conscientious, a medium for keeping on good terms with the magistrates. Such a character was Callistus, one of "the grievous wolves" foreseen by St. Paul when he exhorted his brethren night and day, with tears, to beware of them. How he made himself Bishop of Rome, the holy Hippolytus sufficiently explains.

X.
(Unskilled in ecclesiastical definitions, p. 128.)

It has been sufficiently demonstrated by the learned Döllinger, than whom a more competent and qualified witness could not be named, that the late pontiff, Pius IX., was in this respect, as a bishop, very much like Callistus. Moreover, his chief adviser and prime minister, Antonelli, was notoriously Callistus over again; standing towards him in the same relations which Callistus bore to Zephyrinus. Yet, by the bull Ineffabilis, that pontiff has retrospectively clothed the definitions of Zephyrinus and Callistus with infallibility; thus making himself also a partaker in their heresies, and exposing himself to the anathemas with which the Catholic councils overwhelmed his predecessor Honorius and others. That at such a crisis the testimony of Hippolytus should come to light, and supply a reductio ad absurdum to the late papal definitions, may well excite such a recognition of divine providence as Dr. Bunsen repeatedly suggests.

XI.
(All consented—we did not, p. 128.)

The Edinburgh editor supposes that the use of the plural we, in this place, is the official plural of a bishop. It has been already explained, however, that he is speaking of the provincial bishops with whom he withstood Callistus when the plebs were carried away by his hypocrisy. In England, bishops in certain cases, are a "corporation sole;" and, as such, the plural is legal phraseology. All bishops, however, use the plural in certain documents, as identifying themselves with the universal episcopate, on the Cyprianic principle—Episcopatus unus est, etc. In Acts v. 13 is a passage which may be somewhat explained, perhaps, by this: "All consented...we did not." The plebs joined themselves to the apostles; "but of the rest durst no man join himself to them: howbeit, the plebs magnified them, and believers were added," etc. "The rest" (τῶν δὲ λοιπῶν) here means the priests, the Pharisees, and Sadducees, the classes who were not the plebs, as appears by what immediately follows.

XII. (Our condemnatory sentence, p. 131.)

Again: Hippolytus refers to the action of the suburbicarian bishops in provincial council. And here is the place to express dissatisfaction with the apologetic tone of some writers, who seem to think Hippolytus too severe, etc. As if, in dealing with such "wolves in sheep's clothing," this faithful leader could show himself a true shepherd without emphasis and words of abhorrence. Hippolytus has left to the Church the impress of his character as "superlatively sweet and amiable." Such was St. John, the beloved disciple; but he was not less a "son of thunder." Our Divine Master was "the Lamb," and "the Lion;" the author of the Beatitudes, and the author of those terrific woes; the "meek and gentle friend of publicans and sinners," and the "lash of small cords" upon the backs of those who made His Father's house a "den of thieves." Such was Chrysostom, such was Athanasius, such was St. Paul, and such have ever been the noblest of mankind; tender and considerate, gentle and full of compassion; but not less resolute, in the crises of history, in withstanding iniquity in the persons of arch-enemies of truth, and setting the brand upon their foreheads. Good men, who hate strife, and love study and quiet, and to be friendly with others; men who never permit themselves to indulge a personal enmity, or to resent a personal affront; men who forgive injuries to the last farthing when they only are concerned,—may yet crucify their natures in withstanding evil when they are protecting Christ's flock, or fulfilling the command to "contend earnestly for the faith once delivered to the saints." What the Christian Church owes to the loving spirit of Hippolytus in the awful emergencies of his times, protecting the poor sheep, and grappling with wolves for their sake, the Last Day will fully declare. But let us who know nothing of such warfare concede nothing, in judging of his spirit, to the spirit of our unbelieving age, which has no censures except for the defenders of truth:—

"Eternal smiles its emptiness betray,
As shallow streams run dimpling all the way."

Bon Dieu, bon diable, as the French say, is the creed of the times. Everyone who insults the faith of Christians, who betrays truths he was sworn to defend, who washes his hands but then gives Christ over to be crucified, must be treated with especial favor. Christ is good: so is Pilate; and Judas must not be censured. My soul be with Hippolytus when the great Judge holds his assize. His eulogy is in the psalm: "Then stood up Phinehas, and executed judgment: and so the plague was stayed. And that was counted unto him for righteousness unto all generations, for evermore."

XIII.
(As if he had not sinned, p. 131.)

There is an ambiguity in the facts as given in the Edinburgh edition, of which it is hard to relieve the text. The word καθίστασθαι is rendered to retain (their places) in the first instance, as if the case were all one with the second instance, where μένειν is justly rendered to continue. The second case seems, then, to cover all the ground. What need to speak of men "twice or thrice married," if a man once married, after ordination is not to be retained? The word retained is questionable in the first instance; and I have adopted Wordsworth's reading, to be enrolled, which is doubtless the sense.

This statement of our author lends apparent countenance to the antiquity of the "Apostolic Constitutions," so called. Perhaps Hippolytus really supposed them to be apostolic. By Canon XVII. of that collection, a man twice married, after baptism cannot be "on the sacerdotal list at all." By Canon XXVI., an unmarried person once admitted to the clergy cannot be permitted to marry. These are the two cases referred to by our author. In the Greek churches this rule holds to this day; and the Council of Nice refused to prohibit the married clergy to live in that holy estate, while allowing the traditional discipline which Hippolytus had in view in speaking of a violation of the twenty-sixth traditional canon as a sin. As Bingham has remarked, however, canons of discipline may be relaxed when not resting on fundamental and scriptural laws.

XIV.
(Attempt to call themselves a Catholic Church, p. 131.)

The Callistians, it seems, became a heretical sect, and yet presumed to call themselves a "Catholic Church." Yet this sect, while Callistus lived, was in full communion with the Bishop of Rome. Such communion, then, was no test of Catholicity. Observe the enormous crimes of which this lawless one was guilty; he seems to antedate the age of Theodora's popes and Marozia's, and what Hippolytus would have said of them is not doubtful. It is remarkable that he employed St. Paul's expression, however, ὁ ἄνομος, "that wicked" or that "lawless one," seeing, in such a bishop, what St. Gregory did in another,—"a forerunner of the Antichrist."

XV.
(Callistians, p. 131.)

Bunsen remarks that Theodoret speaks of this sect under the head of the "Noetians." Wordsworth quotes as follows: "Callistus took the lead in propagating this heresy after Noetus, and devised certain additions to the impiety of the doctrine." In other words, he was not merely a heretic, but himself a heresiarch. He gives the whole passage textually, and institutes interesting parallelisms between the Philosophumena and Theodoret, who used our author, and boldly borrowed from him.

XVI.
(The cause of all things, p. 150.)

When one looks at the infinite variety of opinions, phrases, ideas, and the like, with which the heresies of three centuries threatened to obscure, defile, and destroy the revelations of Holy Scripture, who can but wonder at the miracle of orthodoxy? Note with what fidelity the good fight of faith was maintained, the depositum preserved, and the Gospel epitomized at last in the Nicæno-Constantinopolitan definitions, which Professor Shedd, as I have previously noted, declares to be the accepted confession of all the reformed, reputed orthodox, as well as of Greeks and Latins. Let us not be surprised, that, during these conflicts, truth on such mysterious subjects was reflected from good men's minds with slight variations of expression. Rather behold the miracle of their essential agreement, and of their entire harmony in the Great Symbol, universally accepted as the testimony of the ante-Nicene witnesses. The Word was Himself the cause of all created things; Himself increate; His eternal generation implied in the eternity of His existence and His distinct personality.

XVII.
(Tartarus, p. 153.)

I am a little surprised at the innocent statement of the learned translator, that "Dr. Wordsworth justifies Hippolytus' use of this word." It must have occurred to every student of the Greek Testament that St. Peter justifies this use in the passage quoted by Wordsworth, which one would think must be self-suggested to any theologian reading our author's text. In short, Hippolytus quotes the second Epistle of St. Peter (ii. 4) when he uses this otherwise startling word. Josephus also employs it; it was familiar to the Jews, and the apostle had no scruple in adopting a word which proves the Gentile world acquainted with a Gehenna as well as a Sheol.

XVIII.
(For Christ is the God, p. 153.)

Dr. Wordsworth justly censures Bunsen for his rendering of this passage, also for manufacturing for Hippolytus a "Confession of Faith" out of his tenth book. I must refer the student to that all-important chapter in Dr. Wordsworth's work (cap. xi.) on the "Development of Christian Doctrine." It is masterly, as against Dr. Newman, as well; and the respectful justice which he renders at the same time to Dr. Bunsen is worthy of all admiration. Let it be noted, that, while one must be surprised by the ready command of literary and theological materials which the learned doctor and chevalier brings into instantaneous use for his work, it is hardly less surprising, in spite of all that, that he was willing to throw off his theories and strictures, without any delay, during the confusions of that memorable year 1851, when I had the honor of meeting him among London notabilities. He says to his "dearest friend, Archdeacon Hare,…Dr. Tregelles informed me last week of the appearance of the work (of Hippolytus)…I procured a copy in consequence, and perused it as soon as I could; and I have already arrived at conclusions which seem to me so evident that I feel no hesitation in expressing them to you at once." These conclusions were creditable to his acumen and learning in general; eminently so. But the theories he had so hastily conceived, in other particulars, crop out in so many crudities of theological caprice, that nobody should try to study his theoretical opinions without the aid of that calm reviewal they have received from Dr. Wordsworth's ripe and sober scholarship and well-balanced intellect.

General Note.

I avail myself of a little spare space to add, from Michelet's friend, E. Quinet, the passage to which I have made a reference on p. 156. Let me say, however, that Quinet and Michelet are specimens of that intellectual revolt against Roman dogma which is all but universal in Europe in our day, and of which the history of M. Renan is a melancholy exposition. To Quinet, with all his faults, belongs the credit of having more thoroughly understood than any theological writer the absolute revolution created by the Council of Trent; and he justly remarks that the Jesuits showed their address "in making this revolution, without anywhere speaking of it." Hence a dull world has not observed it. Contrasting this pseudo council with the free councils of antiquity, M. Quinet says: "The Council of Trent has not its roots in all nations; it does not assemble about it the representatives of all nations…omni plebe adstante, according to the ancient formula…The East and the North are, almost equally, wanting; and this is why the king of France refused it the title of a council." He quotes noble passages from Bossuet.

**Find this and other great works of the early Church Fathers at lighthousechristianpublishing.com.**

St. Hippolytus

Our Father who art in heaven, hallowed be thy name.
Thy kingdom come, Thy will be done, on earth as it is in heaven.
Give us this day our daily bread and forgive us our trespasses as we forgive those who trespass against us.
And lead us not into temptation, but deliver us from evil, for Thy is the kingdom, the power and the glory.

Amen

Hail Mary full of grace, the Lord is with thee. Blessed art thou amongst women and blessed is the fruit of thy womb Jesus. Holy Mary mother of God, pray for us sinners, now and the hour of our death.

www.ingramcontent.com/pod-product-compliance
Lightning Source LLC
Chambersburg PA
CBHW052205090526
44583CB00017BA/2079